The Environment, International Relations, and U.S. Foreign Policy

The Environment, International Relations, and U.S. Foreign Policy

Edited by Paul G. Harris

GEORGETOWN UNIVERSITY PRESS
Washington, D.C.

Georgetown University Press, Washington, D.C.
© 2001 by Georgetown University Press. All rights reserved.
Printed in the United States of America

10 9 8 7 6 5 4 3 2 1   2001

This volume is printed on acid-free offset book paper.

Library of Congress Cataloging-in-Publication Data

The environment, international relations, and U.S. foreign policy / edited by
Paul G. Harris.
    p. cm.
    Includes index.
    ISBN 0-87840-832-0 (cloth : alk. paper)
    1. Environmental policy—United States. 2. United States—Foreign relations.
3. Global environmental change.   I. Harris, Paul G.
    GE180 E56 2001
    363.7'056'0973—dc21

00-061022

Contents

Tables and Figures

Preface

The Project on Environmental Change & Foreign Policy began at London Guildhall University in early 1998. The primary objectives of the first phase of this ongoing project were to show how environmental changes influence the U.S. foreign policy process; to analyze the actors and institutions—both domestic and international—that constrain and shape U.S. actions on environmental issues; to understand better the central role played by the United States in international efforts to address problems of global environmental change; and to assess U.S. international environmental policies critically. Other objectives of the first phase of the project were to "test the waters" of research in this field; to showcase research that has not been forced into traditional empirical, epistemological, or ontological boxes in the expectation that new areas and issues will be illuminated; to give insight to governmental and nongovernmental practitioners and activists that may improve their understanding of environmental issues in U.S. foreign policy; to get these ideas "onto the street," where they might have some positive effect on policymaking and scholarship; and to enlighten students and laypersons interested in international affairs, U.S. foreign policy, and environmental protection.

Two dozen scholars from several countries contributed to the project's first phase. In achieving the project's objectives, they examined a wide range of important issues related to the role of the United States in global environmental politics. To date, the project has resulted in two books: this volume, dedicated to understanding the place of several different environmental issues in U.S. foreign policy, and a second volume that focuses on the single issue of climate change (global warming) in the context of U.S. foreign policy—*Climate Change and American Foreign Policy* (New York: St. Martin's, 2000). I wish to thank the contributors to this volume for their hard work and perseverance. They and I are grateful to the anonymous referees for their thoughtful and constructive comments, and to all the people at Georgetown University Press for their willingness to give our work the serious consideration we believe it deserves.

Paul G. Harris
Director, Project on Environmental Change & Foreign Policy

The Environment, International Relations, and U.S. Foreign Policy

INTRODUCTION

1 International Environmental Affairs and U.S. Foreign Policy

Paul G. Harris

It is now common to argue that Earth is experiencing important and harmful environmental changes, but this was not always so. Only in recent decades have the connections between human actions and environmental change become widely known. Beginning especially with Rachel Carlson's 1962 book, *Silent Spring*, in which she showed that chemicals introduced into the environment were harming songbirds (and more), Americans started to recognize their impact on the natural world.[1] Subsequently, the U.S. government passed and implemented historically unprecedented legislation that has been effective in reducing and even reversing much of the damage Americans do to their own environment.[2] More recently, Americans have come to realize that adverse environmental changes beyond their borders can threaten environmental protection efforts at home or even dwarf domestic environmental problems in their proportions and consequences. Much more belatedly, they have started to recognize that what they do—in their daily lives, in their industry, and even in their diplomacy—has great impact on the environments of other countries and on the planet as a whole. Thus, environmental issues have, at least on occasion in recent years, moved to the front burner of U.S. foreign policy. They have garnered the attention of policymakers at the highest levels of the U.S. government, including the president and key members of Congress.

This book seeks to illuminate the environmental dimensions of U.S. foreign policy. The contributors highlight some of the areas of environmental change in which the United States has been active, explain why the United States has behaved the way it has in dealing with these issues, and evaluate U.S. international environmental policy from practical and normative perspectives.

For those interested in U.S. foreign policy—that is, the "goals that the nation's officials seek to attain abroad, the values that give rise to those objectives, and the means or instruments used to pursue them"[3]—the value of undertaking such a mission is perhaps obvious. In examining environmental foreign policy, this volume illuminates foreign policy generally. But those interested in the environment, both within the United States and abroad, will also find this project worthwhile. Why? One important reason is that the United States is the world's greatest polluter. For example, its emissions of pollutants that scientists believe contribute to global warming and to the climatic changes that result from global warming surpass those of any other country.[4] Indeed, on a per capita basis, U.S. emissions of these "greenhouse gases" are among the highest in the world. With less than one-twentieth of the world's population, the United States produces nearly one-fourth of the world's greenhouse gases.[5] By reducing its emissions of greenhouse gases, and similarly by reducing its impact on the global environment in countless other ways, the United States can have a vastly disproportionate positive impact on international environmental problems. What is more, with the world's largest economy, it has considerable financial resources that can be directed at environmental problems abroad, and its technological leadership has tremendous potential in this respect.

The United States can also set an example for much of the world. If it leads in the area of international environmental protection efforts, other countries will likely follow.[6] If it fails to lead by acting more robustly to protect the global environment, many other countries will mirror its failure. Thus, the United States can be a leader on international environmental issues, or it can be a "veto state," often determining the success or failure of international environmental cooperation and affecting whether that cooperation leads to effective environmental protection on the ground throughout the world. Finally, many believe that the United States has an ethical obligation—as the world's largest polluter and as the world's wealthiest country—to act both at home and abroad to protect the earth's natural environment and to help those people (and perhaps even other species) adversely affected by environmental changes.

For these and no doubt other reasons, understanding U.S. international environmental policy is central to the entire project of global environmental protection. But understanding the foreign policies of the United States toward the environment is a complex undertaking, not least because the problems are so many and so complex, and because very many actors and forces are involved in shaping those policies. Understanding U.S. foreign policy and the ways in which it affects and is affected by global environmental change is a prerequisite for understanding the larger international environmental debate and the intricacies of global collective action on environmental change. What is more, examining the role of the environment in U.S. foreign policy gives us a better understanding of the foreign policy of the U.S. government generally, which is beneficial for those hoping to understand the role of the United States in other issues that will confront the world in the twenty-first century.

Challenges for U.S. Foreign Policy: Environmental Issues in International Diplomacy

The number of environmental issues directly and indirectly affecting U.S. national interests (and arguably the sentiments of many Americans) is large. This section looks briefly at some of the history of the more prominent issues. Subsequent chapters examine many of these issues in greater historical detail.

Walter Rosenbaum has identified two "eras" in U.S. environmental policy.[7] The first "environmental era" began in the 1960s and extended into the late 1980s, encompassing the Environmental Decade of the 1970s, which saw the most new environmental legislation. Concern for domestic environmental issues rose in the United States during the 1960s, resulting in legislation to improve water quality and to protect wild areas, such as the Clean Air Act of 1963 and the Wilderness Act of 1964. Public concern about environmental issues increased further in the 1970s, and the resulting pressure on politicians and policymakers led to more laws to protect the environment in the United States. During the 1970s, landmark legislation was passed in the areas of air and water pollution, pesticides, endangered species, hazardous and toxic chemicals, ocean pollution, land degradation, wilderness protection, and energy use.[8]

As Rosenbaum argues, the Environmental Decade

> created the legal, political, and institutional foundations of the nation's environmental policies. It promoted an enduring public consciousness of environmental degradation and fashioned a broad public agreement on the need for governmental restoration and protection of environmental quality that has become part of the American public policy consensus. It mobilized, organized, and educated a generation of environmental activists. The environmental movement prospered in a benign political climate assured by a succession of White House occupants tolerant, if not always sympathetic, to its objectives.[9]

However, environmentalists were forced to go on the defensive following the election of Ronald Reagan in 1980. The Reagan administration sought to reduce federal regulations, particularly environmental ones. Although the administration was unable to dismantle the work of the environmental movement in the 1970s, it was able to thwart robust implementation of existing legislation. Furthermore, few new environmental protections were put into place, although the decade is noteworthy for U.S. involvement in international negotiations toward a treaty protecting the earth's stratospheric ozone layer. Reagan's successor, George Bush, was more sympathetic to environmental regulations, having pledged to become the "environmental president." The Bush administration supported environment friendly amendments to the Clean Air Act, and it acceded to amendments strengthening the ozone treaty. In the end, however, the Bush administration's initiatives toward environmental protection were lackluster and few.

The 1990s saw the emergence of a second environmental era. After three decades of trying to combat most environmental problems with their own resources, Americans—and indeed people in other countries—recognized that many of the most pressing environmental issues were ones with causes, consequences, and remedies beyond the sovereign control of the U.S. government or of any other government. This recognition of interdependence among countries meant that international environmental issues became highly salient domestic political issues.[10] Many of the environmental and resource issues that came to prominence domestically in the 1960s and 1970s were also those that moved onto the international agenda in the late 1980s and 1990s. However, rather than focusing on air quality in U.S. cities, activists and policymakers began to look at the consequences of air quality for developing countries and turned their attention to impacts from industrialization on the earth's atmosphere. Rather than remain concerned only with the quality of water in rivers in the United States, concerned individuals focused attention on the quality of water—and the availability of water—in riparian systems covering many countries, and they became much more concerned about the consequences of national river pollution for the world's oceans. Similarly, other formerly domestic concerns spread to international affairs, or at least had close analogies there. According to Rosenbaum, "No transformation in the domestic political conception of environmentalism has more profound future implications than this internationalization of ecological issues."[11]

This transformation was reflected in the intentions and policies of the Clinton administration. Indeed, Clinton and his vice president, Al Gore, campaigned on the environmental theme, and Gore's book, *Earth in the Balance*, demonstrated his sentiments in favor of very strong international environmental regulations.[12] Shortly after Clinton took office, then State Department counselor Timothy Wirth (who was soon to be undersecretary of state for global affairs) declared that the new administration would reestablish the United States as the world's environmental leader: "the United States once again resum[es] the leadership that the world expects of us. . . . [S]ee the changes that we have made related to environmental policy coming out of the disastrous events in Rio just one year ago at the UNCED [United Nations Conference on Environment and Development]. . . . Just a year ago, the United States was viewed as a country not fulfilling its responsibilities, and now we are, on these most difficult issues, once again out in the lead."[13] This assertion was made in repudiation of the preceding decade, in which Republicans in the White House acted to thwart most international action to address global environmental problems. Of course, although many members of Congress—usually Democrats—during the Reagan and Bush administrations supported international environmental protection measures, during the tenure of the Clinton administration many members—usually Republicans—opposed such measures. The upshot is that Clinton was unable to go as far as he and his policy advisors had promised.

Highpoints in International Environmental Diplomacy:
Stockholm and Rio
Until the 1980s and 1990s, the focus of American concern for the environment was largely domestic. Nevertheless, the United States has participated in interna-

tional environmental diplomacy for much of this century, with the most extensive involvement coming in the last three decades. It is party to more than 150 international environmental agreements and treaties, but it joined two-thirds of those since 1970.[14] Much of this new attention to international environmental issues and international efforts to address them arose because environmental issues increasingly were caused—and seen by scientists to be caused—by pollution or its consequences crossing borders and by the realization that international cooperation was needed to address these issues effectively.[15]

Environmental issues truly emerged on the international agenda with the 1972 Stockholm Conference on the Human Environment. The governments of 114 countries sent representatives to Stockholm, although only two heads of state attended. The U.S. government under Richard Nixon was active in pushing the agenda at Stockholm. Governments agreed that their environmental fortunes were interconnected and that they shared a single global commons. Among the important products of the Stockholm conference were the Stockholm Declaration, the establishment of the United Nations Environment Program (UNEP), and the surrounding attention that contributed to the creation of domestic environmental protection ministries.[16] Although the conference was largely devoted to environmental matters, reflecting the preferences of the industrialized developed countries, it also brought attention to questions of development that would be even more salient in future international environmental conferences. The Stockholm Declaration was a set of sometimes conflicting principles—some reasserting sovereignty, others highlighting the need to compromise sovereignty to deal effectively with environmental issues. UNEP soon encountered resistance from developed countries, which wanted to avoid paying for new environmental programs, and from developing countries, which feared that environmental concerns would divert attention away from economic development. Other UN institutions also resisted making UNEP a strong body within the United Nations. They did not want to cede their own new environment-related programs to UNEP.[17] Thus, the Stockholm conference initially had little favorable impact on the earth's environment. Nevertheless, UNEP would eventually take on an important role in international environmental deliberations, and the Stockholm conference raised awareness among publics and governments, including within the United States, about the importance of international environmental cooperation.[18]

Twenty years after the Stockholm conference, diplomats from nearly 180 countries attended the 1992 United Nations Conference on Environment and Development in Rio de Janeiro, making it the largest international conference to that date. Indeed, 118 heads of state spoke at this "Earth Summit," reflecting the growing international interest in environmental issues since Stockholm. The Earth Summit was also noteworthy for the extensive unofficial involvement of nongovernmental organizations, which tried to influence diplomats from the sidelines. Among the products of the Rio summit were the Rio Declaration, a statement of twenty-seven principles that governments agreed to consider as part of efforts to foster sustainable development (the concept of sustainable development is introduced later in this introduction); agreement on conventions dealing with climate change (global warming) and biodiversity (see below), issues that would remain highly contentious and subject to ongoing diplomacy after Rio; establishment of a United Nations Commission on Sustainable Development (CSD), which was intended to promote sustainable development across the UN system and to foster international funding of related programs; Agenda-21, a voluminous statement of UNCED's objectives on all manner of issues related to environment and development; and a weak statement of principles for protecting and managing the world's forests.[19] Permeating UNCED was the demand by developing countries that "new and additional" funds be provided by the developed countries for the purposes of environmentally sustainable development. At Earth Summit II, held in New York in 1997, the focus was whether the Rio summit was a success. It was agreed that UNCED was successful in giving new energy to the goals of the Stockholm conference and that it provided important guidance for environmental programs and stimulated ongoing negotiations on specific important issues such as climate change. But new action on protecting the global environment was incremental, and the commitment by developed countries to provide new aid to the developing world went unfulfilled. Diplomats and environmentalists realized that environmental protection would be a slow, ongoing process.[20]

The U.S. government was active in the Stockholm negotiations, but it took an even greater interest in deliberations surrounding the Rio conference. However, although the United States generally supported the *environmental* agenda at Stockholm, it was much less supportive of the combined environment *and* development agenda at Rio. This weakened support was demonstrated, for example, by the Bush administration's effort to have the Rio Declaration called instead the "Earth Charter," a name that would emphasize the environment objectives of the United States over the development objectives of many other countries, especially those countries in the developing world. The U.S. government was thwarted in other ways at the conference. For example, one of Bush's goals was agreement on a forest convention, but in the end his plans were stifled by developing countries that did not want to relinquish sovereignty over their forest resources. The Bush administration was also opposed to many provisions planned for the biodiversity convention, fearing that they would threaten access of U.S. multinationals to genetic resources abroad and possibly force American corporations to relinquish patent rights. Similarly, the Bush administration opposed the climate convention insofar as it might require the United States to reduce its emissions of heat-trapping greenhouse gases. In the end, it agreed to a relatively weak framework convention that contained only voluntary commitments for the United States and other developed countries to reduce their greenhouse gas emissions to 1990 levels by 2000.[21]

The upshot is that the strong U.S. interest in the Rio conference was frequently directed toward preventing more international regulation in the environmental issue area—notwithstanding President Bush's assertion that he would be the "environmental president." The United States, far from acting as a leader at UNCED, used its influence at Rio to limit the impact of the conference on the U.S. economy. With the advent of President Clinton to the White House, many people expected new, stronger efforts by the United States to implement the objectives of the Earth Summit and of the conventions signed there. Although some movement was clear, it was far from what environmentalists expected and fell well short of the promises made during the Clinton-Gore campaign for the presidency.

Of course, many international efforts were made between Stockholm and Rio—and since—to address environmental issues. Many of these efforts are introduced below, and several are examined in detail in subsequent chapters.[22]

The Atmosphere

Changes to the air and atmosphere threaten human health, national economies, and the natural environment. These problems can be regional, such as air pollution and acid rain that cross national borders, or global, as in the case of stratospheric ozone depletion. Acid rain was one of the prominent early international environmental concerns. Indeed, one reason the UN Conference on the Human Environment was held in Stockholm was the Swedish experience with acid rain that originated in other countries. Acid rain is caused by sulfur dioxide and nitrogen oxide emissions from the burning of fossil fuels and from certain industrial processes. The emissions can travel for hundreds of miles, in the process contributing to reactions in the air that result in rain with high acidity, causing harm to lakes, rivers, and forests. Because the burning of fossil fuels and other common activities causes acid rain, it is a problem in many areas of the world. In 1979, countries signed the Geneva Convention on Long-Range Transboundary Air Pollution, which, along with related agreements and protocols, has met with some success in reducing pollutants that contribute to acid rain, particularly in Western Europe. However, because nitrogen oxide emissions originate largely from motor vehicles, they have been much more difficult to regulate.[23]

Acid rain was prominent on the U.S. environmental foreign policy agenda particularly in the 1980s when the Reagan administration was confronted by the Canadian government over the causes and consequences of acid deposition from smokestack emissions. The Canadians argued that their environment and particularly their eastern lakes were being harmed by sulfur and nitrogen oxide emissions originating in the industrial midwest of the United States. People in the U.S. northeastern states made similar claims. The Reagan administration initially used a delaying tactic—calling for more scientific study to determine the causes of acid rain—but eventually relented by agreeing to enact measures to reduce polluting emissions in the United States. It also signed an international protocol for controlling emissions of nitrogen oxides, which mandated that the United States reduce its emissions of these chemicals to 1987 levels by 1994. Later, the Bush administration agreed in 1990 to amendments to the U.S. Clean Air Act that would substantially reduce sulfur dioxide emissions, and it signed a bilateral agreement with Canada reaffirming these reductions.

Whereas acid rain is a problem facing certain regions of the world, stratospheric ozone depletion has potentially global consequences. Scientists surmised in the 1960s that chlorofluorocarbons (CFCs) and other human-made chemicals could harm the earth's protective ozone layer. Potential consequences of ozone depletion include skin cancers and eye damage in humans. This problem garnered a great deal of attention in the United States in the 1970s and 1980s, contributing to domestic legislation mandating controls on CFCs. Concerns about ozone depletion spread to other countries, and the U.S. government eventually became an advocate of severe restrictions and even elimination of CFCs and other chemicals contributing to ozone depletion. This advocacy resulted in international agreement on the 1985 Vienna Convention for the Protection of the Ozone Layer and the much more robust 1987 Montreal Protocol on Substances that Deplete the Ozone Layer.[24] The Montreal Protocol has been very successful in achieving its objectives, in large measure owing to the willingness of parties to the treaty to strengthen it over time.[25] (See chapters 5 and 7.)

Perhaps the most pressing long-term environmental issue is that of global climate change, variously referred to as global warming or the "greenhouse effect."[26] Climate change results from emissions of greenhouse gases such as carbon dioxide (CO_2) and methane. The most damaging greenhouse gas (in aggregate) is CO_2, which is produced by the use of energy from fossil fuels (e.g., coal, petroleum, and natural gas). Most activities in industrialized countries require the use of energy, most of which derives from fossil fuel sources; thus, most activities contribute to climate change. The vast number and variety of stakeholders with an interest in international regulations related to climate change pose dizzying challenges to policymakers who want to make the changes to transport, industry, and lifestyle that will be required if they are to deal effectively with climate change.[27] Because the potential effects of climate change are great, the need for action is manifest to most knowledgeable scientists. Among the possible effects are increased frequency of severe weather events (e.g., floods, droughts, hurricanes, heat waves), sea-level rise and inundation of coastal areas,[28] and the spread of infectious diseases to areas not previously affected (including the United States).[29]

Concerns about climate change resulted in the 1992 Framework Convention on Climate Change (FCCC), signed at the Earth Summit, in which parties agreed to reduce their greenhouse gas emissions to 1990 levels by 2000.[30] The climate change convention has yet to result in substantial change in state behavior and seems likely to have only small impacts on the problem in the near future, although negotiations to do more have been ongoing. Toward that end, governments agreed to the 1997 Kyoto Protocol to the FCCC in which the developed countries agreed to reduce their emissions of greenhouse gases by about 5 percent by 2008–12.[31] Following their 1998 Buenos Aires Plan of Action, parties to the FCCC pledged in 1999 to agree by November 2000 on the details of implementing the Kyoto Protocol. For its part, the United States has been slow to act on climate change. During the Reagan and Bush administrations, it often sought to prevent mandatory international regulation of greenhouse gas emissions. The Clinton administration was initially more supportive of action, at least rhetorically, but U.S. action toward reducing emissions of gases causing climate change has been incremental at best.[32] Meanwhile, U.S. greenhouse gas emissions continue to rise, already surpassing pledges made at the Earth Summit.

Marine Resources and the Diversity of Species

Marine natural resources have been at risk for decades because of overexploitation and pollution. This fact is reflected at the international level in the many international agreements designed to manage and protect marine resources. Pollution from municipal, agricultural, and industrial wastes dumped into the oceans is addressed by agreements such as the London Dumping Convention and the International Convention for the Prevention of Pollution from Ships (MARPOL).[33] (See chapter 6.) Of particular concern for many environmentalists and governments is the pollution of regional seas, with the Mediterranean being the most visible example. This concern has resulted in negotiation of international agreements under the auspices of the United Nations Regional Seas Program.[34] Most of the world's fisheries are in drastic decline because of overfishing and in some cases because of pollution. Some areas once bountiful in fish are utterly depleted. Hence, governments have endeavored to address these problems with bilateral fishing agreements and broader agreements, notably a 1995 UN-sponsored agreement on straddling and highly migratory fish stocks.

Most prominent of the agreements to protect and manage the oceans is the tortuously negotiated 1982 UN Convention on the Law of the Sea (LOS).[35] This convention establishes parameters for control of maritime territory. Importantly, fish, minerals, and other things found in the sea have traditionally been viewed as resources that exist for the exploitation of humans. This view generally prevails today. Toward this end, the LOS designates 200-nautical-mile exclusive economic zones (EEZs) that give coastal states ownership of the vast majority of the world's fisheries and most of the easily accessible natural resources, specifically petroleum and natural gas. The LOS also clarifies rights of access to resources of the deep seabed beyond EEZs. Those resources are considered the "common heritage of mankind." Although the LOS brought consistency to the management of most ocean natural resources, it failed to mandate extensive protections of natural species, and it did not account fully for migrating fish and marine mammals that move into, out of, and between EEZs. The U.S. government had mixed views on the LOS. It wanted clear rules on access to territorial seas and international straits (a central concern of the U.S. Navy) and sovereignty over resources off its extensive coastlines. However, it did not want to relinquish control of deep seabed resources to "mankind," instead preferring that those resources be exploited to the exclusive benefit of U.S. companies. The U.S. government finally signed the LOS in 1994, but only after the Clinton administration's renegotiation of provisions to give businesses greater access to deep seabed resources.

Any discussion of international cooperation regarding ocean-living resources, even an introductory one such as this, would be incomplete without mentioning whales, dolphins, and sea turtles, three groups of marine animals that have garnered the most public attention and indeed have been the subject of U.S. foreign policy. For centuries, whales were viewed primarily as a marine resource to be exploited. When their numbers declined, countries agreed to the 1946 International Convention for the Regulation of Whaling. However, whale numbers continued to decline, a decline accompanied by increasing public concern about the welfare of these animals. Many people began to think that it was wrong to kill whales at all. As a consequence, a moratorium on whaling was declared by the International Whaling Commission, and the whaling regime has largely moved toward conservation. However, as whale numbers have recovered, pressure has increased from traditional whaling countries (e.g., Iceland, Japan, and Norway) to permit the restart of commercial whaling. The United States, mirroring the concerns of U.S. environmental groups, continues to oppose a return to commercial whaling. (See chapter 10.)

The U.S. government has also pushed for international protection of dolphins and porpoises. In an internationalization of the Marine Mammal Protection Act, it has restricted the imports of tuna caught in ways that do harm to dolphins, leading to major disputes with trading partners and leading to U.S. losses in the tribunal of the General Agreement on Tariffs and Trade (GATT, now the World Trade Organization). Similarly, the United States has placed restrictions on the imports of shrimp caught with nets that do not have turtle excluder devices, mechanisms that prevent endangered turtles from being trapped and drowned in the nets. As in the dolphin case, shrimp-exporting states have challenged these restrictions in international trade tribunals.

One of the biggest international environmental concerns in recent years has been the declining biodiversity of species and the related protection of and access to genetic resources, which are increasingly valuable for the development of new chemicals and pharmaceuticals.[36] Of course, many people are also concerned about the loss of species because they view them as having intrinsic value[37]— hence the visible public campaigns to protect whales, dolphins, sea turtles, panda bears, and so forth. International concerns about endangered species led to the 1973 Convention on International Trade in Endangered Species (CITES). But many threatened species are not well known—or indeed yet known at all to scientists—and many are plants or microbes with potential benefits to humans as chemicals or pharmaceuticals. Concerns about these less-visible aspects of biodiversity resulted in the 1992 Convention on Biological Diversity.[38] Although much work remains, the biodiversity convention started governments, corporations, and other actors on a path to protect the world's biological diversity. A related concern is deforestation, not only the well-publicized cutting of tropical rain forests, but also the decline of diverse forest cover in the developed world.[39] Deforestation sometimes has severe adverse local effects (e.g., loss of topsoil, siltation of rivers, changes to local weather), but it is of particular concern internationally because forests—particularly tropical forests—are rich sources of biodiversity, with many as yet undiscovered or understudied species anticipated to provide the genetic resources for new medicines. Forests of all kinds also act as sinks for CO_2, the chief greenhouse gas, and improve air quality at the local level. Governments are also concerned about the international implications of agricultural practices, soil erosion, and desertification. Indeed, in 1994, many countries agreed to the United Nations Convention to Combat Desertification.[40]

In most of these cases, particularly that of biodiversity, the U.S. government has supported conservation efforts but adamantly defended the rights of American corporations to have access to biological resources and to own and control patents on products produced from those resources.

Hazardous Wastes and Nuclear Pollution

Hazardous wastes, such as toxic industrial materials and low-level radioactive wastes, and questions of how to limit and dispose of them, are important questions for international diplomats. The 1984 Bhopal disaster in India dramatized the potential dangers to human health and the environment posed by hazardous chemicals. Toxic wastes are produced in vast quantities, particularly in the industrialized countries, with the United States far and away the largest producer.[41] These materials were once routinely exported to developing areas of the world, where there are few protections for local inhabitants and environments. This practice continues, although the 1989 Basel Convention and the 1991 Bamako Convention on the transboundary movement of hazardous wastes demonstrate international efforts to limit the movement of hazardous wastes across borders— particularly from the industrialized North to the developing South.[42] Importantly, the largest producers—the United States and Western European countries— have resisted the restrictions of these agreements, and the notion of simply regulating exports of hazardous wastes—instead of stopping them altogether— is abhorrent to many environmentalists and to the governments of developing countries.

Among the most hazardous wastes are those associated with nuclear energy and weapons. Since the early development of nuclear energy and nuclear weapons, governments have been concerned with radioactive fallout and pollution related to nuclear weapons. Although the management of nuclear weapons and related wastes is controlled by the nuclear states themselves, the 1963 partial test ban, which prohibits the testing of nuclear weapons in the atmosphere, oceans, and outer space, has been quite successful in limiting these sorts of tests and associated nuclear fallout.[43] More adversely, fifty years of nuclear weapons development have left vast amounts of nuclear waste in the United States and the former Soviet republics. These wastes pose massive challenges for these countries, particularly for the ones with limited resources for managing the wastes and for surrounding countries potentially affected by them. Governments are also concerned about the disposal or long-term storage of spent nuclear fuel—much of it now crossing international borders to be reprocessed or stored. These issues and related problems fall within the mandate of the International Atomic Energy Agency. Also of great concern are aging nuclear plants of questionable design, particularly plants in eastern and central Europe and the former Soviet republics. Some of these facilities are similar to the plant at Chernobyl, Ukraine, which experienced a meltdown in 1986, spreading radioactive pollution to twenty-odd countries in Europe. Accidents such as the one at Chernobyl and at Three Mile Island, Pennsylvania, led to the 1986 Convention on Early Notification of a Nuclear Accident and the 1986 Convention on Assistance in the Case of a Nuclear Accident or Radiological Emergency. With other Western governments and international organizations, the United States has been concerned that nuclear wastes from weapons development and energy production be managed in a safe manner, and it has provided assistance to former communist countries toward that end.

Population and Consumption

To understand problems of environmental change it is important to consider the related issues of human population and consumption. The concern is with the effects that humans have on the natural environment. More people usually correlate with more environmental damage. By the 1960s, it was recognized that the Earth's population was growing at rates seldom experienced in human history, and authors began warning of a "population bomb" and impending "limits to growth."[44] Although their concerns about the immediate effects of population growth may have been premature, the human population did grow at phenomenal rates in the twentieth century. Indeed, the increased numbers of people on the earth just between the 1992 Earth Summit and the end of the century exceeded the entire human population at the time of the Roman Empire![45] Diplomats— and increasingly nongovernmental organizations interested in population issues— have met on many occasions in an effort to develop international solutions to the problem of population. Among the more prominent meetings was the 1994 Cairo International Conference on Population and Development. The Cairo conference, like other environment-related conferences before it, was characterized by the conflicting goals of developed and developing countries. The former sought limits on population, particularly in the South; the latter sought increased development assistance, which would reduce incentives for large families, and accused the North of a racist campaign to limit the number of nonwhites in the world.[46]

The vast majority of population growth has and will occur in the less-developed countries. It has therefore been common for concerned individuals and politicians to demand that developing countries reduce their sometimes extraordinarily high rates of population growth. Indeed, such efforts have been underway for decades and have begun to bear fruit, particularly in countries that have experienced modest or substantial economic progress in recent years. Although the population will continue to rise by almost one hundred million people per year in coming decades owing primarily to the large numbers of young people in the world, the rate of growth is dropping as countries develop, as family-planning services become widely available, and as women are accorded rights to make decisions about how many children to bear.

The United States became actively involved in population issues in the 1960s, directing foreign aid to international programs designed to limit family size in the developing world. It became the largest contributor of financial assistance to population programs. These efforts continued into the 1980s, but the Reagan administration, equating family-planning programs with abortion, withdrew U.S. support for population-control programs abroad, although much of the assistance continued. President Clinton reversed this opposition to population control in the developing world, at least in the White House, although Congress resisted efforts to fund population-related programs abroad.[47]

But environmental problems are not simply problems of too many people; they are also critically problems of consumption and lifestyle.[48] As the delegates of developing countries argued at the Cairo conference, population is not the only or even the greatest problem, but rather the high levels of often conspicuous consumption among the world's affluent. Vice President Al Gore succinctly identified this problem in a 1993 speech to the United Nations Commission on Sustainable Development. He said that the United States and other developed countries "have a disproportionate impact on the global environment. We have less than a quarter of the world's population, but we use three-quarters of the world's raw materials and create three-quarters of all solid waste. One way to put it is this: A child born in the United States will have 30 times more impact on the earth's environment during his or her lifetime than a child born in India."[49] This problem is not restricted to the United States and other industrialized countries. The world's middle classes are growing rapidly. Although this news is no doubt good in the short term, for it means less people living in poverty, in the longer term it could have devastating environmental consequences if governments do not agree to curb the damage done by the world's affluent people. Nevertheless, one might argue that the United States, as the world's greatest polluter overall and, with only a few rare exceptions, per capita—not to mention as the world's wealthiest country—has a special obligation to reduce American consumption levels and the related environmental impacts, and indeed to help poorer countries cope with the international consequences of high U.S. consumption (see chapter 11).

Environmental Security

These problems of environmental change, as well as others, have led policymakers and analysts to view environment as a problem of security.[50] Conflicts can arise from environmental damage and inequitable distribution of environmental resources, leading to social and political unrest and to environmental refugees.[51] American policymakers and defense officials now perceive that some environmental changes can adversely affect U.S. national security, vital U.S. interests (e.g., access to oil reserves), and the stability of areas where the United States has geopolitical and economic interests.[52] For example, there is concern in some quarters that scarcities of freshwater from overuse and pollution could lead to conflict within and possibly between countries—which is especially the case in the Middle East, where water scarcity could exacerbate existing rivalries between Israel and neighboring Arab countries.[53] There is also concern that conflict could result from differences over how to share and protect water in rivers that pass through more than one country, such as those shared by Turkey, Syria, Iraq, and other countries in the region. Additionally, water shortages in developing countries contribute to internal conflict that harms the well-being of local people and affects the economic and political interests of other countries—including the United States.[54] Such concerns can contribute to U.S. action on international environmental issues. However, sometimes this view can be misdirected because of a tendency on the part of American officials to equate environmental security with national defense, as traditionally defined. Indeed, this attitude could do more harm than good from an environmental perspective. (See chapters 2, 3, and 11.)

Sustainable Development

How can a balance be achieved between environmental viability and economic and human development? Many have suggested that the best means is through actualization of "sustainable development," the theme of UNCED and of the agreements and conventions signed at the Earth Summit. The concept of sustainable development was popularized by the World Commission on Environment and Development (the Brundtland Commission), which was established by the UN General Assembly in 1983 as an outgrowth of the 1972 Stockholm conference. The 1987 report of the Brundtland Commission, *Our Common Future*, emphasized the links between environment, development, and poverty.[55] The report defined sustainable development as environmentally benign development that meets the needs of present generations without impeding future generations from meeting their own needs. The Brundtland Commission was explicit in arguing that the concept of sustainable development must encompass efforts to meet the essential needs of the world's poor, "to which overriding priority should be given."[56] As the report stated, "many forms of development erode the environmental resources upon which they must be based, and environmental degradation can undermine economic development. Poverty is a major cause and effect of global environmental problems. It is therefore futile to attempt to deal with environmental problems without a broader perspective that encompasses the factors underlying world poverty and international inequality."[57]

Underlying the principle of sustainable development is the belief that economic development and related issues of poverty and human well-being cannot be separated from environmental protection. Environmental damage in the long run harms human well-being and contributes to poverty; in turn, people who are living in poverty and lack adequate levels of economic development do more harm to the environment, thereby creating a vicious cycle. By promoting development that simultaneously seeks to minimize harm to the environment, the reasoning goes, it is possible to lift people out of poverty while creating the conditions for long-term environmental protection. The developed countries can also implement sustainable development by making their industries and practices more environmentally benign. Part of the sustainable-development strategy, in which the United States is expected to take a central role, is the provision of new and additional financial and technological resources that will help developing countries raise their living standards while also protecting the natural environment.

Recurring Themes in U.S. Environmental Diplomacy

There are many recurring themes in U.S. involvement in international environmental diplomacy, similar to other areas of U.S. foreign policy. These themes are introduced here. They are elaborated on in subsequent chapters, as are the explanations for them.

The foreign policies of the United States are often directed at protecting the natural environment, a fact that mirrors the growth in concerns about environmental harm within the United States. Robust action by the United States is much more likely if there is clear scientific evidence that the health of Americans or the U.S. economy would be harmed or if there are clear signs that environmental changes are causing substantial human suffering abroad. However, most international environmental issues have rarely presented such acute evidence of immediate harm, at least in the public mind, which is often what counts for policymakers. As a consequence, there is usually a strong tendency for the U.S. government to advocate more research on environmental problems and the potential economic effects of proposed international regulations. This approach delays the formulation of international environmental institutions and associated requirements for national actions, but it can also have the positive effect of increasing certainty surrounding environmental problems, thereby making it easier for politicians to advocate actions.

One of the primary goals of U.S. foreign policy in the environmental issue area (and in others) is to protect or promote the U.S. economy. The U.S. government seeks to limit requirements for the United States to meet internationally mandated regulations, thereby protecting U.S. independence and limiting harm to American businesses. It also prefers that other countries act first, that international actions have limited or no negative impact on Americans, and that these actions not require noticeable changes in American lifestyles and consumption patterns. When the U.S. government does advocate international environmental regulation, the primary goal may not be environmental protections abroad. Instead, it may be trying to create a "level playing field" that requires foreign businesses to operate under the same environmental restrictions as those in the United States. Alternatively—but with similar effect—U.S. foreign policy can be directed at "exporting" U.S. domestic environmental regulations, as in its efforts to protect dolphins and turtles (see chapter 9).

These sometimes conflicting goals—environmental protection versus freedom of action for U.S. businesses—help explain another theme of U.S. foreign environmental policy: North-South differences. U.S. foreign policy seeks to promote environmental or commercial goals favorable to the United States, whereas the countries of the global South, although desirous of clean environments, have their own development and the promotion of North-South economic equity as their central goals. The United States also consistently opposes international environmental agreements that require it to transfer funds to developing countries or that require American businesses to compromise their patent rights.

More broadly, the United States seeks to maintain its sovereignty and to retain its ability to act unilaterally. It resists mandates from international organizations, and it is skeptical of following what it sees as the potential decrees of international bureaucrats. U.S. foreign policy always endeavors to protect U.S. national interests, particularly the most vital ones. Increasingly, however, the global environment has become part of those interests. This change may help explain the incremental embrace of environmental protections by the United States as part of its foreign policy agenda. There is also much evidence in U.S. international environmental policy of the traditional impulse in U.S. foreign policy to help others and to "do good" in the world. The upshot is, however, that U.S. leadership in the international environmental issue area has not been consistent. Sometimes it leads—as in the case of ocean dumping and stratospheric ozone depletion; at others, it resists action, despite possibly severe consequences— as in the case of climate change. Nevertheless, in looking broadly at international environmental diplomacy in recent decades, one can see a gradual U.S. engagement with the world in an increasingly multilateral approach to environmental protection. Thus, as Rosenbaum explains, "on the threshold of the twenty-first century, the U.S. diplomatic trajectory from Stockholm to Kyoto was leading the United States steadily, if unevenly, toward a broadening and deepening commitment to international environmental governance."[58]

Actors and Forces Shaping the International Environmental Policies of the United States

The contributors to this volume highlight the key actors, institutions, and forces shaping U.S. foreign policy on many of these environmental issues. Included among the actors and forces they examine, either directly or indirectly, are the U.S. Constitution, the presidency and executive branch agencies, Congress, the U.S. judiciary, political parties, businesses and nongovernmental organizations, science and economics, media and public opinion, foreign governments, and international institutions. Many other actors and forces prove to be important, depending on the specific environmental issue being addressed by U.S. policymakers. Some of these actors and forces are introduced in the following sections.

The U.S. Constitution

Perhaps the most important force in U.S. foreign policy is the U.S. Constitution. Although it is an eighteenth-century document, Americans and their political representatives constantly refer to it. Most important for our purposes, the Constitution describes the outline—and frequently the detail—of the U.S. government and the ways in which it must operate. Foremost in its prescriptions is the division of the U.S. government into three branches: the legislative branch (Congress), consisting of the House of Representatives and the Senate; the executive branch, headed by the president; and the judicial branch, overseen by the Supreme Court. All three branches of government have a role in the formulation and implementation of U.S. international environmental policy. The Constitution also gives power to the constituent states, which usually have a stake in environmental policy at home and abroad. As Robert Paarlburg points out,

> The U.S. government is particularly susceptible to having divergent international environmental policy preferences, because power is shared across three separate branches (executive, legislative, and judicial) at the federal level, and below that level enormous power remains in the hands of autonomous state and local authorities. Only after executive branch leaders in Washington have developed a sufficiently unified and supportive domestic policy consensus—across all branches and levels of government at home—will they be well positioned to offer effective environmental policy leadership abroad.[59]

The most important impact of the Constitution, however, is the pluralist form of government it created. The American form of democracy is among the most open in the world, providing a myriad of interested individuals and other actors with access to the policy process.

The Congress

Beyond underlying constitutional forces and the existence of the environmental changes themselves, arguably the most important force shaping U.S. international environmental policy is the Congress. It is here that legislation is debated, and it is to the Congress that most stakeholders, both inside and outside the federal government, go to influence policy. Many people believe that the president has prerogative in foreign policy, including that dealing with environmental issues. However, executive branch intentions in the environmental issue area frequently matter much less than legislative branch preferences and support.[60] Congress, after all, passes legislation; it has the ability to tax and spend and to control the president's access to funds; it approves international agreements, and the Senate in particular must ratify all international treaties before they can become part of U.S. law. Ultimately, Congress (usually) mirrors the collective will of the American people.[61] As Paarlburg notes, "it is Congress, not the executive branch or the president, that has final say over U.S. environmental policy, both at home and abroad."[62] (Most of the following chapters examine the impact of Congress on U.S. international environmental policies.)

Party Affiliation

The positions that American policymakers take on international environmental issues are frequently associated with their party affiliation. Although legislators and presidents are free, once in office, to ignore the party's preferences, they often will not do so to ensure that party resources can be brought to bear when they seek reelection. Broadly speaking, one can say that Republican politicians lean toward an anti-environmental approach. They are particularly sensitive to the concerns of businesses, which usually oppose new environmental regulations. (Like party affiliation, the positions of businesses are not always this clearly cut, however.) In contrast, Democratic politicians tend to be more assertive toward environmental regulations, or at least more sympathetic. Environmentalists are generally among their constituents. Although Democrats also want to keep businesses on their side, they must also cater to constituents who favor international environmental agreements and associated national regulations. This being said, Republican administrations—usually viewed as anti-environment and more generally antiregulation (especially if regulation comes from an international organization)—can be proactive in pushing for international environmental action, as was true of the Nixon administration with regard to ocean dumping and of the Reagan and Bush administrations in the case of ozone depletion (see chapters 5 and 6). Many people were not surprised that the Reagan and Bush administrations were often opposed to American action on many international environmental issues, but they were surprised when these administrations were proactive. Alternatively, many people expected the Democratic Clinton administration to favor and actively support international agreements and domestic regulation geared toward environmental protection, but these people were perhaps surprised (some were pleased and some were disappointed) when that administration did not do more.

The President and Executive Branch Agencies

Many of the proposals for environmental legislation, both domestic and international, originate in the White House and in the executive branch more broadly. The president and the agencies he oversees are also responsible for the implementation of federal government policies related to global environmental change. The president can take a lead in proposing international environmental protection efforts or in trying to promote U.S. participation in international environmental instruments and institutions. Indeed, sometimes the executive branch and the president lead the country in this respect (see chapter 6).[63] However, the president must achieve a consensus at home before he or she can lead abroad—despite what many foreigners hope and believe about the president's power to formulate and implement environmental regulations in the United States and to be a leader of international environmental protection efforts.

Many executive branch agencies are involved in U.S. international environmental policymaking and implementation. The most obvious is the Department of State, which has an office of the undersecretary of state for "global affairs," which includes environmental issues, and other branches concerned with international environmental cooperation. The Environmental Protection Agency (EPA) is of course intimately involved in U.S. foreign policy in this area. But less obvious are other agencies, including the Commerce Department and the Department of Defense—among many, if not most, other executive branch agencies. Frequently these agencies have environmental protection in mind, but they are understandably most often concerned with promoting U.S. national interests more broadly defined. Thus, national interests that are perceived to be more important—access to petroleum, economic interests and foreign markets, geostrategic calculations—can distract the United States from using its influence to protect the natural environment abroad (see chapter 4). Executive branch agencies might also be concerned with promoting their own narrow interests. International environmental issues may be seen as vehicles for promoting new programs that justify funding and staffing levels.

The Courts

The legislative and executive branches are not the only core branches of government to become involved in U.S. international environmental policy. Because there is frequently disagreement between Congress and the executive branch agencies charged with implementing statutes, the U.S. courts are frequently called on to interpret U.S. statutes and regulations related to international environmental matters.[64] These disagreements may be about goals, but they may also be simply about interpreting the intent of laws passed by Congress. (Frequently, statutes are ambiguous and give little guidance to executive branch agencies.) The courts may also be called in when industry sues to limit the effects of environmental regulations or when environmental groups sue to make regulations more stringent or to pressure the government to enforce them more rigorously. At these times, the courts decide the degree and nature of U.S. implementation of international environmental agreements or determine the international ramifications of domestic environmental laws and regulations.[65] Thus, the U.S. courts, perhaps surprisingly to many, become important actors in U.S. foreign policy on environmental matters.

Public Opinion

One cannot neglect the role played by the American people. The pluralist nature of American democracy affords people, like other actors mentioned here, substantial access to the policy process. The opinion of the public on issues is perhaps the most important consideration for policymakers. Politicians are interested above all in being reelected. If enough of their constituents are concerned about an issue, they will usually work to promote those concerns in policy. But even unelected bureaucrats are sensitive to public opinion. The views of the public can affect the resources of their agencies, and the bureaucrats are, in the end, beholden to elected officials. For these and additional reasons, the American media has an important role to play. By publicizing adverse global environmental changes, it raises public awareness and thereby shapes the views of the electorate, which can work to stimulate U.S. international environmental activism or to stifle it, depending on the views conveyed by journalists and the effect they have on the public and decision makers. The upshot is that when the media argues that environmental changes adversely affect the interests of Americans, and especially that those changes are also felt by or perceived to harm Americans, policymakers are stimulated to act.

Business Interests

As already indicated, businesses and industry actors (both powerful individual corporations and industry groups) are intimately interested in—and actively try to influence—U.S. international environmental policy. Some of these businesses favor environmental regulation, but more often they are opposed to action on environmental issues. Businesses are potentially very powerful because they have, among other resources, political connections and money to support the election campaigns of politicians. They also have great influence on the U.S. economy and the prosperity of Americans, and they possess (understandably biased) expertise in what are usually complex environmental issue areas. When businesses can credibly point to adverse effects of environmental regulations on jobs and on the overall U.S. economy, members of Congress and the president tend to take their views into account, often to the exclusion of environmental considerations.

However, the influence of businesses can be diluted or constrained when they conflict. Some businesses want international environmental regulation to level the playing field internationally, to bolster demand for their products (e.g., energy-saving equipment), or to protect resources they need (e.g., genetic diversity for biotechnology industries), among myriad other reasons. Many more businesses want to prevent international environmental regulation because they prefer to continue business as usual, delay transitioning to environmentally friendly behavior, or avoid the costs of meeting regulatory requirements. That is, the goal of business (and often of the government) is to force outsiders to comply with environmental restrictions that obtain inside the United States—either for environmental reasons (e.g., in the cases of whales and dolphins) or for economic reasons (to create the level playing field, thereby making other countries' industries subject to the same environmental restraints and costs of U.S. industries). Conflicts that arise among the pro- and anti-environmental goals of industry can stand in the way of their taking a united front against international environmental protection efforts. But when there is little conflict, businesses can have a profound effect on U.S. policy, either for or against environmental protection and associated regulation—depending on their collective and unified preferences (see chapter 7).

Environmental Interests: Nongovernmental Organizations

Nongovernmental organizations (NGOs), both for and against environmental activism, can play an intimate and influential part in U.S. foreign policy on the environment. They are most frequently seen to shape policy from "outside" government. Perhaps their greatest asset is their often large memberships (which for environmental organizations have been stagnant or falling in recent years). By pointing to their members as potential voters who are often willing to vote based largely on environmental questions, environmental NGOs can persuade legislators and the president to listen to their concerns. They actively lobby politicians, frequently asking their members to flood Congress and the White House with mail (these days largely electronic mail). Legislators sometimes go to environmental NGOs for their expertise on particular issues. Indeed, perhaps for this reason, some NGOs are transforming themselves from public advocacy groups into primarily sources of expertise.

NGOs can also influence policy from the "inside." During the 1990s, NGO representatives have increasingly participated in U.S. delegations to international environmental deliberations, sitting alongside American diplomats. Although it would be absurd to believe that they dictate U.S. policy on these occasions, it would also be wrong for us to underestimate the importance of being able to whisper in a delegate's ear during late-night negotiating sessions—or perhaps even to threaten to expose diplomats who are being disingenuous in their public statements in support of environmental goals. Additionally—and very importantly—former members of NGOs, sometimes high-ranking ones, have been appointed to executive branch agencies dealing with international environmental issues. For example, Rafe Pomerance—former environmental activist, former president of Friends of the Earth, and a senior associate of the World Resources Institute (WRI)—was appointed to head the Clinton administration's climate change delegations as deputy assistant secretary of state for environment and development. While at WRI, Pomerance pushed assiduously to persuade the international community that climate change posed a serious threat.[66] Many other individuals with activist environment and development backgrounds became part of the Clinton administration and were active in formulating its climate change policy.

Science and Scientists

The importance of science in initiating and shaping U.S. international environmental policy is inestimable. Although some environmental problems are visible or clearly felt, most are unknown or indeterminate until scientists make the public or policymakers aware of them. And once made aware, policymakers and publics require scientists to inform them of the progress of environmental changes and their impacts (by measuring what has happened or is happening, or by predicting what might happen in the future). For example, the hole in the stratospheric ozone layer over Antarctica was unknown before scientists detected its existence. Similarly, scientists have made the likely causes and possible impacts of climate change a matter of public discourse.[67] Individual scientists can be particularly influential, as, for example, when they testify before Congress or when important politicians read their publications.[68] Groups of scientists—epistemic communities—can influence policy because frequently they have connections to policymakers and bureaucrats.[69] Sometimes scientists can make the government aware of adverse environmental changes, only to find politicians going beyond the scientists' understandings. For example, the Montreal Protocol on ozone depletion was agreed on before there was definitive evidence to support hypotheses about the Antarctic ozone hole.[70] At other times, scientists can present findings only to have them ignored or belittled by politicians, as has been the Republican response to findings of the Intergovernmental Panel on Climate Change. In all cases, scientific findings can be politicized to serve the interests of politicians, businesses, environmentalists, or other actors.[71]

Economics, Trade, and Economists

The U.S. government and Americans are profoundly interested in the vitality of the U.S. economy. Thus, economists are usually involved in all aspects of policy formulation, not least in the area of environmental change.[72] As occurs with the advice of scientists, however, the recommendations of economists regarding environmental issues are often contradictory, and they are frequently focused on economic conditions apart from environmental change per se (short of the extent to which environmental change can be seen as a measurable cost to the economy or to business). Politicians can usually point to economic predictions that support or oppose international environmental regulation. When they do so, as is often the case, they will act on the predictions they believe or those that conform with their other objectives. When the U.S. economy is doing well, U.S. action on international environmental issues is usually more likely; alternatively, when it is doing poorly, U.S. action is usually less likely. This trend of course begs why the Bush administration signed the climate treaty during a recession and why the Clinton administration did little to implement that treaty during perhaps the most extended economic "boom" in contemporary U.S. history. In the end, the United States will prefer action that costs it very little or that even benefits it financially for a time, which largely explains its proactive stance in the late 1980s on international regulation of ozone-destroying chemicals and helps us understand why it is so eager to impose environmental sanctions on other countries (see chapter 9).

Increasingly, changes to the natural environment are tied to trade issues.[73] Environmentalists see economic globalization and the spread of free trade as threats to the environment. They would argue that many developing countries maintain minimal environmental protection regulations in order to attract multinational corporations seeking the lowest production costs. Labor groups fear the export of jobs to countries with minimal environmental protections. Hence, both environmental and labor groups in the United States have pushed for environmental conditions on international trade agreements, notably in the North American Free Trade Agreement (NAFTA) and, as manifested by public demonstrations in Seattle in 1999, in trade agreements associated with the World Trade Organization (WTO).

International Organizations and Foreign Governments

International organizations, institutions, and regimes can influence U.S. foreign policy on the environment. For example, the United Nations has ushered environmental issues onto the international agenda, acting as the stimulus and forum for international deliberations. Simply by making the issues more visible, it can raise the awareness of the American public—witness the hoopla that surrounded the 1992 UNCED Earth Summit in Rio de Janeiro. Also, through agencies such as UNEP and the relatively new CSD, it pushes governments toward implementation of international environmental agreements.[74] International institutions (frequently associated with the United Nations), such as the International Monetary Fund and the World Bank, have become more active in international environmental issues. Sometimes they do so because of U.S. pressure, or, alternatively, they do so and then pull the United States along. A noteworthy example is that of the World Bank, which has grudgingly started to integrate environmental considerations into its funding programs.[75] Other international funding institutions have taken similar steps (see chapter 8). And international "regimes," some formed with the help of U.S. leadership, affect and are affected by U.S. international environmental policy.[76] Examples include the whaling regime surrounding the International Whaling Commission, and the climate change regime, codified in the Framework Convention on Climate Change.[77]

In a somewhat similar vein, foreign governments can influence U.S. international environmental policy. They are of course active in international environmental negotiations, and they sometimes set precedents or goals that the U.S. government finds difficult to oppose actively and visibly. Former prime minister Margaret Thatcher has been credited with pushing the Bush administration to agree to more robust restrictions on the emissions of ozone-destroying chemicals, resulting in the 1990 London amendments to the Montreal Protocol,[78] and the government of Prime Minister Tony Blair helped push the United States to agree to larger cuts in greenhouse gas emissions than it wanted in the 1997 Kyoto Protocol to the climate change convention.

Global Forces

When trying to understand and explain U.S. foreign policy on the environment, one must also consider the impact of several broad forces, chief among which are the environmental changes themselves. Many of these changes are beyond the control of the United States alone and indeed beyond the control of any one set of actors. Regardless of what countries do in the near future, for example, climate change will occur and will affect the interests of the United States as well as the sentiments and the lives of Americans. Its effects will be wide-ranging and cross-cutting, affecting other issue areas and other countries. Similarly, economic globalization is an important force in U.S. international environmental policy. The decay of borders and the challenges to state authority engendered by globalization are intimately connected to global environmental changes. Indeed, one might argue that global environmental change is one of the most profound manifestations of globalization. Furthermore, the spread of free-market economies is having a major impact on the environment; the so-called free hand may be doing much good for people the world over (many will argue this point, of course), but in the long term people may suffer because of the environmental damage that seems inherent in the global spread of capitalism.[79] And there are the "forces" of nascent international norms that bear on questions of U.S. policy toward the global environment, including those norms with ethical content that place limits on the extent to which the United States can continue to place a disproportionate burden on the global environment—and thus hold disproportionate blame for the adverse effects on human well-being that accrue from environmental changes. In the end, it is the very international and global nature of environmental issues that compel the involvement of the U.S. foreign policy establishment.

Simplifying U.S. International Environmental Policy

Explaining and understanding cases of U.S. foreign environmental policy require consideration of a myriad of actors, institutions, and forces. How can we get our minds around these complex cases? How can we organize and manage all the possible variables and explanations? To help us in this task we can turn to theories of international relations and foreign policy. Theory is "a way of making the world or some part of it more intelligible or better understood," or we can define theory a bit more rigorously as "an intellectual construct that helps one to select facts and interpret them in such a way as to facilitate explanation and prediction concerning regularities and recurrences or repetitions of observed phenomena."[80] Thus, theory helps us understand U.S. international environmental policy by simplifying reality and focusing our attention on the actors, institutions, and, indeed, the broader forces that may be most useful for improving our understanding or for explaining a specific case.[81]

Theoretical approaches to foreign policy can be organized into three categories: (1) systemic theories, which emphasize the influence of the international system and the distribution of power within it; (2) societal theories, which focus our attention on U.S. domestic politics and American culture; and (3) state-centric theories, which find answers to questions about foreign policy within the state and within the individuals who work therein.[82] How might these theoretical approaches help explain U.S. international environmental policy? From the perspective of systemic theory, one can argue that the United States joined the UN Convention on the Law of the Sea because it feared that to do otherwise might erode its power. If it did not join the convention, coastal countries might limit access to U.S. Navy ships and submarines, thereby threatening U.S. military flexibility and power vis-à-vis the Soviet Union or other potential enemies. From the perspective of societal theory, when looking at U.S. foreign policy on whaling, one could focus on domestic politics, particularly the influence of NGOs opposed to whaling and the widespread opposition to whaling among the American people. From the perspective of state-centric theory, U.S. policy on climate change could be a function of bargaining and power brokering among interested government agencies, the president and White House, and the Congress.

Other theoretical approaches focus on the roles of regimes and international institutions or on the influence of norms and ideas in explaining U.S. international environmental policy. There can also be ethical considerations in our understandings of that policy, both from human-centered perspectives (e.g., sustainable development as well as human well-being and suffering related to environmental change) and Earth- or environment-centered perspectives (e.g., environmental ethics and "deep ecology"). One could apply these theoretical categories and approaches in different ways, and there are of course many other ways of approaching U.S. foreign policy analytically.

Different analytical approaches to questions of foreign policy, international relations, and environmental change highlight different actors, forces, and processes. It is therefore appropriate that the contributors to this book take many different perspectives to illuminate U.S. international environmental policy. They have their own preferred theoretical frameworks. The upshot is that there are many environmental issues and many actors and forces that influence and are influenced by U.S. foreign policy. What explains the relationships between these issues and actors? Or, what explains U.S. international environmental policy? The contributors to this volume help us answer these questions.

Explanations and Interpretations of U.S. International Environmental Policy

In this volume, contributors look at various environmental issues to illustrate how U.S. foreign policy operates. More specifically, they highlight explanations and causes of U.S. international environmental policy. Many of them also attempt, to varying degrees, to evaluate U.S. policy from practical and normative perspectives.

National Security and Geopolitics: Environmental Issues on the Policy Agenda

Part 2 of the book examines *Realpolitik* in U.S. international environmental policy. Chapters 2 and 3 examine the concept of "environmental security" from practical and critical perspectives, and chapter 4 uses a case study to demonstrate how environmental security and geopolitical considerations influence U.S. foreign environmental policy.

In chapter 2, Braden Allenby argues that environmental security can be defined as the intersection of environmental and security considerations at the national policy level. A relatively new and still somewhat contentious concept, environmental security may be understood as the outcome of several important trends. One is the breakdown of the bipolar geopolitical structure that characterized the Cold War period from the 1940s to the fall of communism in Eastern Europe and the Soviet Union. Another trend, less visible to many in the policy community, is the shift of environmental considerations from "overhead" to "strategic." This process is occurring at many different levels, from individuals and private firms to the national, state, regional, and global policy levels. Taken together, according to Allenby, these trends suggest that environmental security may signal an important evolution of national and international policy systems. If this evolution is to solidify, however, the concept—which has been used to mean different things by different stakeholder communities—must be defined with sufficient rigor to support its operationalization in policy programs.

In chapter 3, Jon Barnett undertakes a highly critical examination of U.S. policy pronouncements that have been informed by the notion of environmental security. His chapter briefly outlines the concept of environmental security and discusses pronouncements on the subject in the U.S. National Security Strategy and from the Department of Defense and the Department of State. According to Barnett, these pronouncements conform to a narrow and nation-centered account of environmental security, consistent with political realism. He argues that the United States selectively interprets environmental security as a means to justify traditional approaches to foreign policy. As such, environmental issues have been co-opted by agency actors hoping to perpetuate roles and their agencies' traditional activities. Nevertheless, Barnett finds some positive ecological potential in the U.S. government's incorporation of environmental security concerns into its foreign policy. It may be an important step toward greater consideration for the environment in the making of foreign policy.

The Caspian Sea is the site of large, newly discovered oil and gas deposits. It is also bedeviled by ecological problems—including pollution, fisheries depletion, and a rising sea level—which are likely to be exacerbated by extensive development of hydrocarbon reserves. In chapter 4, Douglas Blum shows how these changes have posed a dilemma for U.S. foreign policy toward the littoral countries of the Caspian: Is it better to promote collective "environmental security," or should the United States focus on energy extraction for more explicitly self-interested and geopolitical ends? The United States has also taken various steps to address environmental degradation elsewhere in the former Soviet Union and Eastern Europe. In the Caspian, however, despite a number of programmatic statements endorsing environmental protection, U.S. policy has strongly emphasized other objectives: energy security, autonomy for non-Russian actors in the region, isolation of Iran, and projection of American influence. For these reasons, the pursuit of energy exploitation and geopolitically preferable transportation routes has dominated the U.S. agenda. Meanwhile, regional and international efforts to address the Caspian environment have gathered strength. Blum reviews the prospects for multilateral environmental cooperation surrounding the Caspian and suggests that such cooperation offers hope for political stability and economic development in the region. U.S. policy remains malleable and may be responsive to significant changes in global energy markets and regional politics, which tend to support the priority of multilateral cooperation for sustainable development in the Caspian basin.

Domestic and International Politics Shaping
U.S. Global Environmental Policies

The chapters in part 3 examine U.S. international environmental policies by focusing on domestic politics and international influences. Following the broad historical look at local, national, and international aspects of policy regarding stratospheric ozone depletion in chapter 5, subsequent chapters use case studies to focus on the presidency and Congress, business influences, nongovernmental organizations, the courts, and changing bargaining environments in international regimes.

In chapter 5, Srini Sitaraman examines many of the factors that are instrumental in facilitating interstate cooperation on the environment. Realist and neoliberal theories of international relations have focused on the structural causes of interstate cooperation. Relative versus absolute gains, anarchy, issue domains, and international regimes and institutions have received a disproportionate amount of scholarly attention, whereas domestic political processes and factor endowments have not been given sufficient attention. Sitaraman's chapter shows how domestic political processes and different factor groupings in the United States interacted with transnational alliances to influence the negotiation, shape, and structure of the 1987 Montreal Protocol on stratospheric ozone depletion. The U.S. government internationalized the ozone problem by enabling the extension of scientific discourse to the interstate level. Sitaraman shows how domestic political processes and bureaucratic politics affected the final shape and outcome of the Montreal treaty. His chapter demonstrates that the state is a disaggregated entity and that domestic political processes are linked to the external world through a network of intermediary organizations. Sitaraman reveals how U.S. domestic political processes and intragovernmental politics contribute to the formulation of major international environmental agreements. In his analysis, he examines the domestic sources of international environmental policy; the U.S. "internationalization" of ozone depletion; the contested science of ozone depletion; domestic politics and its influence on the shape, structure, and outcome of the Montreal Protocol; and the importance of local, national, and international levels of analysis for our understanding of U.S. international environmental policy and of international environmental cooperation more generally.

In chapter 6, John Barkdull argues that executive branch leadership, specifically the initiative of White House staff, has contributed to U.S. involvement in efforts to prevent ocean pollution. Barkdull's case study sheds light on this matter by focusing on the Nixon administration's negotiation of the 1972 treaty on ocean dumping. The Nixon administration, led by the chairman of the Council on Environmental Quality, Russell Train, transformed a domestic issue—the regulation of dumping of military and commercial wastes in coastal waters by U.S. agencies and citizens—into a matter for international negotiations. Once engaged in international negotiations, the question became whether the United States could achieve a treaty it would accept and how closely the treaty would conform to American preferences. The secret negotiating position of the United States, which Barkdull found in the Nixon Materials at the National Archives, reveals that the United States was highly concerned that the U.S. military retain maximum freedom of action. This goal and others were largely attained, even when the United States would have accepted considerably less. Thus, it appears that U.S. leadership—and particularly leadership by the executive branch—can make a significant difference in the outcome of international environmental treaty negotiations. Furthermore, Barkdull's historical analysis shows that the environmental record of the Nixon administration (if not that of Nixon himself) has been mischaracterized and that the administration was forward looking and proactive in undertaking international environmental legislation—which is not what casual observers expect from a Republican administration. As such, the chapter offers valuable insights for U.S. international environmental policy in the future.

In chapter 7, Robert Falkner argues that state-centric explanations of U.S. foreign environmental policy, which emphasize the autonomy of policymakers, fail to get at the important role corporations play. Falkner discusses various approaches to the study of corporate influence in foreign policy and presents evidence to demonstrate the role of businesses in the making of foreign policy. He examines three environmental cases: ozone-layer protection, climate change, and biotechnology. The "business conflict" model, which emphasizes the fragmentation of and conflicts within the business sector, is contrasted with traditional pluralist and neo-Marxist or structuralist accounts of interest-group politics. Falkner argues that a modified version of the business conflict model best explains corporate influence. It reflects the privileged position of business interests in environmental politics, but it avoids deterministic accounts of corporate dominance by emphasizing competition between opposing business interests. Political alliances between dominant business sectors and the state are identified as essential factors in the evolution of U.S. foreign environmental policy. Most important, the nature of these alliances helps explain why American businesses can alternatively support international environmental regulation, as happened in the ozone case, and oppose such regulation, as evidenced by the response of businesses to international efforts to deal with the problems of climate change and biodiversity.

The community of NGOs has emerged, particularly during the last decade, as an important actor in international environmental relations. NGOs have built public awareness about the environment through conferences and other public activities. More important from the point of view of international relations are their activities aimed at shaping international institutions and international law. In chapter 8, Morten Bøås addresses this issue by looking at NGOs in the United States and their involvement in congressional hearings on multilateral development bank (MDB) activity. Bøås shows how this involvement led to a campaign aimed at making it impossible for U.S. executive directors in MDBs to support projects that could have a major impact on the environment unless an environmental impact assessment (EIA) was made available at least 120 days before the project. The NGO campaign culminated with the Pelosi amendment, which made an EIA in advance of MDB board consideration of projects a requirement for U.S. support. Little more than a year after what originally started as a national campaign in the United States, this procedure was turned into de facto international law when all MDBs made an EIA requirement their standard operating procedure. The chapter documents this process to highlight the transnationalization of U.S. environmental policies, specifically the internationalization of the Pelosi amendment. Bøås also asks the question: What right do interest-based organizations, specifically U.S. NGOs, have to make decisions that affect not only their domestic constituencies, but also people in Africa, Asia, and Latin America?

In chapter 9, Elizabeth DeSombre examines environmental sanctions in U.S. foreign policy. The United States has threatened import restrictions for environmental reasons more often than any other country, with good success generally in accomplishing its stated goals. What appears to be a simple and effective foreign policy tool, however, represents in origin and implementation a number of domestic battles. The sanctions that resulted take a form that, although predictable, no individual proponent would have designed. DeSombre's chapter examines the conflicts present at three stages of U.S. environmental sanctions: their origin, application, and effects. Each of these stages represents a conflict between a set of actors, the outcome of which influences the shape of the sanctions. At the initial stage, the conflict is between environmentalists and industry actors, each of whom wants foreign environmental policy to be used for different ends. Resulting policy takes the form of import restrictions that deny access to U.S. markets to those countries that act in ways the United States deems environmentally unfriendly. This approach protects U.S. industries from products made in ways that do not require the same regulations Americans must follow. Although Congress passes these sanctions, executive branch agencies typically drag their feet when implementing trade restrictions, often interpreting their mandate as narrowly as possible or even refusing to implement the restrictions at all. As a result, a number of the environmental sanctions have been fought in U.S. courts. Congress will sometimes modify its original legislation to limit the discretion agencies have in imposing sanctions. Once the sanctions have been threatened or imposed, the struggle is with the target countries that resist taking the action demanded of them. DeSombre shows that some of the domestic characteristics that influenced the shape of the sanctions also relate to the likelihood that the sanctions will achieve U.S. goals.

In 1946, the United States joined fifteen nations in signing the International Convention for the Regulation of Whaling. Under the convention, the International Whaling Commission (IWC) was created to regulate an industry facing declining demand for whale oil and severe depletion of some whale populations. By the mid-1960s, the focus of the IWC became increasingly preservation oriented, with fewer nations engaged in whaling and with the addition of new nonwhaling members to the convention. This focus led to the polarization of member nations within the IWC—those favoring protection of whales conflicting with those in favor of conservation measures and continued consumptive and nonconsumptive uses. By the mid-1980s, these conflicts peaked when the IWC placed a ban on commercial whaling. That ban is still in effect, although the IWC, with U.S. support, permits whaling by aboriginal groups. In chapter 10, Kristen Fletcher shows how the United States has maintained a stance against commercial whaling, seeking a permanent ban even though international support and science seem to be swaying toward sustainable commercial harvests. She argues that as whale populations improve and the world's whaling policies change, U.S. foreign policy must evolve with them. This conclusion is extremely disturbing for those who wish to see whales protected in perpetuity. Nevertheless, her chapter shows how the U.S. reaction to these international challenges illuminates U.S. whaling policy in particular and its other international environmental policies more generally.

National Interests and International Obligations: A Prescription for U.S. International Environmental Policy

The final part of this book is less analytical than most preceding chapters. Instead, it takes a normative and prescriptive approach to U.S. international environmental policy, recommending a shift in priorities among policymakers so that both U.S. interests and broader normative objectives might be promoted.

In chapter 11, Paul G. Harris argues that the United States can more effectively achieve its foreign policy goals in the environmental issue area, and thereby protect and promote its national interests, by treating other countries, particularly the developing countries, more equitably. Such policies would also promote ethical aims, such as acceptance of American responsibility for the disproportionate adverse impact of the United States on the global environment. Although there has been some movement toward recognition of this idea in its stated policy and behavior, the United States has yet to comprehend fully the extent to which equity may be a fungible power resource in the context of contemporary international affairs. U.S. foreign policy is critical because the United States has the financial, technological, and diplomatic resources that can be brought to bear on environment and development problems. The United States is also the world's greatest polluter. It therefore has the greatest ethical obligation to redress the wrongs of historical and ongoing global pollution. With regard to environmentally sustainable development, it can further its national interests and, coincidentally, promote ethical goals by meeting many of the demands from developing countries for greater international equity. With the foregoing in mind, Harris's chapter examines some of the practical and normative implications of adopting and embracing equity as an objective of U.S. global environmental policy—particularly policy on global climate change—for the United States itself and for the world. It also looks at the implications that such a policy would have for American global power in this new century.

Conclusion

The natural environment is undergoing change, and much of that change is adverse for humans (and for other species). Americans are not immune to these adverse effects. The U.S. government has come to realize that global environmental changes—such as climate change and ozone depletion—can directly affect the interests of the American people. It has also recognized to varying degrees that regional and local environmental problems—such as acid rain, depleted fisheries, and water scarcities—can directly or indirectly affect the economic, political, and security interests of the United States, and that environmental destruction and related human suffering abroad can affect the sentiments of Americans. Environmental changes that reach beyond the borders of countries can seldom be addressed effectively by any one nation, including the United States. These problems require international and even global action if they are to be reduced and mitigated. The world's governments and other important actors cannot deal effectively with environmental changes if the United States does not play an active role. Because the U.S. economy is so large, its diplomatic influence so great, and its contributions to environmental problems so extensive (in short, because it pollutes so much), the United States must be part of international solutions to environmental change. Thus, environmental changes have become a major subject and feature of U.S. foreign policy.

Scholars, practitioners, and activists will therefore want to understand how and why the United States takes the positions that it does on international environmental changes, how these positions can be altered, and whether they deserve to be supported or opposed. Many explanations and interpretations of U.S. international environmental policy can be offered, as the authors of this book demonstrate. Their research and assessments of U.S. international environmental policy not only get us closer to understanding the underlying dynamics of U.S. policy, but also highlight the issues and actors toward which concerned individuals and organizations might wish to focus their energies to protect the natural environment, to promote related U.S. interests, and indeed to promote the interests of other countries and peoples abroad. What is more, these chapters tell us much about U.S. foreign policy more generally, thereby helping us to understand the role that the United States plays in other global issues that concern Americans and people everywhere.

The short conclusion of this book is that there are many actors and forces shaping U.S. international environmental policy. Arguably the best way to understand these actors and forces is to look at how the U.S. foreign policy machine deals with different environmental problems and to undertake such examinations from different theoretical and analytical perspectives. Perhaps foremost among the conclusions of this volume is this: the highly pluralistic nature of U.S. foreign policymaking results in an inevitably large number of players, ranging from individuals to businesses to nongovernmental organizations. The number of local, state (i.e., U.S. "states"), regional, national, and international stakeholders involved in these issues is vast. But the number of actors is not the end of it; the U.S. Constitution created a contentious, multibranch government that does not resolve issues quickly, smoothly, or easily. This convoluted democratic system is compounded by the number and complexity of the problems themselves. Thus, the foreign policies that emanate from Washington are almost inevitably unsatisfactory to all those involved. But understanding the process may help us to raise the level of satisfaction, at least for those on one side of the debate.

When evaluating U.S. international environmental policy (and perhaps U.S. foreign policy more generally), one ought to bear these issues in mind. Neither the president nor any other single actor can have its way without considering the interests and objectives of other actors. Deals must be made, and a consensus must be forged. Neither is easy to do, nor is it always easy to understand.

Notes

1 See Rachel Carlson, *Silent Spring* (New York: Houghton Mifflin, [1962] 1994).

2 Much more remains to be done, of course. Americans continue to do great harm to their own national environment.

3 Charles W. Kegley and Eugene R. Wittkopf, *American Foreign Policy* (New York: St. Martin's, 1996), 7.

4 For the authoritative work on climate change and global warming, see J. T. Houghton, L. G. Meiro Filho, B. A. Callander, N. Harris, A. Kattenberg, and K. Maskell, eds., *Climate Change 1995: The Science of Climate Change* (New York: Cambridge University Press, 1996).

5 Energy Information Administration, *Emissions of Greenhouse Gases in the United States 1996* (Washington, D.C.: Energy Information Administration, 1997); Energy Information Administration, *Annual Energy Review 1996* (Washington, D.C.: Energy Information Administration, 1997).

6 Some countries are way out in front of the United States in the area of international environmental protection, to be sure. And, it should be added, many people and governments do not like it—or at least say as much—when the United States adopts a leadership role on almost any issue, although even they frequently follow that leadership.

7 Walter A. Rosenbaum, *Environmental Politics and Policy*, 4th ed. (Washington, D.C.: Congressional Quarterly, 1998), 11–12.

8 Michel E. Kraft and Norman J. Vig, "Environmental Policy from the 1970s to 2000: An Overview," in *Environmental Policy*, 4th ed., ed. Norman J. Vig and Michael E. Kraft (Washington, D.C.: Congressional Quarterly, 2000),

12–13. See generally Vig and Kraft, eds., *Environmental Policy*, and Samuel P. Hays, *Beauty, Health, and Permanence: Environmental Politics in the United States, 1955–85* (New York: Cambridge University Press, 1987).

9 Rosenbaum, *Environmental Politics*, 11.

10 Cf. Ibid., 14.

11 Ibid.

12 Al Gore, *Earth in the Balance* (New York: Houghton Mifflin, 1992).

13 Timothy Wirth, "World Conference on Human Rights," press briefing, Washington, D.C., 2 June 1993, *U.S. Department of State Dispatch* 4, no. 23 (7 June 1993), available at <http://www.dosfan.lib.uic.edu/ERC/briefing/dispatch/index.html>.

14 Rosenbaum, *Environmental Politics*, 336.

15 The history of international environmental diplomacy through the 1980s is examined in Lynton K. Caldwell, *International Environmental Policy: Emergence and Dimensions* (Durham, N.C.: Duke University Press, 1990), and John E. Carroll, *International Environmental Diplomacy: The Management of Transfrontier Environmental Problems* (New York: Cambridge University Press, 1988).

16 See "Declaration of the United Nations Conference on the Human Environment," UN Doc. A/CONF.48/14 (1972), reprinted in United Nations, *Report of the United Nations Conference on the Human Environment* (New York: United Nations, 1973).

17 Lorraine Elliott, *The Global Politics of the Environment* (London: Macmillan, 1998), 12–13, 108.

18 Mark A. Gray, "The United Nations Environment Programme: An Assessment," *Environmental Law* 20, no. 2 (1990): 291–319.

19 United Nations Conference on Environment and Development, *Report of the UN Conference on Environment and Development: Annex I, Rio Declaration on Environment and Development*, UN Doc. A/CONF.151/26, vol. 1, 12 August 1992; United Nations Conference on Environment and Development, *Report of the UN Conference on Environment and Development: Annex II, Agenda-21*, UN Doc. A/CONF.151/26, vol. 1, 12 August 1992; United Nations Conference on Environment and Development, *Non-Legally Binding Authoritative Statement of Principles for a Global Consensus on the Management, Conservation, and Sustainable Development of All Types of Forests*, UN Doc. A/CONF.151/26, vol. 3, 14 August 1992; United Nations Intergovernmental Negotiating Committee, Framework Convention on Climate Change Secretariat, *United Nations Framework Convention on Climate Change* (Bonn: Climate Change Secretariat, 1992); United Nations Environment Programme, *Convention on Biological Diversity* (Nairobi: UNEP/CBD Secretariat, 1992).

20 Derek Osborn and Tom Bigg, *Earth Summit II: Outcomes and Analysis* (London: Earthscan, 1998).

21 At the time of this writing in early 2000, the United States was anticipated to exceed this target by 13 percent.

22 What follows in the chapter is only a sampling of the most prominent issues. For a more detailed discussion, see, for example, Elliott, *Global Politics;* Gary Bryner, *From Promise to Performance: Achieving Global Environmental Goals* (New York: W.W. Norton, 1997); and Norman J. Vig and Regina S. Axelrod, eds., *The Global Environment: Institutions, Law, and Policy* (Washington, D.C.: Congressional Quarterly, 1999).

23 Rosenbaum, *Environmental Politics*, 352–55.

24 *Montreal Protocol on Substances that Deplete the Ozone Layer, Final Act* (Nairobi: United Nations Environment Program, 1987).

25 See Richard Elliott Benedick, *Ozone Diplomacy*, enlarged ed. (Cambridge, Mass.: Harvard University Press, 1998).

26 See Houghton et al., eds., *Climate Change 1995.*

27 See, for example, William D. Nordhaus, ed., *Economics and Policy Issues in Climate Change* (Washington, D.C.: Resources for the Future, 1998); Ian H. Rowlands, *The Politics of Global Atmospheric Change* (Manchester: Manchester University Press, 1995).

28 Coastal areas of the United States are particularly threatened. During debate on U.S. participation in the climate regime, Senator John Kerry cited the threat posed by climate change to U.S. coastal areas: "between now and the middle of the next century oceans will rise one to three feet and . . . the impact of that will be devastation on the coast of Florida." *Congressional Record*, 25 July 1997, S8119. President Clinton and Vice President Gore made similar statements during visits to Florida in 1997.

29 On potential health implications of climate change, see, for example, A. J. Michael et al., eds., *Climate Change and Human Health* (Geneva: World Health Organization, 1996).

30 "Framework Convention on Climate Change," *International Legal Materials* 31 (1992): 849–73.

31 Of particular note is the 1997 Kyoto Protocol to the FCCC and subsequent international negotiations on its implementation. *Kyoto Protocol to the United Nations Framework Convention on Climate Change*, 10 December 1997, UN Doc. FCCC/CP/1997/L.7/Add.1, available at <http://www.unfccc.de/resources/docs/convkp/kpeng.html>. The Kyoto Protocol is examined in detail in Michael Grubb, *The Kyoto Protocol: A Guide and Assessment* (London: Earthscan, 1999).

32 See Lamont C. Hempel, "Climate Policy on the Installment Plan," in Vig and Kraft, eds., *Environmental Policy*, 281–302. The Project on Environmental Change & Foreign Policy has devoted an entire book to examining climate change in the context of U.S. foreign policy. That book is intended to compliment this one, so we do not go into this topic in great detail in the

present volume. See Paul G. Harris, ed., *Climate Change and American Foreign Policy* (New York: St. Martin's, 2000).

33 The many international agreements to limit or prevent ocean pollution are summarized in Bryner, *From Promise to Performance*, 48–56.

34 For an analysis of how one of these agreements was crafted, see Peter M. Haas, *Saving the Mediterranean: The Politics of International Environmental Cooperation* (New York: Columbia University Press, 1992).

35 For a current summary of the provisions of the United Nations Convention on the Law of the Sea, see R.R. Churchill and A.V. Lowe, *The Law of the Sea*, 2d ed. (Manchester: Manchester University Press, 1999).

36 Dorothy H. Patent and William Munoz, *Biodiversity* (New York: Houghton Mifflin, 1996); Timothy Swanson, *Intellectual Property Rights and Biodiversity Conservation* (New York: Cambridge University Press, 1998); Lakshman D. Guruswamy and Jeffrey A. McNeely, eds., *Protection of Global Biodiversity* (Durham, N.C.: Duke University Press, 1998).

37 Robert Garner, *Animals, Politics, and Morality* (Manchester: Manchester University Press, 1993).

38 United Nations, Convention on International Trade in Endangered Species of Wild Fauna and Flora, Washington, D.C., 3 March 1973, available at <http://www.cites.org/CITES/eng/index.shtml>; United Nations, Convention on Biological Diversity, Rio de Janeiro, 1992, available at <http://www biodiv.org/chm/conv/cbd_text_e.pdf>. Many other agreements related to species protection have been made. See Fridtjof Nansen Institute, *Green Globe Yearbook of International Cooperation on Environment and Development* (New York: Oxford University Press, 1996), 163–64.

39 Leslie E. Sponsel, Thomas N. Headland, and Robert C. Bailey, eds., *Tropical Deforestation: The Human Dimension* (New York: Columbia University Press, 1996).

40 United Nations, Convention to Combat Desertification, Paris, 1994, available at <http://www.unccd.int/convention/text/convention.php>.

41 Elliott, *Global Politics*, 45.

42 Convention on the Control of Transboundary Movements of Hazardous Wastes and Their Disposal (Basel Convention), 1989, available at <http://www.unep.ch/basel/text/con-e.htm>; Convention on the Ban of the Import into Africa and the Control of Transboundary Movements and Management of Hazardous Wastes within Africa, 1991, available at <http://www.ifs.univie.ac.at/intlaw/konterm/vrkon_en/html/doku/waste-af.htm>.

43 The recent failure of the U.S. Senate to support ratification of comprehensive test ban treaty, which would prohibit all nuclear testing, demonstrates the paramount concern with national control and security in this issue area.

44 Paul Erlich, *The Population Bomb* (New York: Ballantine, 1968); D. H. Meadows, D. L. Meadows, J. Randers, and W. W. Behrens, *The Limits to Growth* (London: Earth Island, 1972).

45 As cited by Crispin Tickell, BBC Radio 4, 22 November 1999.

46 For a discussion of international population control efforts, see Barbara Crane, "International Population Institutions: Adaptation to a Changing World Order," in *Institutions for the Earth*, eds. Peter M. Haas, Robert O. Keohane, and Marc A. Levy (Cambridge, Mass.: MIT Press, 1993), 351–93.

47 Indeed, Republicans in Congress are so opposed to family-planning programs that might promote abortion that they have tied this issue to other foreign policy matters, often preventing U.S. action in other areas or preventing funding of completely unrelated programs. In a compromise with Congress regarding funding for the United Nations, the Clinton administration agreed in late 1999 to modest concessions to Republicans opposed to international assistance for family planning generally and for abortion-related programs in particular.

48 Laurie Ann Mazur, ed., *Beyond the Numbers: A Reader on Population, Consumption, and the Environment* (Washington, D.C.: Island, 1994); Garrett Hardin, *Living within Our Limits: Ecology, Economics, and Population Taboos* (New York: Oxford University Press, 1993); and Richard J. Tobin, "Environment, Population, and the Developing World," in Vig and Kraft, eds., *Environmental Policy*, 326–49.

49 Al Gore, "U.S. Support for Global Commitment to Sustainable Development," address to the Commission on Sustainable Development, United Nations, New York City, 14 June 1993, *U.S. Department of State Dispatch* 4, no. 24 (14 June 1993), available at <http://www.dosfan.lib.uic.edu/ERC/briefing/dispatch/index.html>.

50 See, among the many works on environmental security, *Environmental Change and Security Project Report* (Washington, D.C.: Woodrow Wilson International Center for Scholars, annual); Geoffrey D. Dabelko and P. J. Simmons, "Environment and Security: Core Ideas and U.S. Government Initiatives," *SAIS Review* 17 (winter–spring 1997): 127–46; Jessica Tuchman Mathews, "Redefining Security," *Foreign Affairs* 67 (1989): 162–77; Thomas Homer-Dixon, "On the Threshold: Environmental Changes as Causes of Acute Conflict," *International Security* 16, no. 2 (1991): 76–116; Norman Myers, *Ultimate Security: The Environmental Basis of Political Stability* (New York: W. W. Norton, 1993); Thomas Homer-Dixon, "Environmental Scarcities and Violent Conflict: Evidence from Cases," *International Security* 19, no. 1 (summer 1994): 5–40.

51 Elliott, *Global Politics*, 219–41.

52 See White House, *The National Security Strategy* (Washington, D.C.: U.S. Government Printing Office, 1994), and subsequent summaries of national security strategy.

53 See Peter Gleick, "Water and Conflict," and Miriam Lowi, "West Bank Water Resources and the Resolution of Conflict in the Middle East," Occasional Paper 1, Project on Environmental Change and Acute Conflict (Sep-

tember 1992); Natasha Beschorer, *Water Instability in the Middle East* (London: International Institute for Strategic Studies, 1992); David Brooks and Stephen Lonegran, *Watershed: The Role of Fresh Water in the Israeli-Palestinian Conflict* (Ottawa: International Development Research Center, 1994).

54 See, for example, Aaron T. Wolf, *Hydropolitics along the Jordan River* (New York: United Nations, 1995); World Bank, *Fostering Riparian Cooperation in International River Basins* (Washington, D.C.: World Bank, 1997); Ben Crow, David Wilson, and Alan Lindquist, *Sharing the Ganges* (London: Sage, 1995).

55 World Commission on Environment and Development (the Brundtland Commission), *Our Common Future* (Oxford: Oxford University Press, 1987). See also United Nations, *Agenda-21 Earth Summit: United Nations Program of Action from Rio* (New York: United Nations, 1992). There are many evaluations of the notion of sustainable development in principle and practice. See, for example, Sharachchandra M. Lélé, "Sustainable Development: A Critical Review," *World Development* 19, no. 6 (June 1991): 607–21; and Gary Bryner, "Agenda 21: Myth or Reality," in Vig and Axelrod, eds., *The Global Environment*, 157–89.

56 Brundtland Commission, *Our Common Future*, 43.

57 Ibid., 3.

58 Rosenbaum, *Environmental Politics*, 338.

59 Robert Paarlburg, "Earth in Abeyance: Explaining Weak Leadership in U.S. International Environmental Policy," in *Eagle Adrift: American Foreign Policy at the End of the Century*, ed. Robert J. Lieber (New York: Longman, 1997), 149.

60 See Paarlburg, "Earth in Abeyance."

61 For highlights of recent actions by Congress in the environmental issue area, see Michael E. Kraft, "Environmental Policy in Congress: From Consensus to Gridlock," in Vig and Kraft, eds., *Environmental Policy*, 121–44.

62 Paarlburg, "Earth in Abeyance," 144.

63 See Norman J. Vig, "Presidential Leadership and the Environment: From Reagan to Clinton," in Vig and Kraft, eds., *Environmental Policy*, 98–120.

64 For a more detailed discussion of the role of the courts in U.S. environmental policy, see Lettie McSpadden, "Environmental Policy in the Courts," in Vig and Kraft, eds., *Environmental Policy*, 145–64.

65 See particularly chapter 9 in this volume, and, for a more general treatment, Richard Oliver Brooks and Thomas M. Hoban, eds., *Green Justice: Environment and the Courts* (Boulder, Colo.: Westview, 1996).

66 Philip Shabecoff, *A New Name for Peace: International Environmentalism, Sustainable Development, and Democracy* (Hanover, N.H.: University Press of New England, 1996), 152.

67 See S. George Philander, *Is the Temperature Rising? The Uncertain Science of Global Warming* (Princeton: Princeton University Press, 1998).

68 President Clinton is believed to have read a book citing the dangers of climate change while his administration's most crucial climate change policies were being formulated: Ross Gelbspan, *The Heat Is On: The High Stakes Battle over Earth's Threatened Climate* (New York: Addison-Wesley, 1997). The president was reportedly seen carrying the book during his 1997 summer holiday.

69 Epistemic communities are networks of knowledge-based experts "with recognized expertise and competence in a particular domain and an authoritative claim to policy-relevant knowledge within that domain or issue-area." They help countries identify their interests, frame the issues for collective debate, propose specific policies, and identify salient points for negotiation. Peter M. Haas, "Introduction: Epistemic Communities and International Policy Coordination," *International Organization* 46, no. 1 (1992): 1–35, quote from 3.

70 See Benedick, *Ozone Diplomacy.*

71 On the complicated relationship between science and policy, see Sheila Jasenoff, *The Fifth Branch: Science Advisers as Policymakers* (Cambridge, Mass.: Harvard University Press, 1990).

72 See Thomas G. Ingersoll and Bradley R. Brockbank, "The Role of Economic Incentives in Environmental Policy," in *Controversies in Environmental Policy,* ed. Sheldon Kamieniecki, Robert O'Brien, and Michael Clarke (Albany: State University of New York Press, 1986), 210–22; Terry Anderson and Donald Leal, *Free Market Environmentalism* (Boulder, Colo.: Westview, 1991); A. Myrick Freeman III, "Economics, Incentives, and Environmental Regulation," in Vig and Kraft, eds., *Environmental Policy,* 190–209; and Rosenbaum, *Environmental Politics.*

73 See David Vogel, "International Trade and Environmental Regulation," in Vig and Kraft, eds., *Environmental Policy,* 350–69.

74 See, for example, Bryner, *From Promise to Performance,* chap. 4; Elliott, *Global Politics,* chap. 4; and Thomas G. Weiss, David P. Forsythe, and Roger A. Coate, *The United Nations and Changing World Politics* (Boulder, Colo.: Westview, 1997), part 3.

75 For critical assessments of World Bank environmental progress, see Bruce Rich, *Mortgaging the Earth: The World Bank, Environmental Impoverishment, and the Crisis of Development* (Boston: Beacon, 1994), and Kevin Danaher, ed., *50 Years Is Enough: The Case Against the World Bank and the International Monetary Fund* (Boston: South End, 1994).

76 International regimes can be defined as accepted principles, norms, rules, and decision-making procedures around which international actors' expectations converge in a given issue area. See Stephen D. Krasner, *International Regimes* (Ithaca: Cornell University Press, 1983), and, generally, Volker Rittsberger, *Regime Theory and International Relations* (Oxford: Clarendon, 1997).

77 See Harris, *Climate Change and American Foreign Policy.*

78 Benedick, *Ozone Diplomacy*, 169.

79 It is worth pointing out that the major alternative that has been tried—communism—has an even worse record of environmental destruction.

80 Paul R. Viotti and Mark V. Kauppi, *International Relations Theory* (Boston: Allyn and Bacon, 1999), 3.

81 On the differences between understanding and explaining, see Martin Hollis and Steve Smith, *Explaining and Understanding International Relations* (New York: Oxford University Press, 1991).

82 John Barkdull and Paul G. Harris, "Approaches to Understanding U.S. International Environmental Policy," unpublished paper for the Project on Environmental Change and Foreign Policy, 2000. Cf. G. John Ikenberry, David A. Lake, and Michael Mastanduno, eds., *The State and American Foreign Economic Policy*, special issue of *International Organization* 42, no. 1 (1988).

NATIONAL SECURITY AND GEOPOLITICS

2 New Priorities in U.S. Foreign Policy: Defining and Implementing Environmental Security

Braden Allenby

A number of new national security policy issues have arisen since the end of the Cold War.[1] One of the more interesting ones, from the perspectives of policy and practice, is the effort to integrate previously separate policy structures of national security and the environment to create a new focus area: *environmental security*. This chapter reviews the development of the concept of environmental security and suggests means by which such a policy can be operationalized. This discussion is placed in the context of U.S. policy evolution and the leading role the United States has assumed in defining and implementing environmental security. However, the general principles are broadly applicable.

Environmental security is a relatively new and still somewhat contentious concept. Conceptually, it may be defined as the intersection of environmental and national security considerations at a national policy level, but its operational implications are still poorly defined. It has come to the fore recently for several reasons. The most obvious is the breakdown of the bipolar geopolitical structure that characterized the Cold War, a process that allowed previously repressed issues and interests to surface. A second, more subtle, reason is the continuing shift of the environment from an "overhead" to a "strategic" concern for society. This process is occurring at many different levels, from implementation of Design for Environment methodologies within firms to continuing attempts to integrate environmental and trade considerations in the World Trade Organization (WTO). Taken together, these trends suggest that environmental security may be an important evolution of national state and international policy systems. A necessary first step, however, is to define the concept with sufficient rigor to support an operational program. That is the purpose of this chapter.

Initially, the idea of environmental security may well strike one as novel, perhaps even a trifle oxymoronic. It arises predictably, however, from the combination of a world increasingly perceived as environmentally constrained with one where the previous stability generated by the ideological confrontation between capitalism and communism has broken down.[2]

And broken down it has, along a number of critical dimensions. On the environmental side, human activity is increasingly understood as fundamentally affecting a number of basic global and regional physical, chemical, and biological systems in a process that, thanks to demographic and economic growth, is accelerating.[3] On the economic side, similar discontinuous evolution is marked by increasing globalization, the rise of the service and knowledge-based economy, and a concomitant change in patterns of work and the social contracts that previously linked workers with firms.[4] On the geopolitical side, the end of the bipolar geopolitical Cold War structure, with its defining conflict between capitalist and communist global ideologies, has led to a more fragmented, complex world as previously submerged local and regional tensions emerge, often explosively. Not only are these regional perturbations difficult to manage in themselves, but they are complicated by important shifts in institutional authority, which has led to a still unclear shift in governance patterns from one dominated by national states to one characterized by a balance among a number of institutions, including nongovernmental organizations (NGOs), transnational corporations and capital markets, and more complex communities of interest (see figure 2.1).[5]

Taken together, such trends suggest that human societies are moving toward a globalized economy and society that will not be more homogeneous, but rather more complex in the technical sense. There will be more communities, defined in

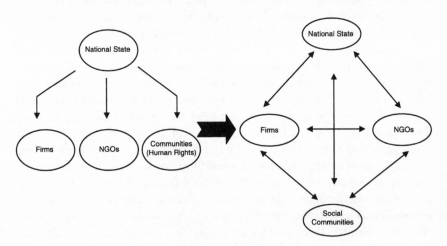

Figure 2.1.   Evolution in International Governance Systems.

The international governance system, based on the primacy of the national state, is evolving into a far more complex structure with many more competing stakeholders. In addition to the state, these stakeholders include private firms, NGOs, and communities of all kinds.

terms of both traditional geographical space and, increasingly, common interests defined in cyberspace; there will also be more units, systems, interests, political and social entities, and technology clusters at many different levels. As a result, of course, many more interrelationships will exist among them. As a general matter, then, substantially more sophisticated policy structures will be required to define and manage the interests of national states in such an environment.

To complicate matters further, consider for a moment the policy structures that the concept of environmental security potentially impacts, such as foreign policy, security policy, environmental policy, and science and technology policy. For a number of reasons, all of these generally function in the short term—perhaps years—and focus on the interests of a specific geographic area. Many of the natural and human systems with which national security and environmental policy in the broadest sense must deal, however, lie far beyond these intuitive boundaries.[6] Stratospheric ozone depletion, for example, will require decades to mitigate. The natural systems whose perturbations cause global climate change have responses measured on timescales ranging from (possibly) decades to centuries to millennia. Loss of genetic biodiversity is permanent. On the human side, the evolution of successful institutions, such as national states, also occurs over decades and centuries. As societies, economies, and human activity generally become more complex even in the short term, it is increasingly critical to develop pragmatic policy systems that integrate gracefully and robustly over very disparate temporal and spatial scales, particularly where a rapid and accelerating rate of change and the inherent complexity of the systems involved make planning and prediction even more difficult than usual. This process, which is still little understood, has been called "adaptive management."[7]

Environment as Strategic

If the concept of environmental security is to make any sense, it is necessary to understand the evolution of environmental issues and policy from an historical "overhead" position to one that is "strategic" for individuals, firms, and states. Increasingly, it is recognized that environmental issues can no longer be thought of as ancillary, but should be considered integral components of industrial, social, political, and economic systems. This dynamic—the movement of environment from overhead to strategic—occurs at many different scales within firms, industrial sectors, and society itself. Used in this sense, overhead issues are those that are ancillary to primary functions, whereas strategic issues are those that are viewed as integral to the primary activity (table 2.1). For a firm, putting an air scrubber on a manufacturing facility to limit emissions is overhead, but changing product designs and business plans in response to changing European product management initiatives is strategic. Each case may differ in detail, but there is a fundamentally similar logic to each. Looked at this way, the integration of environmental considerations into the national security apparatus can be seen

Primary Activity	Time Frame	Focus of Activity	Endpoint	Relation of Environment to Economic Activity	Example
Remediation, compliance	Past focus	Individual site, media, or substance	Reduce local anthropocentric risk	Overhead	Superfund cleanup, scrubbers for stack emissions
Industrial ecology, Design for Environment	Present/future focus	Materials, products, services, and operations during life cycle	Global sustainability	Strategic and integral	Product takeback; Blue Angel ecolabel

Table 2.1. Environment as Strategic.

Environmental issues are evolving from being overhead to strategic for firms, institutions, and society as a whole. In part, it is this dynamic that has generated the concept of environmental security, because some environmental issues become recognized as potentially affecting the stability and core interests of the national state.

as only one example, albeit an important one, of a broader transition in social governance of environmental issues.[8]

On a social level, the transition of environmental issues from overhead to strategic inevitably results in a certain level of conflict with existing legal and policy structures. This outcome is not surprising because such structures—including, for example, those dealing with consumer protection, government procurement, antitrust, trade, or, in this case, national security—have generally been created over the years without any explicit consideration of their environmental implications and are thus not environmentally efficient. In effect, the environmental externalities associated with existing legal and policy regimes have been invisible to such institutions.[9] Increasingly, however, the difficulty of mitigating complex environmental perturbations—such as loss of biodiversity and habitat; stratospheric ozone depletion; degradation of water, soil, and atmospheric resources and sinks; and global climate change—has made the need to integrate environmental dimensions into existing legal systems more apparent, if not easier.[10] Ignoring environmental externalities imposed by existing legal and regulatory structures is no longer acceptable.

The critical barriers to such policy evolution are frequently not economic, legal, or technological, but cultural. For example, consider the conflicts and misunderstandings that have arisen as the world's trading system, embodied in entities such as the WTO and the North American Free Trade Agreement (NAFTA) zone, struggles to combine free trade and environmental protection. The trade community—which had heretofore dealt with environmental requirements, if it dealt with them at all, as protectionist trade barriers—is having to come to terms with environmentalists. The latter, in turn, have tended to view the global economy, and thus trade, as somewhat suspect in itself, but also as an ideal tool to impose extraterritorial environmental requirements. Using trade in this way is, however, strongly constrained by international law, which, being based on the foundation of the absolute sovereignty of the national state, significantly limits the ability to impose one country's environmental values on another through trade.[11] Moreover, elements of both groups are also beginning to understand that free trade, economic development, and environmental protection are all valid policy goals, but it may not be possible to optimize all at the same time.[12] How to evaluate the inevitable trade-offs has not yet been determined, but the dialog to date reflects different mental models prevalent in each community, more than disagreement over specifics.[13]

Another example is provided by the experience of the U.S. electronics industry as it attempted to reduce use of chlorofluorocarbons (CFCs) in manufacturing in accordance with the Montreal Protocol, which was intended to reduce stratospheric ozone depletion. This attempt generated significant conflict with an important customer of that sector, the U. S. military.

The military in most countries is a large purchaser of goods and complex weapons systems, and the manufacturing, design, and maintenance of these products is usually governed by complex sets of contracting, procurement, and operating requirements. In the United States, such requirements are embodied in military specifications (MILSPECs) and military standards (MILSTDs). These requirements have been drawn up over the years to ensure appropriate performance of products and systems under the extreme conditions of military use and have virtually never had any environmental inputs. They form a powerful and complex cultural and legal system.

Stratospheric ozone depletion, on the other hand, is a by now classic example of unanticipated impact of human economic activity on fundamental natural systems. In this case, anthropogenic gases, primarily CFCs, which are quite stable, were found to be migrating to the upper atmosphere. There, subject to energetic sunlight, they released chlorine, which, in turn, catalyzed the destruction of stratospheric ozone. Stratospheric ozone in appropriate concentrations in the stratosphere is important because it blocks highly energetic sunlight from hitting the earth's surface, where it can cause significant damage to living things.[14] Once this relationship was understood, the international community accordingly crafted a response, the Montreal Protocol, which aimed to eliminate the production and use of CFCs.

CFCs, however, were not just a routine emission from certain industrial processes. Rather, they were at the time a critical material in electronics and metal piecepart manufacturing, as well as being important for maintenance of high-performance technology systems. They were thus critical to the operational integrity of the military forces of the United States.[15] This relationship created conflict between two previously unrelated regulatory structures: environment and MILSPECs/MILSTDs. In fact, because of cross-referencing in government, industrial, and commercial documents, and because of the use of the rigorously tested MILSPECs and MILSTDs as industry standards around the world, it has been estimated that half of all CFC-113 use worldwide for the manufacture of electronics circuit boards was driven by U.S. MILSPECs and MILSTDs.[16] Moreover, the MILSPEC/MILSTD system is extremely complex. For example, review of requirements to use CFCs embedded in these specifications and standards involved searching more than 600,000 pages of technical documents, and one testing requirement for passive electronics devices referenced to 1,700 other documents.[17] Thus, it is perhaps not surprising that when the U.S. electronics industry began to phase out ozone-depleting substances pursuant to the Montreal Protocol, the single biggest barrier to prompt phaseout was not technical, not economic, not scientific—but MILSPECs and MILSTDs.

Integrating the military procurement system with environmental policy objectives in this case did not imply ignoring the procurement system and specifications or reducing performance requirements. After all, the policy rationale for MILSPECs and MILSTDs—robust performance under adverse conditions—was both strong and continuing. Rather, the process involved the integration of environmental and performance requirements into a new generation of

MILSPECs and MILSTDs, which would meet the goals of both environmental and military procurement policy. This process continues today, in research projects such as one that identifies alternatives to sealants containing heavy metals and that is funded under the Strategic Environmental Research and Development Program (SERDP, a Department of Defense research program operating in collaboration with the Department of Energy and the Environmental Protection Agency).[18] This is a useful example of what environmental security might look like in practice. It also illustrates that environmental security itself is but one example of a dynamic occurring in many areas.

Post–Cold War Evolution of National Security

National security is, almost by definition, the function that is the most critical for many national states. As in the case of environmental issues, this policy structure is evolving rapidly and, for those involved in the process, unpredictably. It is characteristic of the evolution of complex systems that their future states are unpredictable. That this basic principle is not as well understood as perhaps it should be is in large part a product of the way we perceive history. When we look back, it appears reasonable to us that the system should have evolved the way it did. If we look forward, as national security and environmental policymakers are now, the unpredictability is all too evident.[19] In particular, two major assumptions that have supported the traditional view of security—that the national state is relatively absolute and, since the beginning of the Cold War, that the conflict between capitalism and communism in various forms defined global geopolitics— are, at least in their absolute forms, becoming less valid.

Under these circumstances, the Cold War–operating definition of national security based on a bipolar world and primarily on military confrontation is for many too limited. Accordingly, a number of suggestions for expansion of the concept have been made, focusing primarily on economic security and environmental security.[20] This chapter focuses on environmental security, not economic security, which is to some extent analytically separable. From a conceptual perspective, at least, it seems true that if environmental issues and perturbations are strategic to a society, one would expect them to become a prominent dimension of national policy.[21]

National security issues arise, virtually by definition, in the context of the interests of a specific state. For that reason, and because interest in this concept has been high in U.S. policy circles, this chapter can focus on U.S. initiatives and interests. These initiatives and interests should be regarded as illustrative, however, both because they are in a very early stage of development and because conceptually similar approaches can be applied by any other state.

U.S. policy has indeed begun to evolve in response to these recent challenges. Thus, in 1996, the administration noted: "our current decisions regarding the environment and natural resources will affect the magnitude of their security risks over at least [twenty to thirty years]. . . . Even when making the most generous allowances for advances in science and technology, one cannot help but conclude that population growth and environmental pressures will feed into immense social unrest and make the world substantially more vulnerable to serious international frictions."[22] In a subsequent major speech at Stanford University on 9 April 1996, Secretary of State Warren Christopher noted that "our administration has recognized from the beginning that our ability to advance our global interests is inextricably linked to how we manage the Earth's natural resources," and accordingly recognized the need to "contend with the vast new danger posed to our national interests by damage to the environment and resulting global and regional instability." Secretary of State Madeleine Albright subsequently strongly reaffirmed that policy shift in *Environmental Diplomacy: The Environment and U. S. Foreign Policy:* "Not so long ago, many believed that the pursuit of clean air, clean water, and healthy forests was a worthy goal, but not part of our national *security.* Today environmental issues are part of the mainstream of American foreign policy."[23] Vice President Gore added that "Our foreign policy must now address a broad range of threats—including damage to the world's environment—that transcend countries and continents and require international cooperation to solve," and that this step represented "an important turning point in U.S. foreign policy—a change the President and I strongly support."[24] Thus, it is fair to conclude that, at least for the Clinton administration, the need for an environmental dimension to foreign policy is increasingly recognized and accepted (see chapter 4 of this volume).

It is less clear that the dimensions of this requirement, the means by which it can be institutionalized in existing policy structures, and the gradations between foreign policy concerns and national security interests have been adequately worked out. After all, there are many resource scarcities and environmental perturbations around the world, most of which will impact the United States only minimally. In 1995, for example, the National Science and Technology Council (NSTC) identified a number of potential issues, including climate change, ozone depletion, ocean pollution, and the possibility of "large numbers" of environmental refugees that it felt constituted "a broad class of global threats evident in the post–Cold War world [that would] affect our nation's security."[25] Unlike the State Department's *Environmental Diplomacy* report, which referenced "foreign policy," the NSTC report was titled *National Security Science and Technology Strategy.* Many, at least in the traditional security community, would take the position that this subject is overbroad for a national security agenda rather than just a foreign policy agenda. Incidents and issues in each of these areas might indeed raise security concerns, but clearly in most cases they will not.[26]

The root cause of this confusion appears to be threefold: (1) the understandable confusion that marks a period when previous policy regimes and structures are undergoing rapid change, as discussed above; (2) the ambiguity of the term *national security;* and (3) failure to draw a strong enough line between the broad category of foreign policy and the more restricted category of national security. To speak to the second point, it is apparent that *national security* itself is an ambiguous term: people tend to define it according to their internal mental models. Goldstone suggests a reasonable approach:

> There is only one meaningful definition of national security, and it is not inherently military, environmental, or anything else. Variations of that definition guided us throughout the cold war, and long before. That definition goes something like this: A "national security" issue is any trend or event that (1) threatens the very survival of the nation and/or (2) threatens to drastically reduce the welfare of the nation in a fashion that requires a centrally coordinated national mobilization of resources to mitigate or reverse. While this seems common sense, it is clear from this definition that not any threat or diminution of welfare constitutes a national security threat; what does constitute such a threat is a matter of perception, judgment, and degree.[27]

The ambiguity between foreign policy and security interests can be confusing; it is a fertile source of unnecessary disagreement between environmental and security communities. It is very important to differentiate between the perspectives of a global view—where one views human security or, more broadly, biological security as a whole—and of a national state view, which focuses on the interest of the state rather than on global systems (see figure 2.2). Within the context of the national state, it is also necessary at a minimum to differentiate further between national security issues and foreign policy issues. In general, situations that proximately involve national security as defined by a particular state will be only a subset of the broader totality of the foreign policy interests of the state.

In this regard, it is probably fair to say that most initial attempts to expand the Cold War concept of national security to include other dimensions, such as environment, have perhaps been too inclusive. Many considerations and issues have been included that realistically do not have significant potential to impact the security of the United States or its citizens substantially and adversely. For example, the NSTC *National Security Science* report includes promotion of "sustainable development" as a policy response; given the broad ambiguous and broad scope of this concept, it is difficult to identify environmental issues that would *not* be included.[28] Conversely, little consideration has been given to excluding issues that, even if they may have such impacts, may not be appropriately managed by the national security apparatus for a number of reasons, such as institutional capability.

For example, the Clinton administration has defined three goals in its national security strategy, including not just achieving the traditional military security

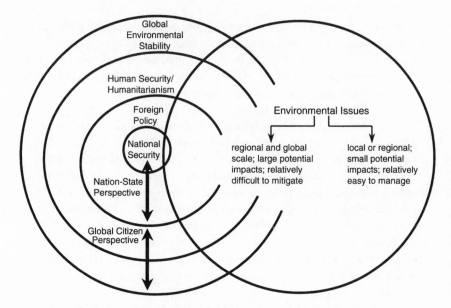

Figure 2.2.   The Intersection of Environmental and Security Issues.

goal but also "promoting prosperity at home," which explicitly includes the promotion of sustainable development and ultimately of democracy and stability.[29] This definition encompasses a broad range of potential threats and issues, including but not limited to economic development and trade. Moreover, by including the concept of sustainable development, virtually all regional or global environmental perturbations can be captured. Such expansive definitions of security have perhaps unnecessarily impeded acceptance of the fundamental legitimacy of the concept of environmental security, particularly in the security community, which tends to favor traditional military definitions.[30] Equally problematic, the failure to clarify issues and concerns can, as the trade example indicates, lead the environmental and national security communities to talk past each other and to become fixated on perceptual rather than real differences.

Accordingly, a more rigorous definition of the concept of environmental security is important, both because such a definition makes the concept easier to operationalize and because it increases the legitimacy of the concept, particularly with the national security community. Creating such a definition requires both a more robust intellectual structure and the integration of applicable science and technology with the policy structure (traditionally a weak point of the U.S. Department of State).[31] If nothing else, such understanding could reduce unnecessary conflict by identifying issues that can be resolved through empirical assessment and greater scientific and technological knowledge, without recourse to ideological conflict. The following sections sketch out one way in which this understanding might be accomplished.

Institutional Aspects of Environmental Security

At least the potential clash in underlying cultures between environmentalists and members of the national security community is apparent. Environmental NGOs often tend to be liberal, open, and nonhierarchical. They also tend to have a global rather than the national state perspective, as well as some aversion to technology and traditional military activities. Conversely, the national security community in most countries is conservative, insular, heavily focused on military threats and challenges, secretive, and powerful; it also tends to focus on short-term, obvious problems. Culturally, such security communities are among the least likely to embrace environmental considerations and, when they do, to do so only in a mission-oriented context.[32]

Beyond the question of different institutional cultures lies another often overlooked factor: institutional capacity. Even if an environmental perturbation may pose a significant threat to a national state, it may still not be a national security issue if it falls outside the competency and culture of the national security community and its component institutions. For example, assume for argument's sake that anthropogenic global climate change is both real and can be shown to have such substantial negative impacts on the United States that it clearly meets usual operational definitions of national security threats. An argument can still be made that it is not a "national security" issue, although it may have relevant dimensions.[33] In this case, the scientific and technological research and development capabilities necessary to understand and respond to the phenomenon would reside broadly throughout the civilian research community, not within traditional security organizations (the Department of Defense and the CIA, for example). Moreover, the scientific process most likely to result in rapid development and deployment of relevant knowledge would be the traditional one of open dialog and peer review, not the more secretive one that tends to characterize science and technology within the security community. The National Science Foundation, not the Department of Defense, would be institutionally and culturally better positioned to support such a program, which does not mean that the security establishment might not have some specific concerns. For example, would any critical allies or areas of the world likely be destabilized by sea-level rise? It does mean that the issue, taken as a whole, is not best managed by the security community, nor viewed in its totality as a "national security" issue.

To ensure that these cultural and institutional capability issues are captured, a three-part test to determine whether an environmental issue or perturbation should be considered an environmental security issue may thus be proposed:

1. Are the potential impacts of the environmental perturbation in question substantial enough to be considered a national security threat?
2. Are the links between the environmental threat and the relevant impact(s) relatively certain and proximate?
3. Even if the environmental threat is substantial, certain, and proximate, is the national security apparatus institutionally and culturally the most capable of mounting an effective response? And if so, to all or only to selected dimensions of the threat?

An Environmental Security Taxonomy

Given this test, the next question is whether it is possible to define the concept better, making it both easier to implement and less contentious ideologically. In doing so, it will be important both to recognize the role of and to enhance the development of appropriate science and technology (S&T) capabilities. This recognition will also support the creation of a filter mechanism that can provide at least a conceptual taxonomy to enable issue identification and prioritization. Resources, financial and human, are always constrained. Common sense thus dictates the policy principle that, all things being equal, investment in relevant S&T should be directed primarily at creating a targeted S&T base to support specific critical elements of the environmental security mission, rather than be scattered across all potential foreign policy issues.

There are any number of ways to generate an analytical framework that supports the evolution of the environmental security concept into operational programs and projects. One useful way is to view the concept as an amalgam of four conceptually separate components: resource security, energy security, environmental security, and biological security ("REEB"; see figure 2.3).

1. *Resource security* involves both local or regional competition for scarce resources and patterns of resource flows and use. Resource issues in either category become a resource security concern if they have the potential to give rise to political or military conflict of security concern to the relevant state. Current examples include competition for water resources in areas such as the Middle East;[34] the dispensation of arable land in areas such as Chiapas, Mexico;[35] or the management of flows of nuclear materials to avoid proliferation of weapons of mass destruction.[36]

2. *Energy security* involves the identification and maintenance of access to energy sources necessary to support the continuation of economic and military activities of the United States. Although military conflict deriving at least in part from competition over secure energy sources has already occurred (e.g., the Gulf War), public interest in energy security as an issue has waned because many people assume that energy security is already assured or too expensive to maintain.[37] Energy markets are, however, increasingly unstable, and thus energy

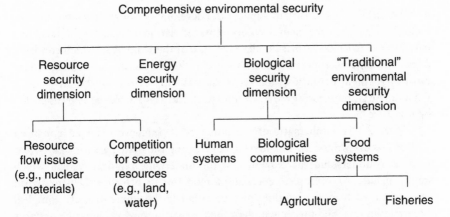

Figure 2.3. Dimensions of Environmental Security.

Environmental security as a category can be parsed into several dimensions, thus facilitating analysis and reducing unnecessary confusion.

security must be regarded as an increasing concern, especially as global economic activity and concomitant competition for energy resources accelerate.[38]

3. *Environmental security* involves the maintenance of environmental systems whose disruption would likely create national security concerns for the relevant state. Examples might include releases of nuclear material in one state that substantially impact other states,[39] or environmental degradation in one locality that is so intense as to generate substantial population migration or other dangerous conditions in other states.[40]

4. *Biological security* involves maintaining the health and stability of critical biological systems whose disruption would likely create national security implications for the United States. The two most obvious classes of systems are human populations and food systems, including crops, livestock, and fisheries. A less-obvious class consists of biological communities of various kinds, such as wetlands, forests, or critical habitat, which frequently provide important "natural infrastructure" functions, such as flood control or fisheries breeding areas. A particularly difficult set of issues in this latter class arises when activity in one country affects an internal biological community, whose disruption has extraterritorial effects. Thus, for example, deforestation of the upper reaches of a watershed for a major river might reduce the ability of that biological community to absorb and retard storm water, in turn generating unprecedented flooding in downstream nations (as with India and Bangladesh).

This particular way of parsing environmental security is obviously reflective of underlying physical and biological systems. It thus makes apparent the need to build an S&T capability to support the development of the resource, energy, biological, and environmental components of national security. In fact, this parallels the national security policy structure of the Cold War, which consisted of two closely linked primary components: an S&T base that provided military capability, threat definition, and technological support for collaborative threat reduction (e.g., monitoring treaty compliance); and a policy component supported by that base.[41]

Figure 2.4 is a schematic of the policy/S&T framework for an enhanced national security mission. The first step in creating the S&T base for a particular issue is to understand the dynamics of the underlying physical system, which might include, for example, generating a model of its behavior. Depending on the system, such model building may be either fairly simple or quite complex. For example, one might wish to understand potential future precipitation patterns and water-management systems in Asia as part of a confidence-building program with the goal of ensuring that crop failures and food shortages do not result in destabilizing population migrations.[42] Such a model would need to include a number of submodels covering a wide spatial and temporal scale (see figure 2.5).[43]

As understanding of the system is gained, metrics by which one can track and evaluate its evolution over time can be developed. Ideally, such metrics will be supported by sensor systems providing real-time system dynamics data and will offer the ability to predict when the system might be approaching instability. This prediction is particularly important because human systems tend to be predicated on the assumed stability of underlying natural systems, and much human effort is essentially aimed at engineering such stability in inherently variable systems. Thus, for example, much of the manipulation of rivers in the Middle East is intended to stabilize their annual supply of water at the highest possible level (these riverine systems are by nature highly unstable), as well as to expropriate as much of the resource as possible.[44] Instabilities in natural systems— such as precipitation patterns, changes in groundwater flow, or other perturbations that either increase the interannual variability or reduce the amount of water that can be reliably produced—can under these circumstances generate the potential for resource scarcity conflict.

Finally, understanding the physical systems relevant to a possible security issue provides an opportunity for development of mitigation technologies and strategies before the potential conflict develops. In fact, with luck, the issue can be identified, defined, and resolved within the context of a collaborative S&T effort without rising to the policy dimension at all. For example, if crop failure resulting from changes in precipitation patterns is a concern, an entire set of mitigation efforts is possible, depending on the timescale. With several years' warning, new crops and cultivars can be introduced that are more robust under the predicted conditions. Even with less warning, water recycling, demand reduction, and water-storage technologies can be deployed. Appropriate food transpor-

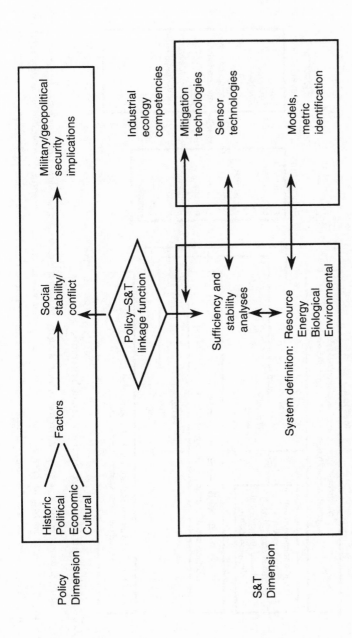

Figure 2.4. Industrial Ecology Environmental Security Model.

In general, environmental security considerations will be only one component of a complex reality. Nonetheless, by identifying and segregating issues that can be addressed through deployment of science and technology (S&T), the potential for conflict may be reduced. Note in particular the need to ensure that policy and environmental security S&T are coordinated: for a number of reasons, this linkage is difficult to develop and maintain.

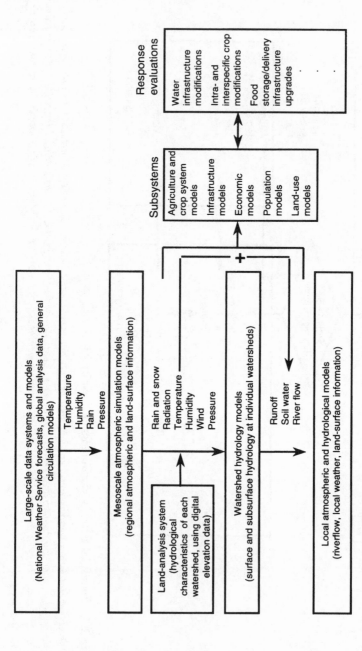

Figure 2.5. Hydrologic/Agriculture System Model Schematic.

The science and technology required to support environmental security policies is not trivial, as this example shows. It involves understanding systems that operate at very different temporal and spatial scales, and the appropriate response can be very complex as well. Source: B. R. Allenby, "Environmental Security: Concept and Implementation," International Political Science Review 21, no. 1 (2000), 17.

tation, storage, and distribution facilities can be prepared. Other countries could respond by planting more grain for export to buffer the anticipated additional demand.

One would anticipate that the above process will be only a part of the policy response because it is likely that in many cases the national security effects of perturbations will arise only when they occur in conjunction with more traditional indicators of national state instability.[45] This conjunction, however, offers its own challenge, as experience indicates that the linkage between the S&T and policy dimensions, although conceptually apparent, is frequently weak or less effectual than possible.[46] It is therefore worth emphasizing at the outset the need to establish a clear linkage function between the S&T and policy dimensions (as in figure 2.4).

An environmental security taxonomy such as suggested here can also be used to develop methods to identify and prioritize potential environmental security issues. To begin with, the regions of primary interest to a state can be combined with the classes of issues discussed above to generate a space of potential concerns. The number of these concerns can be winnowed down using both general principles and case-specific assessment. Environmental insults that are of long duration, have broad and severe geographic impacts, and are technically difficult and expensive to mitigate will be of more concern than others, ceteris paribus.[47] Using such guidelines, it is possible to construct a matrix linking five geographic areas of self-evident critical geopolitical interest to the United States—China, Mexico, the former Soviet Union, Southeast Asia (including India and Pakistan), and the Middle East—with the four REEB categories (see table 2.2). Within this framework, examples of issues that would appear to be the most pressing are identified. Similar matrices could easily be generated for other countries.

Conclusion

Environmental security is a concept reflecting both the increased complexity and challenge of anthropogenic environmental perturbations and the post–Cold War geopolitical environment. It is increasingly discussed as a component of national policy in countries such as the United States, but is yet both somewhat ill-defined and contentious. This discussion has therefore suggested a test by which issues fitting that category may be identified, proposed a more rigorous definition of the components of the enhanced national security mission, and illustrated a way in which these two processes can be easily used to identify and prioritize potential environmental security issues. This is only a beginning; in particular, continued dialog and understanding among stakeholders, both within and among national states and international institutions, should be encouraged. Managing a more complex world is neither trivial nor impossible, but it is a difficult challenge, as questions of environmental security demonstrate.

Region	Resource security	Energy security	Environmental security	Biological security

China	nuclear materials
	commodity
	  consumption patterns
	water
		petroleum demand
		petroleum supply
		nuclear energy systems
			environmental costs
			  of economic growth
			environmental refugees
				crop stability and
				  food-demand growth
				population stability

Mexico	water
	land distribution
			environmental costs
			  of economic growth
			  refugees
				crop stability
				pathogen systems
				population stability

Former
Soviet Union
	nuclear materials	nuclear energy–
		  production technology
			environmental costs of
			  economic growth
			nuclear waste issues
				population stability

Southeast Asia	nuclear materials water	petroleum demand petroleum supply nuclear energy systems	environmental refugees	pathogen systems crop stability and food-demand growth
Middle East	nuclear materials water	petroleum supply	environmental refugees	

Table 2.2.   Environmental Security Prioritization: U.S. Perspective.

This matrix presents a simple way in which potential environmental security issues can be identified. Although this illustrative schematic is based on a U.S. perspective, the method can be expanded and deployed by any state.

Notes

1 I wish to thank Deborah Petrocy for assistance in compiling the tables and figures for this chapter. The opinions expressed are mine, not necessarily those of AT&T, Columbia University, or Lawrence Livermore National Laboratory.

2 Braden R. Allenby, "Environmental Security as a Case Study in Industrial Ecology," *Journal of Industrial Ecology* 2, no. 1 (1998): 45–60; Jessica T. Mathews, "Redefining Security," *Foreign Affairs* 68 (1989): 162–77.

3 See, e.g., B. L. Turner, W. C. Clark, R. W. Kates, J. F. Richards, J. T. Mathews, and W. B. Meyer, eds., *The Earth As Transformed by Human Action* (Cambridge: Cambridge University Press, 1990); Lawrence Livermore National Laboratory, *Industrial Ecology: Energy and Transportation, Engineering, Modeling, and Environment*, UCRL-LR-124625 (Livermore, Calif.: LLNL, 1996).

4 See, e.g., P. F. Drucker, "The Global Economy and the Nation-State," *Foreign Affairs* 76, no. 5 (1997): 159–71; T. Judt, "The Social Question *Redivivus*," *Foreign Affairs* 76, no. 5 (1997): 95–117; J. T. Mathews, "Power Shift," *Foreign Affairs* 76, no. 1 (1997): 50–66; W. B. Wriston, "Bits, Bytes, and Diplomacy," *Foreign Affairs* 76, no. 5 (1997): 172–82.

5 This pattern is not often recognized. The climate change negotiations, for example, assume the same primacy of nation-states that has marked the past several hundred years of diplomacy, despite the obvious importance of firms, nongovernmental organizations, and geographical and interest communities to any viable outcome. See B. R. Allenby, *Industrial Ecology: Policy Framework and Implementation* (Upper Saddle River, N.J.: Prentice-Hall, 1999); R. Cooper, *The Post-modern State and the World Order*, Paper No. 19 (London: Demos, 1996); S. Sassens, *Losing Control: Sovereignty in an Age of Globalization* (New York: Columbia University Press, 1996); Mathews, "Power Shift."

6 Allenby, *Industrial Ecology*. The difficulty of generating policy structures whose timescale is the same as the environmental perturbations that they are intended to address is discussed throughout L. H. Gunderson, C. S. Holling, and S. S. Light, eds., *Barriers and Bridges to the Renewal of Ecosystems and Institutions* (New York: Columbia University Press, 1995).

7 See Gunderson, Holling, and Light, eds., *Barriers;* Allenby, *Industrial Ecology.* The concept of "adaptive management" introduced in Gunderson, Holling, and Light is not limited to the firm or to NGOs, but is intended as a new mechanism for managing complex systems.

8 Indeed, this dynamic is a principal driver behind the evolution of the new field of industrial ecology and of the implementation of industrial ecology principles through such practices as Design for Environment (DFE) and Life Cycle Assessment (LCA). B. R. Allenby and D. J. Richards, eds., *The Greening of Industrial Ecosystems* (Washington, D.C.: National Academy Press, 1994);

R. Socolow, C. Andrews, F. Berkhout, and V. Thomas, eds., *Industrial Ecology and Global Change* (Cambridge: Cambridge University Press, 1994); T. E. Graedel and B. R. Allenby, *Industrial Ecology* (Upper Saddle River, N.J.: Prentice-Hall, 1995); Allenby, "Environmental Security." Interestingly enough, the U.S. Department of Defense, in collaboration with the U.S. Environmental Protection Agency and Department of Energy, has a research program that looks at how industrial ecology principles may be applied to military operations and systems (the Strategic Environmental Research and Development Program, or SERDP). See SERDP Scientific Advisory Board, *Annual Report to Congress: Fiscal Year 1997* (Washington, D.C.: SERDP, 1998).

9 The degree to which institutions, as well as individuals, have limited perception, especially during periods of rapid and discontinuous change, is generally not appreciated. See, generally, N. Luhmann, *Ecological Communications*, trans. J. Bednarz Jr. (Chicago: University of Chicago Press, 1989).

10 See Gunderson, Holling, and Light, eds., *Barriers*.

11 R. V. Hartwell III and L. Bergkamp, "Environmental Trade Barriers and International Competitiveness," *Environmental Law Review* 24 (1994): 10109–115.

12 R. Repetto, "Trade and Environmental Policies: Achieving Complementarities and Avoiding Conflicts," in *WRI Issues and Ideas* (Washington, D.C.: WRI, July 1993).

13 A. C. Raul and P. E. Hagen, "The Convergence of Trade and Environmental Law," *Natural Resources and Environment* 8, no. 2 (1993): 3 *et seq.*

14 For an accessible treatment of the atmospheric science, see M. B. McElroy and R. J. Salawitch, "Changing Composition of the Global Atmosphere," *Science* 243 (1989): 763–70; for a broader treatment including possible biological effects, see, e.g., University Corporation for Atmospheric Research (UCAR), *Reports to the Nation on Our Changing Planet: Our Ozone Shield* (Boulder, Colo.: UCAR, 1992).

15 E. T. Morehouse Jr., "Preventing Pollution and Seeking Environmentally Preferable Alternatives in the U. S. Air Force," in Allenby and Richards, eds., *Greening*, 149–64.

16 Ibid.

17 Ibid.

18 See 10 U.S. C. Sec. 2901.

19 See chapter 9, "Complex Systems," in Allenby, *Industrial Ecology*, 131–46. The increasing complexity of the modern environment for decision makers raises a number of issues regarding institutional competency that are generally not recognized or appreciated. In business, for example, the inadequacy of the individual to manage dynamic complexity has led to the concept of the "learning organization," an idea that few firms have been able to understand, let alone implement. See, e.g., P. M. Senge and J. D. Sterman, *Systems*

Thinking and Organizational Learning: Acting Locally and Thinking Globally in the Organization of the Future (Cambridge, Mass.: MIT Sloan School of Management).

20 See for example M. Renner, *National Security: The Economic and Environmental Dimensions*, Worldwatch Paper no. 89 (Washington, D.C.: Worldwatch, 1989); Executive Office of the President, *A National Security Strategy of Engagement and Enlargement* (Washington, D.C.: Executive Office of the President, 1996); U. S. Department of State, *Environmental Diplomacy: The Environment and Foreign Policy*, Department of State Publication no. 10470 (Washington, D.C.: Department of State, 1997); Mathews, "Redefining Security." The executive office publication speaks of "national security," whereas the Department of State refers to "environmental diplomacy." Nonetheless, the environmental issues identified by the executive office as part of a "national security" strategy—which include degradation of air, water, land, fisheries, and other resources; drought; pollution; deforestation; loss of biodiversity; ozone depletion; desertification; ocean pollution; climate change; and population growth—are so broad and encompassing that one is challenged to identify an environmental issue of any consequence that is *not* listed (26). To some extent, then, these two documents can be read as demonstrating that the necessary boundary between what is critical for the United States—a security issue—and what is merely good and useful to do—a diplomacy issue—has yet to be drawn.

21 T. Homer-Dixon, J. H. Boutwell, and G. W. Rathjens, "Environmental Change and Violent Conflict," *Scientific American* (February 1993): 38–45; T. Homer-Dixon, "Environmental Scarcities and Violent Conflict: Evidence from Cases," *International Security* 19, no. 1 (1994): 5–40; B. R. Allenby, T. J. Gilmartin, and R. F. Lehman II, eds., *Environmental Threats and National Security: An International Challenge to Science* (Livermore, Calif.: Lawrence Livermore National Laboratory, 1998); Mathews, "Redefining Security."

22 Executive Office of the President, *National Security Strategy*, 26.

23 U. S. Department of State, *Environmental Diplomacy*, 2.

24 Ibid., 1.

25 U. S. National Science and Technology Council (NSTC), *National Security Science and Technology Strategy* (Washington, D.C.: NSTC, 1995).

26 See, e.g., M. Levy, "Time for a Third Wave of Environment and Security Scholarship?" *Environmental Change and Security Project Report* 1 (spring 1995): 44–46; M. Levy, "Debate," *Environmental Change and Security Project Report* 2 (spring 1996): 58–60. This concern was also apparent in my discussions of this issue during my tenure at Lawrence Livermore National Laboratory.

27 J. A. Goldstone, "Debate," *Environmental Change and Security Project Report* 2 (spring 1996): 66–71, at 66.

28 National Science and Technology Council, *National Security Science*, 45–47; on the ambiguity of the sustainable-development concept, see Allenby, *Industrial Ecology*, chap. 3.

29 Executive Office of the President, *National Security Strategy*.

30 R. Fleishman, "Environmental Security: Concept and Practice," *National Security Studies Quarterly* (summer 1995): 11–16; Levy, "Debate," *supra* n. 26.

31 A. Lawler, "State Department Sees S&T Weakness," *Science* 280 (1998): 998–99; A. K. Solomon, "The Science and Technology–Bereft Department of State," *Science* 282 (1998): 1649–50; D. Malakoff, "Gibbons Joins Effort to Boost Science at State," *Science* 286 (1999): 391.

32 For example, an initial Department of Defense report on environmental security deals almost completely with short-term issues that might impact unit readiness, and, based on my experience as a member of the Strategic Environmental Research and Development Program Scientific Advisory Board, that program focuses, at best, on pollution prevention, despite its stated goal of addressing "environmental security" concerns. U. S. Department of Defense, Office of the Under Secretary of Defense, Acquisition and Technology, *Report of the Defense Science Board Task Force on Environmental Security* (Washington, D.C.: Defense Science Board, 1995); SERDP Scientific Advisory Board, *Annual Report to Congress*.

33 See, for example, the World Resources Institute discussion of global climate change: although the concept of energy security is raised, the scope of the discussion clearly indicates that a targeted, national security type of research program would be entirely inadequate to the scale and complexity of the research and development required to respond to that phenomenon. J. J. MacKenzie, *Climate Protection and the National Interest: The Links among Climate Change, Air Pollution, and Energy Security* (Washington, D.C.: World Resources Institute, 1997).

34 See, e.g., D. M. Liverman and K. L. O'Brien, "Global Warming and Climate Change in Mexico," *Global Environmental Change* (1991): 351–64. P. H. Gleick, "Water and Conflict," *International Security* 18, no. 1 (1993): 79–112; K. Kelley and T. Homer-Dixon, *Environmental Scarcity and Violent Conflict: The Case of Gaza* (Toronto: AAAS/University of Toronto, 1995).

35 P. Howard and T. Homer-Dixon, *Environmental Scarcity and Violent Conflict: The Case of Chiapas, Mexico* (Toronto: AAAS/University of Toronto, 1995).

36 See, e.g., Center for Strategic and International Studies (CSIS) Global Organized Crime Project, *The Nuclear Black Market* (Washington, D.C.: CSIS, 1996); V. Percival and T. Homer-Dixon, *Environmental Scarcity and Violent Conflict: The Case of South Africa* (Toronto: AAAS/University of Toronto, 1995); V. Percival and T. Homer-Dixon, *Environmental Scarcity and Violent Conflict: The Case of Rwanda* (Toronto: AAAS/University of Toronto, 1995).

37 See, e.g., V. A. Stagliano, "The Ghost of OPEC in Energy Security Policy," *Resources* (spring 1995): 6–9.

38 K. E. Calder, "Asia's Empty Tank," *Foreign Affairs* 75, no. 2 (1996): 55–69; J. J. Romm and C. B. Curtis, "Mideast Oil Forever," *Atlantic Monthly* (April 1996): 57–74.

39 There are a number of reasons why nuclear material flows are difficult to manage. Some involve past social priorities: when national survival is deemed to be at stake, experience demonstrates that environmental issues come a distant second to operational ones. Some involve the policy and institutional structures within which nuclear materials are managed: in particular, the mix of relatively open commercial and highly secretive military domains through which nuclear materials migrate is a significant barrier to the communication and information systems required for rational management of such flows. Managing and mitigating the resultant waste streams and inadvertent contamination are difficult and expensive processes. See D. J. Bradley, C. W. Frank, and Y. Mikerin, "Nuclear Contamination from Weapons Complexes in the Former Soviet Union and the United States," *Physics Today* (April 1996): 40–45; J. K. Schafer, T. H. Isaacs, and L. D. Ramspott, "Nuclear Materials," in Allenby, Gilmartin, and Lehman, eds., *Environmental Threats*, 267–80.

40 P. Gizewski and T. Homer-Dixon, *Environmental Scarcity and Violent Conflict: The Case of Pakistan* (Toronto: AAAS/University of Toronto, 1996).

41 R. F. Lehman II, personal communication, 4 October 1999.

42 Progress is already being made in linking new understanding of climactic patterns, such as the El Niño and Southern Oscillation (ENSO) events, with potential mitigation efforts. R. Showstack, "Scientists Aim to Translate El Niño Data into Mitigation Efforts," *Eos* 78, no. 39 (1997): 417 *et seq.*

43 In this sense, the S&T base required for environmental security can be understood as a component of the broader effort to develop the capability to engineer earth systems, and economic and social systems can be seen as integrated entities. B. R. Allenby, "Earth Systems Engineering: The Role of Industrial Ecology in an Engineered World," *Journal of Industrial Ecology* 2, no. 3 (1999): 73–93.

44 P. H. Gleick, "Water in Southern Africa and the Middle East," in Allenby, Gilmartin, and Lehman, eds., *Environmental Threats*, 189–204.

45 See Homer-Dixon, Boutwell, and Rathjens, "Environmental Change"; G. D. Dabelko and P. J. Simmons, "Environment and Security," in Allenby, Gilmartin, and Lehman, eds., *Environmental Threats*, 19–34.

46 Although the United States has recognized that there has been a dramatic increase in the number of foreign policy issues requiring S&T competence, it has proven difficult in practice to strengthen the linkage between foreign policy and national security, on the one hand, and relevant S&T capabilities on the other.

47 See, generally, Allenby, *Industrial Ecology*.

3 Environmental Security and U.S. Foreign Policy: A Critical Examination

Jon Barnett

The United States is the world's largest economy, has the world's largest military, and produces more greenhouse gases than any other country. For this reason, the ways in which the United States engages with the problem of environmental degradation are crucial for the survival of the planet. Importantly, the concept of environmental security is now integral to the environmental diplomacy of the United States, and a number of its policy pronouncements have been informed by the notion of environmental security. This chapter seeks to discuss these pronouncements from a broad critical and normative perspective. It focuses on the U.S. National Security Strategy, the U.S. Department of Defense, and the U.S. Department of State. It argues that the United States selectively interprets environmental security to justify its traditional approach to world affairs, but that there is nevertheless some positive potential in this incorporation of environmental security into foreign policy.

The Concept of Environmental Security

The notion of environmental security is contested.[1] It is a function of the confla-tion of the two terms—*environment* and *security*—that are themselves imprecise. One of the pervasive difficulties with environmental security is a lack of agreement on the definition of the problem that it supposedly addresses. In this sense, environmental security is the answer to an unspecified question.[2] The problem that environmental security addresses can be crudely categorized in three principally different, but not necessarily exclusive, ways. First, environmental degradation may impact on *national* security through transborder flows of hazardous sub-stances (the radioactive plume released after Chernobyl is an obvious example); a decrease in the health of a nation's populace (from toxins in the food chain, cancers arising from ozone depletion, vector-borne diseases, and so on); a decline in the natural capital base for economic activity (less timber, oil, genetic diversity, water, and so on); influxes of environmental refugees; domestic unrest because of declining economic growth and struggles over increasingly scarce environmental resources; declining access to markets and materials if environmental degradation contributes to civil strife in foreign markets; and the possibility of international conflicts over common property resources (fish and water are two common examples).[3] In this view, then, environmental security is one of a comprehensive array of sectoral threats to *national* security. Understood in this way, environmental security is consistent with strategic concerns about warfare and territorial integrity. This first approach to environmental security, the *environment and security* view, is influenced by both political-realist and liberal international relations theory.[4]

A second way of conceiving of environmental security is as the risks that human activities pose to the health and resilience of the biosphere, which is sometimes referred to as *ecological security*.[5] Thus, biodiversity loss, climate change, deforestation, and even nuclear power are human-induced problems that threaten the functional integrity of the biosphere. Although consistent with deep green philosophy, few authors assert that this conception of environmental security is about protecting the rights of nature above the rights of humans. Instead, advocating security of the biosphere is seen as means to protect the habitat of all life forms, including humans, and to promote peace. Peace and environment are seen to be related because the domination and degradation of nature is both the means and by-product of the domination of people by more powerful people. This second approach is called the *securing the environment* view.[6]

Alternatively, in the approach that this chapter favors, environmental security can be seen as a problem for *human* security. This position is an essentially normative one asserting that environmental degradation has little meaning beyond that of the rights of present and future generations to live in a healthy and stable environment. The inverse concept of environmental *in*security is central to this approach, defined as the vulnerability of people to the effects of environmental degradation.[7] Environmental insecurity occurs wherever ecological problems exacerbate the social impact of economic processes affecting underdevelopment. Understood in this way, environmental insecurity is evident, for example, in the 3 million deaths per year from diarrheal diseases as a result of unsafe drinking water, in the estimated 20,000 pesticide-related deaths per year, and in the 4.7 million deaths per year from tuberculosis and malaria.[8] This approach has strong resonance with the notion of environmental justice.[9]

Beginning in 1983, but more significantly after the end of the Cold War, a number of articles relating environmental degradation to national security appeared in influential U.S. policy journals such as *International Security, Foreign Affairs, Atlantic Monthly,* and *Foreign Policy*.[10] Of these articles, Ullman's "Redefining Security" and Kaplan's "The Coming Anarchy" appear to have had the most influence on the shape of contemporary U.S. environmental security policy. According to Dalby, "Kaplan is in some ways a continuation of long-established lines of argument. But he is new in that his powerful articulation of environment as the cause of threats to national security has updated Malthusian themes and brought the 'environmental security' policy discussions forcefully to the attention of a wider public."[11]

Ullman's "Redefining Security" is not dissimilar in its discussion of Third World poverty as an engine for armed conflict and illegal immigration. He suggests that environmental degradation is "likely to make Third World governments more militarily confrontational in their relations with the advanced, industrialised nations."[12] Both Kaplan and Ullman have a particular view of environmental problems. Both downplay the differentiated impacts of inappropriate development that affect people, and both ignore the differences of responsibility for this underdevelopment, pollution, and resource depletion. Instead, environmental degradation is seen simply as an independent source of external danger to developed states, particularly the United States.

With such powerful articulations of environmental degradation as an instigator of outside threats to the United States, and with the high degree of compatibility between these theories and existing U.S. security theory, it is not surprising that U.S. foreign policy eventually took environmental security on board. Dabelko and Simmons set the context: "The number of U.S. government and scholarly endeavors exploring the issues of environment and security, or "environmental security," is proliferating. . . . Many senior figures in the Clinton Administration have embraced environment and security ideas. While these ideas have not produced a common policy agenda or focus, numerous rhetorical statements and government initiatives addressing the environment in the context of U.S. security interests have appeared since 1993."[13]

The Clinton administration has created a number of high-level positions to deal with matters of environmental security, including a senior director for global environmental affairs at the National Security Council, a national intelligence officer for global and multilateral issues at the National Intelligence Council, elevating environmental management to the level of deputy undersecretary within the Department of Defense and an undersecretary for global affairs within the Department of State.[14]

Recent statements and initiatives that incorporate the notion of environmental security can be loosely attributed to the National Security Strategy, the Department of Defense, and the Department of State. Given that these departments are mutually reinforcing and overlap in their promotion of U.S. security interests, this categorization should be seen as a loose one that helps facilitate discussion. The interpretation and deployment of environmental security by these three institutions are discussed in the next section.

The U.S. National Security Strategy (NSS)

The U.S. National Security Strategy (NSS) is the most important unclassified statement of U.S. security policy. The NSS has made reference to environmental degradation as a security issue since 1991, and it has figured in subsequent strategies, including the 1998 National Security Strategy titled *A National Security Strategy for a New Century*.[15] The overall tone of the 1998 NSS is established in its preface: "At this moment in history, the United States is called upon to lead— to organize the forces of freedom and progress; to channel the unruly energies of the global economy into positive avenues; and to advance our prosperity, reinforce our democratic ideals and values, and enhance our security" (iv). The goal of the National Security Strategy is "to ensure the protection of our nation's fundamental and enduring needs: protect the lives and safety of Americans, maintain the sovereignty of the United States with its values, institutions and territory intact, and promote the prosperity and well-being of the nation and its people" (5). Within this context, environmental issues are embedded within a suite of "new, complex challenges":

> The same forces that bring us closer increase our interdependence, and make us more vulnerable to forces like extreme nationalism, terrorism, crime, environmental damage and the complex flows of trade and investment that know no borders. (iii)

> We seek a cleaner global environment to protect the health and well-being of our citizens. A deteriorating environment not only threatens public health, it impedes economic growth and can generate tensions that threaten international stability. To the extent that other nations believe they must engage in non-sustainable exploitation of natural resources, our long term prosperity and security are at risk. (5)

> Crises are averted—and U.S. preventative diplomacy actively reinforced—through U.S. sustainable development programs that promote voluntary family planning, basic education, environmental protection, democratic governance and the rule of law, and the economic empowerment of private citizens. (8)

Environmental problems are mentioned in the second of the three categories of national interest described in the NSS. These categories prioritize issues of concern to the United States. The first category, *Vital Interests*, includes the maintenance of territorial integrity, economic well-being, and critical infrastructures, and all three are to be defended using military might "unilaterally and decisively" when necessary (5). The second category, *Important National Interests*, includes issues that do not affect national survival but do affect national well-being and "the character of the world in which we live" (5). Issues explicitly mentioned include the flow of refugees and the state of the global environment. In order to protect these important national interests, the United States will use its resources "insofar as the costs and risks are commensurate with the interests at stake" (5). "Resources" in this sense refers to the integration of foreign assistance, diplomatic, military, and intelligence capabilities. The third and least important category is *Humanitarian and Other Interests*, which includes providing disaster relief, supporting democratization, promoting development, and promoting human rights (5). Thus, environmental degradation is a second-tier security issue, and although dealing with this "Transnational Threat to U.S. Interests" (6) has not so far involved the use of force (diplomatic and legal mechanisms have been the preferred avenues), the use of force is not explicitly ruled out in the NSS.

That the environment figures in the NSS leaves no doubt that the environment is now a security issue for the United States. By virtue of the dominant influence of the United States in world affairs, all nations will need to be familiar with the concept of environmental security to navigate their way in the global political arena successfully. Although frequently global in name, the environmental security agenda is nevertheless one led by the United States. It is therefore extremely important to try to understand what U.S. policy means when it talks of environmental security. The NSS sees environmental degradation as a "threat" that is not distinguished from other sources of vulnerability such as extreme nationalism, terrorism, and crime. Indeed, environmental degradation is seen not merely as a threat, but also as a "danger" to U.S. security: "Environmental threats do not heed national borders and can pose long-term dangers to our security and well-being" (13). This presentation of environmental risks as threats and dangers likens the problem of environmental degradation to problems where harm is more deliberately imposed by Others from the outside. Further, the NSS normalizes environmental danger by likening it to an objective risk. However, all risks are subjective. What the NSS views as threatening and dangerous is only that which might threaten U.S. interests, such as an influx of environmental refugees or environmentally induced conflicts. Exactly how these perceived dangers threaten the United States is not made clear: they are existential rather than specific threats.

This construction of external dangers is integral to the delineation of Us from Other and to the subsequent engendering of the nation.[16] Hence, the question "Insecurity how?" is never adequately answered in the NSS. At least part of the answer is that the foreign policy community is still fundamentally concerned about environmental degradation restricting "access to foreign markets" and undermining "American competitiveness" (both subsections of the 1998 NSS). Thus, rather than being the primary concern, environmental insecurity can be read as coda for the metaconcern of declining opportunities for economic growth.

The environmental security perspective of the NSS is strongly linked with the "environment and security" view. This is not surprising given that Kaplan's "Coming Anarchy" "played a catalytic role in bringing the environment-conflict thesis to the attention of the highest levels of the Clinton Administration and the larger Washington policy community."[17] In the first instance, the NSS is concerned with "natural resource scarcities" that "often trigger and exacerbate conflict" (13). This influence of the environment-conflict thesis on U.S. national security thinking was underlined by Eileen Claussen, former senior director for global environment affairs at the National Security Council: "From my perspective, the environment and security relationship builds in part on important linkages between resource scarcity and conflict."[18] Further, President Clinton has referred to the likely outcome of "terrorism, tension and war" if environmental degradation is not halted.[19] However, despite an extensive literature on the subject, it is by no means clear that environmental degradation will result in any increase in violence, particularly between nation-states.[20]

References in the NSS to "stability" (and hence instability) are assumed to mean a concern for violent conflict (reflecting the influence of realist theory), but also more for general political unrest and hence disturbances in the operation of the global market (reflecting the influence of liberal theory). Yet the most frequent and most probable forms of international conflict are not likely to involve direct violence, but will instead take the form of exacerbated diplomatic and trading tensions between North and South—which will arise from the deprivations generated by the U.S.-led global economy—superimposed on the tensions of environmental diplomacy.[21] Such tensions may yet escalate if the United States is careless in its engagement with the South as it seeks to secure the environmental interests it perceives to be important. The NSS can be read as a discursive primer for more cavalier forms of engagement, as suggested by the aforementioned reference to those "nations [that] believe they must engage in non-sustainable exploitation of natural resources" and that are seen to present risks to U.S. security and prosperity (5).

That these nonsustainable resource uses are clearly seen as a threat to U.S. security again reflects the influence of the "environment and security" approach of the NSS. So, according to the NSS, "Environmental threats such as climate change, ozone depletion and the transnational movement of hazardous chemicals and waste directly threaten the health of U.S. citizens" (13). Thus, the United States is the central referent object of security, and ecological and humanitarian problems that transpire outside the United States are of secondary importance. This attitude reflects an ongoing problem of viewing environmental degradation from within the national frame of reference as established by Kaplan and Ullman. Insofar as there is some truth to the "global" nature of environmental degradation, this state-centered approach leads to diminished policy.[22] For example, the NSS has a subsection on "promoting sustainable development abroad" as a means to enhance U.S. interests, but much less is said about promoting sustainable development at home despite the enormous contribution of the United States to environmental change.[23]

There is a danger that what the United States ostensibly appears to fear most (refugees and conflicts) is likely to be reified by its own national security policy discourse. From the perspective of those in the South, the contradictions of injustice exposed by the environmental insecurity of the many requires not a defense of northern territory and prosperity, but a radical and profound change in modern institutions and beliefs. In dialectical terms, the security/defense discourse of the NSS turns a blind eye to these contradictions and the immanent possibility of radical change. The long-term success of such a strategy is an open question, but what is more certain is that continuing to defend U.S. prosperity will see more exploitation of people and ecosystems in the industrializing world and consequently more insecurity for the many in the name of the security of the few.

Despite these problems, the 1998 NSS is notably more benign and informed with respect to environmental problems than the 1996 and 1997 strategies. The 1996 NSS went so far as to countenance the possibility that there might be competition between nations for "dwindling reserves of uncontaminated air."[24] Although the context of the 1998 NSS is still very much national security from threats emanating from the outside, there is significantly greater awareness of the measures required to promote environmental security as human security, including increasing aid and promoting family planning and education. The NSS also aims to implement the Program of Action on population growth developed at the 1995 Cairo conference, and it seeks to achieve Senate ratification of the Convention on Biodiversity, the Convention on the Law of the Sea, and the Convention to Combat Desertification. So, however rhetorical the understanding and however questionable its achievements, the 1998 NSS nevertheless demonstrates a more sophisticated understanding of the causes of environmental degradation and of the means to lessen them than did its predecessors. This is a welcome sign of a gradual shift in the approach of the United States to global environmental problems.

Counterbalancing these positive developments, however, is an increasingly strong free-trade agenda (between 1996 and 1998) that was arguably contrary to the goals of environmental security. Economic and energy security still take priority over environmental security in the U.S. strategic vision. Also of concern is the repeated reference in the NSS to the need to promote "American values" as a means to enhance "both our security and prosperity" (2), suggesting not merely an intolerance of difference, but the desire to impose uniformity as a security imperative. Given that the United States is the biggest consumer and polluter in the international community, a world shaped in its image would be far from environmentally secure. Finally, it is alarming that the United States considers that its nuclear weapons "serve as a hedge against an uncertain future, a guarantee of our security commitments to allies and a disincentive to those who would contemplate developing or otherwise acquiring their own nuclear weapons" (12).

The U.S. Department of Defense (DOD)

In his 1995 annual report to Congress, the U.S. secretary of defense asserted that "environmental security is now an essential part of the U.S. defense mission and a high priority for DOD."[25] The involvement of the U.S. Department of Defense (DOD) in environmental security began in 1990 when Senator Sam Nunn, chair of the Senate Armed Forces Committee, said: "There is a new and different threat to our national security emerging—the destruction of our environment. The defense establishment has a clear stake in countering this growing threat. I believe that one of our key national security objectives must be to reverse the accelerating pace of environmental destruction around the globe."[26]

Nunn used a particular discursive strategy, namely the reference to "global" environmental problems as *threats*, therefore implicitly justifying military involvement in defense. However, it is less than obvious how the U.S. military might help reverse the accelerating pace of environmental destruction around the globe. There are potential roles for the military with respect to environmental degradation, but none justify continued high levels of expenditure on the military, and few would make a genuine contribution to reducing environmental degradation.[27]

Also in 1990, then senator Al Gore published a paper calling for a Strategic Environment Initiative (SEI).[28] Gore stated that "the global environment has ... become an issue of national security" and proposed that what was required was "a mobilization of talent and resources usually reserved only for the purposes of national defense."[29] Gore is one of the most thoughtful of high-level officials speaking on environmental security. He argued that radical changes in the meaning and implementation of development are required if environmental degradation is to be halted. His SEI proposal was consistent with the policy integration idea of sustainable development in that it sought to cut across all policy sectors. He identified energy research and development policy as the sector most urgently requiring reform, seeking to reverse the funding priorities of the U.S. Department of Energy, which in 1990 devoted two-thirds of its budget to defense-related programs and only one-fifth for energy research and development.[30] However, Gore was reluctant to draw on funds from defense to finance environmental policies. This reluctance explains in part why his otherwise commonsense proposals were ultimately reduced to a set of narrow military and foreign policy responses.

Following Nunn's and Gore's appeals, in November 1990 the U.S. Congress allocated U.S.$200 million to the Strategic Environmental Research and Development Program (SERDP) operated by the Department of Defense.[31] The aim of SERDP is "to harness some of the resources of the defense establishment ... to confront the massive environmental problems facing our nation and the world today."[32] It has four functions: (1) to promote research of relevance to the DOD and the Department of Energy (DOE) to enable them to meet their environmental obligations; (2) to identify outcomes of this research and technologies developed by the DOD and DOE, which "would be useful" (read saleable) to other governmental and private organizations; (3) to supply other governmental and private organizations with data and data-handling mechanisms for use in environment-related research and development; and (4) to identify technologies developed by the private sector that might be of use for the DOD and the DOE.[33] The implicit function of the SERDP seems therefore to make sure that DOD and DOE compliance with environmental regulations is cost effective and that any potential marketing possibilities from DOD and DOE research and development are exploited. This commercial function is revealed by then secretary of defense William Perry's report to Congress: "The Department's [technology] strategy is to . . . expedite the use and commercialization of these technologies."[34]

In 1993, the Department of Defense upgraded the division responsible for environmental matters to the level of deputy undersecretary. The division's official title is the Office of the Deputy Under Secretary of Defense (Environmental Security) (DUSD[ES]), subordinate to the Office of the Deputy Under Secretary of Defense for Acquisition, Technology, and Logistics. Initially, DOD involvement in environmental matters was domestically oriented and not linked to security as such. This involvement began in 1984 with the establishment of the Defense Environmental Restoration Account.[35] A number of legislative acts progressively forced the DOD and the DOE to comply with environmental legislation. The two most important were the 1986 Superfund Amendments and Reauthorization Act and the Federal Facilities Environmental Compliance Act of 1992.[36] Hence, much of the impetus for the DOD's environmental activities was not internally driven but externally imposed.

This imposition of compliance is clearly revealed in the first of the DUSD(ES)'s "overriding and interconnected goals," which is "to comply with the law."[37] The other three goals are:

To support the military readiness of the U.S. armed forces by ensuring continued access to the air, land and water needed for training and testing;
To improve the quality of life of military personnel and their families by protecting them from environmental, safety, and health hazards and maintaining quality military facilities;
To contribute weapons systems that have improved performance, lower cost, and better environmental characteristics.[38]

What is being secured in this variant of environmental security is the military readiness of the armed forces rather than the security of the state (as the NSS would have it), let alone the citizens of that state. The threat here is the possibility that environmental degradation might undermine the effectiveness of the U.S. military by limiting access to training areas or by detracting from the health and welfare of military personnel. The nature of the DOD's response is consistent with the reactive and rhetorical position many other sectors and government agencies throughout the world have adopted in response to environmental concerns and laws.

The reference to weapons systems with "better environmental characteristics" is ambiguous, but in his report Perry suggests that DOD is seeking to "incorporate environmental security considerations into all aspects of weapon system acquisition, maintenance and operations."[39] The aim seems to be to factor environmental benefits and costs into the purchasing of weapons systems. Perry uses phrases such as "where possible" and "as feasible," which suggests that this goal is rhetorical more than practical.[40] It is difficult to see a secretive weapons negotiation process devoting much attention to the environmental characteristics of the weapon in question. Indeed, where environmental characteristics may be given most attention is in the ability of the weapon to *destroy* life rather than to conserve it. This goal of developing "environmentally benign" weapons is further problematized by the U.S. nuclear arsenal.[41]

These criticisms having been made, it must be acknowledged at least tacitly that if there is to be a military, it might as well be one that seeks to minimize its environmental impacts. If the U.S. DOD has to use twenty-five million acres of land and own the "largest federal archaeological collection in the world," it is a small blessing that it now acknowledges its environmental responsibilities.[42] However, these responsibilities should be met through substantial action. In the absence of, say, a substantial redistribution of funds and personnel, it seems that the DOD is using environmental security (a term that ideally suits their needs) to promote its (questionable) green credentials and to marginalize the efficacy of scholars and social movements critical of the Pentagon's environmental record.[43]

Looking beyond the borders of the United States, the DUSD(ES) asserts that it has "a vibrant and growing role in enhancing international environmental security."[44] The Pentagon is seeking to extend its environmental security activities to other regions. Thus, "The U.S. military's role in environmental protection is manifold: it demonstrates leadership in the U.S. and abroad, helps guarantee access to the air, land and water needed to train U.S. forces[,] and helps promote environmentally sustainable behavior on the part of other militaries around the world."[45] Moreover, "DOD's view of 'environmental security' [also comprises] . . . understanding where environmental conditions contribute to instability and where the environment fits into the war and peace equation; bringing defense-related concerns to the development of national security; [and] studying how defense components can be used as instruments of U.S. global environmental policy."[46]

Thus, the Pentagon sees itself as a promoter of sustainability and a leader in environmentally responsible behavior among militaries. This claim is made unselfconsciously, in spite of Renner's observation that the Pentagon is very likely the largest consumer of energy of any organization in the world and is therefore most likely the world's largest producer of greenhouse gases.[47] Further, such claims ignore the point that this damage transpires for no productive outcome other than the dubious need to maintain an extraordinarily large military. The leadership that the U.S. military apparently demonstrates is therefore highly suspicious. It may indeed be an ecologically modern military, but it is nevertheless the world's most powerful military, has the largest stockpile of nuclear weapons, and has the largest budget of any military in the world.

When "access to the air, land and water needed to train U.S. forces" is applied to environmental security within the United States, it is tenuous because many military training areas have significant environmental contamination and lie adjacent to the homelands of indigenous people.[48] However, when understood in terms of "international activities," as it is in the citation above, it can be read as a desire to enclose other people's lands for the purpose of military training. On this point, it is also worth noting that although the DOD may be working toward cleaning up its bases at home and prides itself on reducing its record of violations of domestic law, there is no similar commitment with respect to cleaning up existing and former U.S. bases abroad. Perry's nine-page report to the president and Congress devotes only seven lines to the issue of overseas bases, as opposed to one and a half pages to "restoring DOD Facilities" at home.[49] Of these seven lines, the salient points are that "DOD will *consult* with the host nations on environmental compliance and clean up" and that for the most part "funding ... will be *negotiated* with the host nation" (my emphasis).[50] So, according to Seigel, "the official position of the U.S. government is that it is not generally obliged to clean up hazardous wastes at foreign military bases."[51] A genuine commitment from the United States to "global" environmental security issues would entail a specific and unambiguous program of action to clean up its overseas bases.

The desire to understand where "environmental conditions contribute to instability" is consistent with the NSS in its adherence to the "environment and security" interpretation of environmental security. This confluence between the NSS and the DOD strengthens the links between military and environmental security, which suggests new reasons to maintain military readiness and so a further reason to forestall budgetary cutbacks. The possibility of a peace dividend is reduced when the impossibility of peace is constantly proven through these discourses of danger. So for as long as the emphasis remains on military solutions, one can assume that there is a pervasive lack of genuine will to redress environmental insecurity.[52]

The environmental assistance given to other militaries around the world is not given according to need but according to traditional geopolitical dictates.[53] For example, the environment has been a key element of the continuation of the North Atlantic Treaty Organization (NATO) beyond the end of the Cold War. Former NATO secretary general Manfred Worner was particularly revealing, saying that "no other NATO country, in our traditional division of labor, equals the United States in its global responsibilities."[54] The "responsibility" to which Worner refers is "to be the purveyor of stability, not only vis-à-vis East and Central Europe, but also to the world at large."[55] This statement can be read as the search for new reasons for old orders, what Worner himself calls a "shift . . .

in the rationale for our defense."[56] Worner refers to "the immense conflict potential that is building up in Third World countries, characterized by . . . climate shifts and the prospect of environmental disaster," which suggests that the environment now figures as part of the rationale for the northern "management" of global affairs.[57] Thus, for Dalby, "this NATO understanding of the post Cold War world is clearly one of the persistence of 'Northern' institutions as the core political arrangements from which the rest of the world can be 'managed.' . . . [T]he theme of a select few managing the world's affairs is clear."[58] This is precisely the outcome that those in southern states feared would result when environmental matters began to be understood as security issues.[59] It should be noted that these managerial ambitions run counter to existing green theory, which argues for local responses and local autonomy.

Bearing in mind Dalby's observation that adding the environment into traditional geopolitical security formulations merely perpetuates the notion of "threats from the South" to justify further the hegemony of the North, it is instructive to look at DOD-NATO environmental security initiatives. The U.S. DOD is involved in:

a bilateral agreement on environmental protection within the militaries of Norway, Sweden, Poland, and Russia;
a NATO pilot study on environmental aspects of reusing former military lands;
a NATO pilot study on environmental management systems;
a NATO pilot study on "environmental security in an international context";
an Arctic military environmental cooperation program with Norway and Russia;
a Baltic Sea initiative;
NATO's Committee for Challenges to a Modern Society;
a trilateral agreement with Canada and Australia on environmental security issues;
an Asia-Pacific Defense environmental security initiative to open up a military environmental venue for cooperation with Pacific Rim countries.[60]

The DOD considers that it is "earning a reputation for strong environmental leadership within NATO." Following the critical reasoning above, environmental security can be seen to be strongly complicit in the extension of NATO and the managerial agenda of the United States.[61]

The tangible initiatives thus far have focused on Eastern Europe, largely through the auspices of NATO/U.S. confidence-building approaches. The reason for this focus may lie in the discourse of danger that has always served to justify the realist approach to security, where containment and engagement are seen to be required, and environmental security is one means for NATO to achieve these goals.[62] In contrast, the impoverished South, although scripted in most of the literature as a barbaric Other, has less capacity to threaten the North. Hence, despite the efforts of some authors to understand the South as a threat in terms of refugee flows, declining access to valuable resources, and potential (if vague) disruption to "international security," these threats are by no means as real in the realist imagination as the threat from the usual enemy in Eastern Europe.[63] So there is no action to help the South, and the lack of clear economic returns no doubt compounds the disincentives for doing so.

It appears, then, that using environmental security as means to reach out to other nations through military institutions is geopolitical-speak for environmental security as means to both construct and contain threatening Others. For the DOD, the problem of environmental insecurity is still fundamentally the problem of realpolitik. Ethical concerns are absent, and "the Good" is understood in a highly parochial (i.e., not universal) way. Further, in that military activities create environmental insecurities for people living within the United States, this sense of the Good often does not apply to the very people the state alleges to protect. More importantly, although two-thirds of the world's people may well face greater insecurity and deprivation in the future, this potentiality is not seen as sufficient cause for substantial action. In this context, environmental security is not about the environment; it is about security.

Therefore, it seems that efforts to build peace, however feeble, only focus on those who threaten the capitalist peace. The following question must then be raised: Is the best path to world peace not to arm the "South"? Would a proliferation of the means of violence expose the ethical interruption that realpolitik creates? One would hope not; the logic of violence should not be used to overcome violence. Such an immanent critique clearly has its limitations in this context. This discussion, however, points to the limitations of the self-interest rationality prevalent in much of the environmental security literature: to wit, we should act because it is in Our (the National) interest. If this remains the strategy of environmental security and of environmental foreign policy more generally, then motivating discourses of danger will have to be constantly re-created in a way disturbingly similar to the way in which threats are sought out by strategic planners to justify militarized national security. Indeed, the two logics are wholly interdependent.

The U.S. Department of State

The U.S. State Department became formally involved in environmental security in 1996 when then secretary of state Warren Christopher delivered a landmark speech at Stanford University.[64] The Stanford speech is laden with references to the effect of environmental degradation on U.S. interests and security. Christopher identifies two principal reasons why environmental issues must be incorporated into U.S. foreign policy: "First, environmental forces transcend borders and oceans to threaten directly the health, prosperity and jobs of American citizens. Second, addressing natural resource issues is frequently critical to achieving political and economic stability, and to pursuing our strategic goals around the world." He goes on to add that "The United States is providing the leadership to promote global peace and prosperity. We must also lead in safeguarding the global environment on which that prosperity and peace ultimately depend." This argument is similar to the claim to global managerialism present in NATO post–Cold War security doctrine. It also misleadingly scripts "environmental forces" as threats in the same "environment and security" way that the NSS does. The question "Whose security?"—or in this case, "Whose peace and prosperity?"—must be asked. The answer is arguably less the peace and prosperity of all people and more the peace and prosperity of the United States and its allies. Further, the question "Insecurity how?" remains unanswered; again, the threats are existential.

A notable feature of Christopher's Stanford speech is the way in which it manages to transfer responsibility for environmental problems away from the United States and onto the "globe" via a continued recourse to threats to the national interest. For example, "Across the United States, Americans suffer the consequences of damage to the environment far beyond our borders. Greenhouse gases released around the globe by power plants, automobiles and burning forests affect our health and our climate, potentially causing many billions of dollars in damage from rising sea levels and changing storm patterns." Christopher does not mention that 24 percent of the offending greenhouse gases come from the United States alone or that it produced 213,620,000 metric tons of hazardous wastes between 1991 and 1994 (as opposed to 7,000,000 in France and 9,100,000 in Germany).[65]

In his speech, Christopher indicates the degree to which military power is involved in affecting U.S. "strategic goals": "In carrying out America's foreign policy, we will of course use our diplomacy *backed by strong military forces* to meet traditional and continuing threats to our security, as well as to meet new threats. . . . But we must also contend with the vast new danger posed to our national interests by damage to the environment and resulting global and regional instability" (my emphasis). This passage reveals the linkage of military diplomacy with environmental degradation and instability, suggesting that the military has a potential role to play in managing (anticipated) environmental induced conflicts.

The latent economic agenda in U.S. foreign policy is evident in Christopher's speech. For example, he talks of the "enormous stake in consolidating democratic institutions and open markets" in the United States (also a strong theme of the NSS). Democracy and free markets are twin pillars of contemporary U.S. foreign policy, yet the two are by no means mutually dependent. An "open" economy need not respect the rights of its people; indeed, arguably, a government that opens its economy may be negligent in its responsibilities to its people. Further, opening the economy to the global market is not necessarily what democracies do. Nevertheless, the free-market ideology has continued to pervade U.S. foreign policy under the guidance of Christopher's successor, Madeleine Albright. The economic self-interest goes further. Christopher points out that "American businesses know that a healthy global environment is essential to our prosperity" and that "Protecting the environment also opens new business opportunities. We are committed to helping U.S. companies expand their already commanding share of a [U.S.]$400 billion market for environmental technologies."[66] Thus, a part of the rationale for DOD involvement in Eastern Europe and for the SERDP becomes clearer.

Christopher's speech unveiled the State Department's Environmental Initiative for the Twenty-first Century, which involves creating alliances between the various divisions of the State Department as well as various forums on issues and in "key regions" and progressively establishing "environmental opportunity hubs" in key embassies. One of the objectives for these "opportunity hubs" is to "help U.S. businesses sell their leading edge environmental technology."[67] The initiative also introduced the "partnership for environment and foreign policy" program, which seeks to promote greater cohesion on environmental issues among the various divisions of the State Department.

A key part of the Environmental Initiative is the production of an annual report, the first of which was issued in 1997. From an environmental perspective, this first annual report is a far more encouraging document than Christopher's early speech. The inside/outside theme is far less evident, although it has by no means disappeared. However, there is now some degree of recognition of the U.S. contribution to global environmental problems. What is also encouraging is a sense of the "borderless." For example, "The State Department now operates on the premise that countries sharing common resources share a common future and that neighboring nations are downstream and upwind, not just North and South or East and West, of each other. Threats to a shared forest, a common river, or a seamless coastline are forcing countries to expand their existing bilateral relationships to include environmental issues, and to create new regional frameworks to confront and combat shared environmental challenges."[68]

This is not to say that the State Department has completely reformed itself; its efforts must still be read in the context of the National Security Strategy, and Christopher's early speech as part of the U.S. managerial ambitions. However, what is striking here is the presence of a global outlook that seems to depart from the practical geopolitical imagination underlying earlier pronouncements.[69] There is a certain ecological sensibility in the reference to "downstream and upwind," for example, which indicates either a better awareness of ecological realities or a more sophisticated green spin. Timothy Wirth, the former undersecretary of state for global affairs, displayed a similar ecological sensibility: "Simply put, the life support systems of the entire globe are being compromised at a rapid rate—illustrating our interdependence with nature and changing our relationship to the planet."[70]

Finally, although Secretary of State Albright was less concerned with environmental issues than Christopher, she too displayed a more benign and informed approach to environmental problems. In her 1998 Earth Day speech, for example, she mentioned security and conflict only once, made partial recognition of the U.S. responsibilities, and included a humanitarian theme.[71] These signs of a shift in sensibility are encouraging, but more strident reforms are necessary to break away from the still dominant nation-centered and realist approach to environmental security.

Interpreting Environmental Security Discourse in U.S. Foreign Policy

The NSS, DOD, and State Department interpret environmental security in a way that maintains the legitimacy of the U.S. government in the face of pressing environmental problems. By deploying a green rhetoric—however vacuous—the state makes a token gesture to placate the concerns of the general public and to forestall a crisis of legitimacy.[72] This gesture completely fails to engage with environmental problems themselves. Green theory tells us that environmental insecurity is a product of capitalism, militarism, industrialization, and instrumental reason, yet these agencies' approach to environmental security is to deploy "a complex repertoire of responsibility and crisis-displacement strategies" that ignore these contradictions of modernity.[73]

The U.S. approach to environmental security maintains legitimacy by a combination of symptom amelioration, token gesturism, the "greening" of legitimating political ideology, and the displacement of the crisis in a variety of different directions: either downward into civil society; or upward onto a global political agenda: or, indeed, sideways in presenting the crisis as another body's (e.g., state's) legitimization problem.[74] These various tactics are evident in U.S. environmental security discourse. The lethargic effort to clean up contaminated bases "at home" (but not abroad) is indicative of the "symptom amelioration" tactic. The "greening of political ideology" is most clearly manifest in the environment-conflict discourse, which is fundamentally consistent with realist international relations theory. There appears to be little evidence for displacement downward into civil society (perhaps not surprising given the enormous variety of nongovernmental groups vying for legitimacy in domestic U.S. politics). However, the tactic of displacing problems up to the global level is clear, particularly in the State Department's pronouncements. That this global rhetoric also opens up the possibility of the United States as global manager and policeman further enhances the lure of this tactic. Finally, displacement sideways to present environmental degradation as someone else's legitimization problem is apparent in the references to instability and political upheaval that intertwine with the environment-conflict discourse. For the U.S. government, then, environmental security is used to preserve legitimacy, avoid radical reform, and distract attention from the contradictions of the modern world for which the United States is inextricably responsible. Such continued strategies of displacement are "dysfunctional long-term tendencies" that render the United States "a profound threat to global security."[75]

All of these approaches to environmental security interpret the environment as a direct or indirect threat to U.S. interests. Talking in terms of "threats" in this way confuses environmental problems with military problems—which is an inappropriate way to understand environmental problems, particularly given that "threat" in security discourse is a potent symbol of deliberate and malignant danger to the inside emanating from the outside. In this respect, the environment becomes another danger that helps constitute the sense of "us" necessary for nationalism and state legitimacy. Talking in terms of global threats blurs the distinctions between subject and object, and cause and effect, in ways that obscure the U.S. complicity in environmental degradation. This environmental security policy discourse evades the most salient point about national security and environmental degradation: that the country most complicit in "global" environmental degradation is the United States itself.

Talking in terms of threats is a discursive tactic that simultaneously downgrades the interdependence of environmental problems while excluding from consideration the role of U.S. businesses, consumers, and government in generating environmental problems. Campbell is succinct in his assessment of this discourse of threats and Others:

> One of the effects of this interpretation has been to reinscribe East-West understandings of global politics in a period of international transformation by suggesting that the "they" in the East are technologically less sophisticated and ecologically more dangerous than the "we" in the West. This produces a new boundary that demarcates the "East" from the "West." . . . But environmental danger can also be figured in a manner that challenges traditional forms of identity inscribed in the capitalist economy of the "West." As a discourse of danger which results in disciplinary strategies that are deterritorialized, involve communal cooperation, and refigure economic relationships, the environment can serve to enframe a different reading of "reasoning man" than that associated with the subjectivities of liberal capitalism, thereby making it more unstable and undecidable than anti-communism.[76]

It is precisely these implications of deterritorialization, communal cooperation, and refiguring economies that threaten the U.S. security elite and so are denied and excluded in their environmental security pronouncements.

Another failing of the "threat" discourse is that it focuses attention on issues "only when crises are imminent, by which time it is often too late for effective interventions and corrective measures."[77] This is another example of what Prins calls the environmental Catch-22: by the time environmental problems are unambiguously overt, it is too late to rectify them; yet, alternately, unless the problems are immediately pressing, there is insufficient motivation for action by mainstream political institutions.[78] Thus, the particular state- and military-centered interpretation of environmental security by the U.S. policy community ignores a telling implication of environmental problems for politics: that long-term and fundamental reforms are required to address the underlying structural causes of environmental degradation.

Underlying this presentation of environmental problems as threats is a recurrent conflation of threat with risk. Environmental security in this sense represents the state's particular highly politicized assessment of risk rather than any scientific account of the actual risks. There is little correlation between the two. The U.S. government's assessment of risks is far less a matter of credible scientific assessment and far more a matter of the politics of identity and Otherness. Thus, "the response of individual states to environmental pathologies is often determined by contingent political factors as opposed to informed risk assessments."[79] The challenge for the environmental movement, according to Hay, is "not only to continue to provide such informed risk assessments, but also to expose the distortions imposed by the state's own consequence-risk calculus."[80] This chapter has sought to expose these distortions.

Conclusion

The U.S. security policy community has narrowly interpreted the concept of environmental security to serve its long-standing institutional position as guardian of the national interest.[81] Dabelko and Simmons call this approach a "classic bureaucratic effort to retain comparable budgetary outlays and reap public relations benefits."[82] Pirages calls the U.S. response "cosmetic" and "timid," arguing that environmental security has "not revamped foreign policy and security thinking."[83]

Underlying these initiatives and pronouncements on environmental security is a resistance to meaningful change and a defense of the current order. As Dalby notes, "in so far as security is premised on maintaining the status quo it runs counter to the changes needed to alleviate many environmental and economic problems because it is precisely the status quo that has produced the problems."[84] The policy responses discussed in this chapter are not the new foreign and security policies we might have expected to flow from the concept of environmental security. Rather, they are consistent with the usual approach to foreign policy based on the usual inside/outside rationality. For the United States, environmental security is about securing the very lifestyles and institutions that degrade the environment against the risks associated with this same degradation. Thus,

President Bush's comment at the Rio Earth Summit in 1992—that American lifestyles were not negotiable—still holds true.

U.S. environmental security policy does not help to minimize the causes of environmental insecurity; indeed, it seems fundamentally implicated in their perpetuation. It also does not recognize that fundamental long-term changes in the structure of the global political economy are required, and it does not recognize that if any single country needs to implement this reform, it is the United States itself. Instead, it suggests that the best way to secure against threatening Others is to prepare for war: the irony in this strategy of securing against violence by advocating violence is by now well known. But preparing for war is a significant cause of the very environmental degradation the U.S. military finds so threatening, and so the outcome is a continued spiraling downward toward violence and environmental insecurity.

Weighed against these negative features of U.S. environmental security policy are two principal positive outcomes. First, that environmental concerns now figure in U.S. national security reasoning suggests that the policy community is at least attentive to environmental concerns, even if it interprets them in overly narrow and parochial ways. More importantly—and perhaps the most valuable function of the concept of environmental security—this inclusion of environmental security creates a common point of dialogue between the green movement and national security planners. The incorporation of environmental security into U.S. foreign policy therefore serves an extremely important epistemic function that offers the possibility of a more benign and environmentally effective U.S. foreign policy.

The second positive aspect of U.S. environmental security policy is that there is a discernible shift toward a more sensitive and benign understanding of environmental problems in both the NSS and State Department pronouncements. Between 1996 and 1998, the NSS dropped a number of references to environmental degradation as a threat, and it has downplayed the possibility of environmental degradation leading to violent conflicts. More importantly, the NSS now recognizes the need for noncoercive forms of diplomacy and for the ratification of existing international conventions and treaties. Over the same short period, the State Department has also developed a more sophisticated approach to environmental problems, and it has downplayed the inside/outside theme that has traditionally underwritten foreign policy. However, there is a danger that the Pentagon's self-congratulatory, vague, and militaristic interpretation of environmental security will counteract these small positive gains made by the NSS and the State Department.

The future utility of the concept of environmental security in U.S. foreign policy is thus still unclear, as is the future contribution of the United States to genuine global peace and security. What is clear, however, is that through the deployment of environmental security in U.S. foreign policy, both the future of the concept and the future of the planet are intertwined.

Notes

1 For a comprehensive review of environmental security, see Jon Barnett, *The Meaning of Environmental Security* (London and New York: Zed, 2001).

2 Lothar Brock, "The Environment and Security: Conceptual and Theoretical Issues," in *Conflict and the Environment*, ed. Nils Gleditsch (Dordrecht: Kluwer, 1997), 17–34.

3 A broad coverage of these themes can be found in Norman Myers, *Ultimate Security: The Environmental Basis of Political Stability* (New York: W. W. Norton, 1993). See also Thomas Homer-Dixon, "On the Threshold: Environmental Changes as Causes of Acute Conflict," *International Security* 16 (1991): 76–116; Peter Gleick, "Environment and Security: The Clear Connections," *Bulletin of Atomic Scientists* 47 (1991): 17–21.

4 Lorraine Elliott, *The Global Politics of the Environment* (New York: New York University Press, 1998). On the relationship between realist and idealist/liberal theory, I support Robert Walker's view that the overstated theoretical opposition or "great debate" between the two serves as a "substitute for serious theoretical reflection and critical engagement" about the state of world politics. Robert Walker, *Inside/Outside: International Relations as Political Theory* (Cambridge: Cambridge University Press, 1993), quote at 107. There is a conflation of both realist and liberal views in the National Security Strategy.

5 A sample includes: Patricia Mische, "Ecological Security and the Need to Reconceptualize Sovereignty," *Alternatives* 14 (1989): 389–427; Patricia Mische, "Security Through Defending the Environment: Citizens Say Yes!" in *New Agendas for Peace Research: Conflict and Security Reexamined*, ed. Elise Boulding (Boulder, Colo.: Lynne Rienner, 1992), 103–19; Katrina Rogers, "Ecological Security and Multinational Corporations," *Environmental Change and Security Project Report* 3 (1997): 29–36.

6 Elliott, *Global Politics*.

7 Barnett, *Meaning of Environmental Security*.

8 Anne Platt, "Confronting Infectious Diseases," in *State of the World 1996*, ed. Lester Brown (London: Earthscan, 1996), 114–32; Lester Brown, Christopher Flavin, and Hal Kane, *Vital Signs 1996–1997: Trends That Are Shaping Our Future* (London: Earthscan, 1996).

9 See, for example, Robert Bullard, ed., *Unequal Protection: Environmental Justice and Communities of Color* (San Francisco: Sierra Club, 1994).

10 Richard Ullman, "Redefining Security," *International Security* 8 (1983): 129–53; John Cooley, "The War over Water," *Foreign Policy* 54 (1984): 3–26; Jessica Mathews, "Redefining Security," *Foreign Affairs* 68 (1989): 162–77; Norman Myers, "Environment and Security," *Foreign Policy* 74 (1989): 23–41; Homer-Dixon, "On the Threshold"; Joyce Starr, "Water Wars," *Foreign Policy* 82 (1991): 17–36; Peter Gleick, "Water Conflict: Freshwater Resources and

International Security," *International Security* 18 (1993): 79–112; Robert Kaplan, "The Coming Anarchy," *Atlantic Monthly* 273 (1994): 44–76; Marc Levy, "Is the Environment a National Security Issue?" *International Security* 20 (1995): 35–62.

11 Simon Dalby, "The Environment as Geopolitical Threat: Reading Robert Kaplan's 'Coming Anarchy,'" *Ecumene* 3 (1996): 471–96, quote at 475.

12 Ullman, "Redefining Security," 142.

13 Geoff Dabelko and P. J. Simmons, "Environment and Security: Core Ideas and U.S. Government Initiatives," *SAIS Review* 17 (1997): 127–46, quote at 128.

14 Dabelko and Simmons, "Environment and Security," 128; Gerald Thomas, "U.S. Environmental Security Policy: Broad Concern or Narrow Interests," *Journal of Environment and Development* 6 (1997): 397–425.

15 William Clinton, *A National Security Strategy for a New Century* (Washington, D.C.: White House, October 1998). Subsequently cited in the text by page number.

16 See, for example, Walker, *Inside/Outside;* Simon Dalby, "American Security Discourse: The Persistence of Geopolitics," *Political Geography Quarterly* 9 (1990): 171–88; David Campbell, *Writing Security: United States Foreign Policy and the Politics of Identity* (Manchester: Manchester University Press, 1992).

17 Dabelko and Simmons, "Environment and Security," 136.

18 Eileen Claussen, "Environment and Security: The Challenge of Integration," *Environmental Change and Security Project Report* 1 (1995): 40–43, quote at 40.

19 William Clinton, "Remarks on Earth Day 1994," cited in *Environmental Change and Security Project Report* 1 (1995): 51.

20 A principal finding of the most substantial research project into environmental degradation and conflict is that environmental degradation is highly unlikely to be a factor in armed conflict among nations. For a summary of this research, see Thomas Homer-Dixon and Valerie Percival, *Environmental Scarcity and Violent Conflict: Briefing Book* (Toronto: University of Toronto, 1996). For skeptical readings of the thesis that environmental degradation will induce violent conflict, see Barnett, *Meaning of Environmental Security*, and Nils Gleditsch, "Armed Conflict and the Environment: A Critique of the Literature," *Journal of Peace Research* 35 (1998): 381–400.

21 As Richard Falk suggested as long ago as 1971, and as has been reflected in every major international conference on the environment since Stockholm in 1972. Richard Falk, *This Endangered Planet: Prospects and Proposals for Human Survival* (New York: Random House, 1971).

22 Although note the way representations of environmental problems as uniformly global mask real discrepancies in responsibility and impact and tend to be used to promote the agendas of the North at the expense of the South. See Wolfgang Sachs, ed., *Global Ecology: A New Arena of Political Conflict* (London: Zed, 1993).

23 Indeed, the discussion of sustainable development itself is confused: "Environmental and natural resource issues can impede sustainable development efforts and promote regional instability" (*National Security Strategy* [1998], 33). Hence, sustainable development here means sustainable *economic* development, or else the writers of the NSS are unaware that *ecologically* sustainable development is precisely about these "environmental and natural resource issues," which, as written, are axiomatic.

24 William Clinton. *U.S. National Security Strategy of Engagement and Enlargement* (Washington, D.C.: White House, 1996), 26.

25 William Perry, *An Annual Report from the DOD to the President and Congress of the U.S. on Environmental Security*, available at <http://es.epa.gov/program/p2dept/defense/ann-rpt.html> 1995, 1.

26 Quoted in Gordon MacDonald, "Environmental Security," *IGCC Policy Brief* 1 (February 1995): 2.

27 See, for example, Jon Barnett, "In Defense of the Nation-State: Securing the Environment," *Sustainable Development* 6 (1998): 8–17; Kent Butts, "Why the Military Is Good for the Environment," in *Green Security or Militarized Environment?* ed. Jyrki Kakonen (Dartmouth: Brookfield, 1998), 83–110; Julian Oswald, "Defense and Environmental Security," in *Threats Without Enemies*, ed. Gwyn Prins (London: Earthscan, 1993), 113–34.

28 Al Gore, "SEI: A Strategic Environment Initiative," *SAIS Review* 10 (1990): 59–71.

29 Ibid., quotes at 60 and 63.

30 Ibid., 66.

31 Thomas, "U.S. Environmental Security Policy."

32 Cited on the SERDP homepage, <http://www.serdp.org/>. The SERDP steering council is comprised of six representatives from DOD, three from DOE (a long-standing partner in the U.S. nuclear weapons program), one from the Environmental Protection Agency (EPA), and one from the Coast Guard. For a fuller discussion of SERDP, see Thomas, "U.S. Environmental Security Policy."

33 SERDP homepage.

34 Perry, *Annual Report from the DOD*, 3–4.

35 Ibid.

36 Ibid.; Thomas, "U.S. Environmental Security Policy."

37 Office of the Deputy Under Secretary of Defense (Environmental Security), *Environmental Security Mission* (Washington, D.C.: Office of the Secretary of Defense, 1997), available at <http://www.acq.osd.mil/ens>.

38 Ibid.

39 Perry, *Annual Report from the DOD*, 3.

40 Ibid.

41 Ibid.

42 Ibid.

43 See, for example, Michael Renner, "Assessing the Military's War on the Environment," in *State of the World 1991*, ed. Lester Brown (New York: W. W. Norton, 1991), 132–52; Joni Seager, *Earth Follies: Coming to Feminist Terms with the Global Environmental Crisis* (New York: Routledge, 1993); Valerie Kuletz, *The Tainted Desert: Environmental Ruin in the American West* (New York and London: Routledge, 1998).

44 "Update on Governmental Activities, Department of Defense," reported in *Environmental Change and Security Project Report* 2 (1996): 132.

45 Ibid.

46 Ibid., 133.

47 Renner, "Assessing the Military's War on the Environment."

48 Valerie Kuletz documents the proximity of U.S. nuclear weapons program sites to places where Native Americans live in the U.S. Southwest. Kuletz, *Tainted Desert.*

49 Perry, *Annual Report from the DOD.*

50 Ibid., 9.

51 Lenny Seigel, "Overseas Contamination: The Pentagon's Record," *Environmental Change and Security Project Report* 2 (1996): 15–17, quote at 16.

52 Jyrki Kakonen, "The Concept of Security: From Limited to Comprehensive," in *Perspectives on Environmental Conflict and International Politics*, ed. Jyrki Kakonen (London: Pinter, 1992), 146–55.

53 See Simon Dalby, "Threats from the South: Geopolitics, Equity, and 'Environmental Security,'" in *Contested Grounds: Security and Conflict in the New Environmental Politics*, ed. Dan Deudney and Richard Matthew (Albany: State University of New York Press, 1999), 155–85.

54 Manfred Worner, "Global Security: The Challenge for NATO," in *Global Security: North American, European, and Japanese Interdependence in the 1990's*, ed. Eric Grove (London: Brassey's, 1991), 100–105, quote at 101. For a more comprehensive and thoughtful critique of Worner's plans for NATO, see Dalby, "Threats from the South."

55 Worner, "Global Security," 102.

56 Ibid.

57 Ibid., 103

58 Dalby, "Threats from the South."

59 See Somaya Saad, "For Whose Benefit? Redefining Security," in *Green Planet Blues: Environmental Politics from Stockholm to Rio*, ed. Ken Konca, Michael Alberty, and Geoff Dabelko (Boulder, Colo.: Westview, 1995), 273–75.

60 "Update on Governmental Activities, Department of Defense," reported in *Environmental Change and Security Project Report* 2: 134.

61 Perry, *Annual Report from the DOD*, 9.

62 On discourses of danger, see Graeme Cheeseman and Robert Bruce, eds., *Discourses of Danger and Dread Frontiers: Australian Defence and Security Thinking after the Cold War* (St. Leonards: Allen and Unwin, 1996).

63 See Ullman, "Redefining Security"; Cooley, "The War over Water"; Myers, "Environment and Security"; Gleick, "Water Conflict"; and Kaplan, "The Coming Anarchy."

64 Warren Christopher, "American Diplomacy and the Global Environmental Challenges of the 21st Century," address at Stanford University, 9 April 1996, available at <http://dosfan.lib.uic.edu/text.html>.

65 United Nations Development Program, *Human Development Report 1998* (New York: Oxford University Press, 1998), 202–3.

66 Christopher, "American Diplomacy."

67 Ibid.

68 United States Department of State, *Environmental Diplomacy: The Environment and U.S. Foreign Policy*, available at <http://www.state.gov/www/global/oes/earth.html>, 1997.

69 On practical geopolitics, see Geraoid O'Tuathail and John Agnew, "Geopolitics and Discourse: Practical Geopolitical Reasoning in American Foreign Policy," *Political Geography* 11 (1992): 190–204.

70 Timothy Wirth, "Address to the National Press Club, 12 July 1994," cited in *Environmental Change and Security Project Report* 1 (1995): 54.

71 Madeleine Albright, "Earth Day 1998: Global Problems and Global Solutions," available at <http://secretary.state.gov/www/statements/1998/980421.html>, 1998.

72 For the classic discussion of legitimacy, see Jürgen Habermas, *Legitimation Crisis* (London: Heinemann Educational, 1976).

73 Colin Hay, "Environmental Security and State Legitimacy," in *Is Capitalism Sustainable? Political Economy and the Politics of Ecology*, ed. Michael O'Connor (New York: Guilford, 1994), 217–31, quote at 221. Hay interprets environmental security as the goal of securing the environment.

74 Ibid., 221.

75 Ibid., 227.

76 Campbell, *Writing Security*, 197.

77 Dabelko and Simmons, "Environmental Security," 142.

78 Gwyn Prins, "Politics and the Environment," *International Affairs* 66 (1990): 711–30.

79 Hay, "Environmental Security and State Legitimacy," 226.

80 Ibid., 226.

81 Thomas, "U.S. Environmental Security Policy," 397–425.

82 Dabelko and Simmons, "Environmental Security," 132.

83 Dennis Pirages, "Demographic Change and Ecological Security," *Environmental Change and Security project Report* 3 (1997): 37–46, quote at 37.

84 Simon Dalby, "The Politics of Environmental Security," in *Green Security or Militarized Environment?* ed. Jyrki Kakonen (Dartmouth: Brookfield, 1994), 25–53, quote at 33.

4 Geopolitics, Energy, and Ecology: U.S. Foreign Policy and the Caspian Sea

Douglas W. Blum

The Caspian Sea has received a great deal of attention for its sizable deposits of oil and gas. Much less attention has been paid to the deteriorating condition of the Caspian's ecology. Nevertheless, much like the more publicized problems of the Aral Sea, the Caspian is increasingly beset by environmental degradation. Pollution and fisheries depletion have increased, often dramatically, since the end of the Soviet Union, while an elevation of the sea level from 1978 to 1996 has compounded the problem of pollution and created others of its own. Lamentably, the development priorities embraced by the bordering states have so far relegated environmental protection to the bottom of most policy agendas.

American policymakers are thus confronted by a dilemma. Given the preferences of the region's ruling elites and a strong wish to curry their favor, Washington has been led to make similar trade-offs. In seeking to encourage marketization and regional penetration by U.S.-based oil companies, U.S. policymakers have tended to deemphasize environmental issues as well. Because of the prestige of the United States, as well as the resources at its disposal, this policy has profound environmental consequences.

As this chapter argues, the development of U.S. policy has been predicated on prevailing conceptions of national interests, especially economic and geostrategic interests linked to energy extraction. More subtly, U.S. policy is geared to traditional realist concerns for relative power and therefore retains a rather anachronistic, zero-sum quality. Yet, such policy assumptions and preferences are not set in stone. A number of international developments may help to change American calculations, such as the depressed market for oil and secular shifts in the domestic politics of key Caspian states. With the lowered profitability of oil and the decline of political threats, established policy may be reevaluated. At the same time, new opportunities may arise, particularly those involving long-term stability and environmental protection.

I begin this chapter with a brief description of the major environmental problems in the Caspian Sea. Next, I analyze U.S. environmental policy and competing policy preferences in the region. I then place U.S. environmental policy in a broader context by discussing the alternative projects currently underway in the Caspian basin. The existence of such alternatives both sharpens the policy trade-off and opens up new possibilities for constructive engagement in the environmental arena. Finally, I evaluate the significance of recent developments in international politics, which bear on U.S. international environmental policy-making in the future.

Caspian Environmental Problems

The three main types of environmental problems in the Caspian Sea are fisheries depletion, water pollution, and a rise in sea level.[1] These problems are linked to additional problems because the rise of the sea together with pollution threatens the viability of coastal wetlands and places the biodiversity of the region in serious jeopardy. Water pollution, moreover, is likely to result in diminishing tourism and may even cause widespread public health problems. These health problems are partly linked to the danger of radioactive exposure because the Caspian borders several old sites of underground nuclear detonations in Kazakhstan.[2]

The depletion of fish stocks is a new phenomenon in the Caspian Sea and is a direct result of the collapse of the Soviet Union. During the Soviet period, quotas for the Soviet Union were enforced, and poaching operations were kept to a minimum. However, with the emergence of four new and impoverished bordering states, overfishing has become rampant. The most highly publicized related problem is the threat to the sturgeon population, because the Caspian is responsible for 80 to 90 percent of the world's sturgeon catch (and caviar production). In addition to overfishing, Caspian fisheries are further depleted by pollution.[3]

The latter two problems—pollution and sea-level rise—are not new. Pollution has been on the rise for years, a cumulative result of the Soviet command system with its output quotas and lax environmental enforcement. The two leading sources of water pollution in the Caspian basin are offshore oil rigs and waste discharge from the Volga as well as from towns on or near the Caspian coast.[4] The increase in oil and gas extraction and transportation has already had a discernible effect on the level of pollution, which may worsen dramatically if economic conditions are conducive to further energy development.[5]

The rise of the sea level, too, began under Soviet rule. Between 1978 and 1996, the Caspian rose more than two meters. Since then, it has started to subside—merely another cycle in an endless and poorly understood process of fluctuation.[6] Unfortunately, Soviet bureaucrats did not factor such changes in water level into their planning, as a result of which extensive industrial facilities, thousands of hectares of cultivated land, and entire communities have been inundated. Although the water is now apparently receding, the damage already done is enormous.

The key point for our purpose is that the extent and interconnectedness of Caspian environmental problems are such that unilateral state efforts are bound to be inadequate. Natural resources such as fish stocks and clean water are classic "common pool" resources, the management of which is not amenable to piecemeal measures. Furthermore, the causes of environmental problems in the Caspian basin are dispersed and wide-ranging, including point-specific effluents as well as major estuaries and microeconomic actors together with major oil companies. The same may be said of flood-control efforts: management efforts in one area may have effects on other areas. Consequently, only well-coordinated state actions can offer any hope of success.

U.S. Policy toward the Caspian Region in the Post-Soviet Period

During the past several years, environmental protection in the Caspian basin has received a fair amount of attention in official U.S. policy. The issue has been raised repeatedly in programmatic statements by senior officials.[7] Moreover, not only has it been raised with regard to the Caspian itself, but the Clinton adminis-tration's staunch support for the proposed Baku-Ceyhan pipeline has frequently been justified on environmental grounds. Citing Turkey's anxiety over the pros-pect of a disastrous spill in the Bosphorus, leading officials have promoted the Ceyhan route as an environmentally safe alternative to other pipelines exiting onto the Black Sea.[8]

Yet, official rhetoric aside, the only program funded by the U.S. government is the Caspian Environmental Partnership, sponsored by the U.S. Agency for International Development (USAID) and intended to link together educational institutions, regulatory agencies, and nongovernmental organizations (NGOs). The goal is to provide technical expertise, legal infrastructure, and political support for robust environmental regulation in the energy sector, as well as to make provisions for oil spill cleanup.[9] The first strand of the partnership unites American universities and private firms with their regional counterparts for the purposes of exchanging scientific-technical information as well as providing insights into how American institutions work and relate to governments. The regulation component is geared toward drafting clear and consistent legal guide-lines, including rules and standards for offshore drilling. The NGO component, finally, is intended to foster independent oversight and accountability mechanisms in the long run by helping to establish a vibrant civil society.

For political reasons, however, the partnership is limited in geographic scope: Section 907 of the Freedom Support Act prevents U.S. aid to the Azerbaijan government, and the absence of diplomatic relations precludes involvement with Iran.[10] Perhaps even more striking from an environmental standpoint, the partnership is narrowly focused on problems directly connected with oil and gas exploitation and does not encompass the wider set of issues affecting the Caspian, as outlined above. Thus, rather than taking a broad ecological perspective, U.S. assistance is tied to more fundamental political goals.

Interestingly, this approach stands in contrast to the Clinton administration's fairly significant efforts elsewhere in the former Soviet Union and Eastern Europe, much of which originated in U.S.-Russian relations under the Gore-Chernomyrdin Commission. In Lake Baikal, the Aral basin, Chernobyl, and numerous other areas, the U.S. government (acting through agencies such as the U.S. Geological Survey and the National Science Foundation) has provided financing and expertise to promote environmental conservation and cleanup. Indeed, the Gore-Chernomyrdin Commission established an environmental working group for Caspian Sea problems. Despite this early investigative project and the subsequent USAID program, such efforts have fallen well short of the more extensive program designed for the Aral Sea.[11]

In addition to the overall paucity of attention, there has also been little systematic effort in the United States to integrate ongoing environmental protection measures in the Caspian region. One notable exception is a scientific research project organized jointly by the United States and Turkey, which addresses a broad range of environmental issues, including the interrelationship between social, economic, political, and ecological processes. This project has been launched under the auspices of the North Atlantic Treaty Organization (NATO) independently of the littoral states. Although the latter have been invited to participate, any high-level involvement in planning and implementation is dubious given NATO's imprimatur, particularly for Russia and Iran.[12]

Although the Clinton administration endorses both private-sector development and ecological preservation efforts, it does not assume primary responsibility for their enactment or for the coherence of the overall regulatory framework that results. More importantly, the prevailing political orientation prevents Washington from participating in fully inclusive multilateral projects. In fact, U.S. policy has at times inhibited the emergence of such initiatives, as the case of Technical Entrepreneurs Intrapreneurs Network (TEIN) shows. A nonprofit agency based in the United States, TEIN is intended to promote environmentally sustainable development through small-scale entrepreneurship. Yet, as part of the U.S. G-7 Global Inventory Project, TEIN accepts official government policy regarding the Caspian and therefore seeks participation from all states except Iran. From an environmental perspective, the usefulness of such piecemeal, noninclusive efforts is inevitably limited.

In sum, Washington's approach involves *relatively* active environmental intervention in many areas of the former Soviet Union, but very limited and highly politicized engagement in the Caspian Sea. And yet the Caspian has become a magnet for interventionist efforts. As discussed in the following section, a number of significant cooperative ventures for Caspian environmental protection have emerged during the past several years. It is important to have some familiarity with these ventures in order to appreciate the range of opportunities and policy options available to the United States should it wish to pursue them.

Caspian Environmental Protection: Regional Policies, Initiatives, and Institutions

What options exist for implementing environmental protection measures, should U.S. policy preferences begin to shift in this direction? The range of available alternatives includes limited, bilateral efforts already under way, as well as more ambitious (and more difficult to control) multilateral projects. This section briefly reviews the various initiatives that have been undertaken to manage Caspian environmental problems and links these initiatives with the underlying political dynamics of the region.

State Environmental Programs

All of the littoral states have made efforts to launch environmental protection programs in the Caspian. Yet such efforts have varied greatly in terms of scope and sophistication. Not surprisingly, Russia has concentrated far more resources in this direction than have the other states because of its far higher level of scientific and technical expertise. Unfortunately, economic crisis has distracted state attention from environmental protection, which is widely regarded as an unaffordable luxury. Consequently, regardless of the extent of careful planning and analysis, state agencies are unable to ensure that approved projects actually come to fruition. Even when the measures involved do not generate political disagreement, such as combating sea-level rise, state monies are not often forthcoming.[13]

Environmental concerns have recently become somewhat more pronounced in Azerbaijan as the Caspian Environmental Program (CEP) has begun to attract notice. At the same time, official environmental standards (described in the next section) have been relaxed for oil companies operating offshore in order to facilitate foreign investment for oil drilling and transportation.[14] The prevailing priorities are thus clearly revealed: environmental implementation is to be strengthened, but only on the condition that it not jeopardize energy extraction. Still, significant legal changes have been enacted to promote administrative compliance with existing regulations and to improve enforcement.[15] The chairman of the State Committee for Ecology and Environment Protection, Ali Hasanov, made a number of public statements about the importance of undertaking measures for the Caspian region, and the committee organized meetings and projects focusing on conservation and pollution prevention.[16] The leading consortium involved in extraction has implemented environmental regulations as well.[17] Similar efforts—for essentially similar reasons—have been undertaken by Iran and Kazakhstan, albeit to a lesser extent.[18] Only Turkmenistan's efforts have been negligible so far, which, again, reflects both a lack of priority and the state's utter impoverishment.[19]

International Organizations, Regional Programs, and the Caspian Environmental Program

A number of highly visible international organizations have launched independent environmental efforts in the Caspian basin. For the most part such initiatives have been carefully focused to address a single set of problems in a given area, rather than attempting to deal with a broad range of issues that straddle state borders. The World Bank, for example, has provided loans for specific projects in Russia, Kazakhstan, and Azerbaijan, including environmental cleanup, sturgeon restocking, and pollution monitoring.[20] NATO's Infrastructure Logistics and Civil Emergency Planning Division has been providing advice to Azerbaijan on environmental security (i.e., handling oil spills and similar accidents). The Global Environment Facility (GEF) has funded several individual projects, such as a local water-purification plant in Kazakhstan.[21] The European Economic Commission has offered to assist the littoral states in undertaking ecological surveys.[22] And the Soros Foundation has provided funding for environmental education and is attempting to organize an international movement to protect the Caspian from pollution as a result of oil and gas exploitation.[23] But by far the most comprehensive and organized project is the Caspian Environmental Program.

The CEP includes all of the littoral states together with the World Bank, the United Nations Development Program (UNDP), the United Nations Environment Program (UNEP), and the European Union. Nominally a $100 million program, it includes sweeping overall objectives—ideally to be embodied in a regional framework convention—as well as specific National Action Plans. The CEP has drafted a conceptual framework for coordinated work in pollution monitoring, fisheries management, conservation of wetlands and endangered wildlife, and coastal-zone protection and rehabilitation, especially in areas affected by flooding from sea-level rise prior to 1997.[24] In addition, the CEP focuses on long-term goals by attempting to strengthen institutional capacity (including NGO activity) at the local, national, and regional levels. In short, it is a classic international environmental regime, focusing on neofunctional integration and incorporating current understandings of the institutional and social requirements for attaining robust cooperation.[25] Formally launched only in 1998, the program faces massive bureaucratic, financial, and political obstacles, and it is still far too early to assess its prospects for success.

It is not too early, however, to assess the U.S. government's position regarding the CEP. Although no official attitude was articulated, the Clinton administration did not warmly endorse the program.[26] In part, this attitude may be attributed to the overriding priority attached to energy extraction and geopolitical competition. Environmental concerns are dwarfed, in Washington's perspective, by the short-term political and economic stakes in this volatile post-Soviet region. The realization of such interests might be hampered by the existence of any stringent regime under external control, especially if it inhibited rapid extraction. In addition, the inclusive regional membership of the CEP—especially its inclusion of Iran—places it outside the purview of U.S. government policy. In order to appreciate the future prospects of this policy, we must review both its origins and the factors likely to affect its development.

Caspian Energy and U.S. Geopolitical Objectives

The emergence of the essentially extractive agenda of the United States for the Caspian may be dated to late 1993, with the announcement of the "deal of the century" to develop massive deposits off the coast of Azerbaijan. Although the phrase was hyperbolic, the fact that a consortium of major oil companies had been licensed to explore offshore fields generated a flurry of excitement. Not only was the quantity of hydrocarbons apparently quite large, but the fact that Azerbaijan was willing to act alone in developing these reserves meant that Russian control was no longer absolute, which in turn signaled the onset of an intense round of competition for access to undersea oil and gas deposits. With the sudden surge of interest in the region, the Clinton administration began to support U.S.-based multinational corporations (MNCs) in the frenzied international bidding for partnership in various consortia.[27] In addition to direct efforts to join the Caspian energy boom, the administration and Congress have also pursued the grandiose transportation and development project known as the Silk Road initiative (or TRACECA), which will greatly facilitate extraction and export of energy resources as well as boosting other Caspian investments.

Leading administration officials and other politicians have rationalized the aggressive exploitation of Caspian energy in terms of preventing excessive dependence on the Persian Gulf. Accordingly, the strategy of achieving "energy security" involves source diversification so as to ensure an adequate supply of oil and gas to key international markets.[28] The primary concern is not so much the United States, which imports only 18 percent of its oil from the Persian Gulf, but rather Japan and Western Europe. As such, the U.S. strategy is a response to the lessons of recent history, including the oil shocks of the 1970s and Iraq's invasion of Kuwait. Without a doubt, cheap oil has subsidized the growth of the developed world in the late 1980s and the 1990s. In addition, U.S. policy has reflected expectations—prior to the Asian economic crisis—of sharply increasing global demand for oil.

It should also be noted that U.S. policy dovetails with the self-interest of a significant group of political elites. A critical role in shaping U.S. Caspian policy has been played by former high-ranking officials with ties to MNCs working in the region.[29] In urging that the extraction of Caspian resources become a national priority and that steps be taken to counter Russian and Iranian influence, these well-placed individuals have simultaneously advanced their own fortunes. Yet, it would be simplistic and perhaps overly paranoiac to suggest that such personal connections reveal a hidden agenda or a policymaking cabal. On the contrary, many of these same figures have been quite outspoken and candid in defending U.S. interest in pursuing energy security. Such a position and indeed such widespread involvement in the energy industry reflect a sincere conviction that—to modify the old adage—what is good for Exxon is good for America.

Besides energy extraction, U.S. policy in the Caspian is strongly affected by geopolitical calculations.[30] The main elements of this geopolitical agenda are opposition to Iran and containment of Russian influence. A secondary objective is the promotion of full autonomy for the region's former Soviet states, which in turn provides a vehicle for Washington's efforts to extend influence. Although a thorough analysis of these issues is beyond the scope of this chapter, a general discussion may be useful for locating environmentalism in a broader, regional policy perspective.

The anti-Iranian thrust in U.S. policy is not new; it dates to the wave of Islamic fundamentalism that swept Ayatollah Khomeini to power in 1979, culminating in the seizure of hostages at the U.S. embassy. Subsequent American efforts have been directed at containing Islamic fundamentalism and, specifically, Iranian influence. This policy was more recently underscored by the Iran and Libya Sanctions Act (signed in 1996 and modified in 1997), which prevents companies from investing more than $20 million per year in Iran. In this way, the Clinton administration attempted to isolate and pressure Iran (while selectively granting exemptions for Kazakhstan and Turkmenistan and for participants in the South Pars project, including the French oil company, Total). Despite the moderation of Tehran's domestic and foreign policy following the emergence of the Khatami government, the Clinton administration was extremely cautious in reevaluating its Iranian policy.[31]

A second geopolitical aspect of U.S. policy is opposition to Russian hegemony. In part, this opposition is indistinguishable from U.S. political and military support for the newly independent states (see below). But an additional component involves official endorsement for the Baku-Ceyhan main export pipeline, which would circumvent Russian soil. The stated rationale for this position is to avoid excessive reliance on Russia. Beneath this concern, however, lurk deeply embedded fears about resurgent Russian expansionism.[32] At first blush, the prospects for overt political and military dominance by Moscow may appear illusory, given the miserable level to which the country's fortunes have sunk in the aftermath of the currency crisis and default in the fall of 1998. Nonetheless, extreme nationalist elements within the Russian strategic elite have consistently used various stratagems to further their interests, including the use of military pressure to compromise President Eduard Shevardnadze's control of Georgia and provision of clandestine military support for Armenia in its struggle over Nagorno-Karabakh. Even in the aftermath of the financial collapse, it is a commonplace to encounter nostalgia for Moscow's past glory and assertions of Russia's continued "great power" status. Although U.S. conduct—including in the former Yugoslavia as well as in the Caspian region—has contributed to the reemergence of aggressive jingoism and anti-American sentiment, such attitudes have a deeply entrenched constituency in Russian society.[33]

A third prominent theme in U.S. policy is the encouragement of independence (and, nominally, the promotion of democracy) for Kazakhstan, Azerbaijan, and Turkmenistan. As already suggested, promoting autonomy for the former Soviet states offers a way of advancing U.S. oil interests and containing Russian expansionism. This approach involves concrete as well as symbolic forms of American support (most blatantly obvious in the Clinton administration's attempts to rescind Section 907 of the Freedom Support Act).[34] Militarily, such support includes U.S.-led peacekeeping exercises in the Black Sea, Caucasus, and Central Asian regions; offers of direct military assistance; and overtures for more active NATO cooperation through the Partnership for Peace program.[35]

All three U.S. goals—containment of Iran, containment and limited engagement with Russia, and autonomy for the former Soviet states—are intimately bound up in the tangled pipeline politics of the region. Officially, Washington has steadfastly endorsed construction of multiple pipeline routes. Without reviewing the extraordinarily complicated options and calculations involved in this matter, the key point is that multiple pipelines, as interpreted by Washington, would avoid complete reliance on Russian routes (thereby reducing Russian influence) and would entirely avoid Iranian soil.[36] The Clinton administration specifically favored east-west routes, including a main export pipeline running from Baku to Ceyhan, Turkey, on the Mediterranean Sea. In addition, the administration endorsed the idea of a trans-Caspian line (or lines) laid on the deep-sea floor.[37] Such efforts are intended to enhance the ability of the former Soviet states to extract and transport oil and gas independently (i.e., without Russian or Iranian approval) and preferably in conjunction with U.S.-based MNCs. Ostensibly, energy extraction offers these states a path to development and democratization.[38]

Similarly, the United States has attempted to influence the outcome of a legal dispute over the ownership of Caspian natural resources. Again, the issues are highly complex, but the fundamental question is whether these resources are owned separately or jointly by the littoral states. The Clinton administration called for division of the sea into exclusive national sectors, and Energy Secretary Bill Richardson intervened in regional negotiations between Azerbaijan and Turkmenistan to promote resolution of the legal debate on these terms.[39] The purpose of such efforts is to foster the realization of a pipeline regime preferred by the United States and to promote inclusion of American firms in future energy contracts.

The crucial issue for the purpose of this chapter is how such U.S. policies affect the Caspian ecology and the prospects for regional cooperation. The simple answer is that such influence is sharply negative, at least insofar as it impedes the emergence of a multilateral environmental regime. First, the trans-Caspian pipeline poses significant dangers in its own right, particularly if its contents are oil.[40] U.S. officials have taken the position that such difficulties can be managed with the best available technology and with oil company support of a regional environmental protection fund.[41] In addition, U.S. political intervention on behalf of the trans-Caspian pipeline impedes agreement on a legal status that would be compatible with a sound environmental regime. On the contrary, bilateral division of the seabed—and possibly of the water column as well—between Azerbaijan and Turkmenistan undermines the process of multilateral negotiation within the structure established by the Caspian Environmental Program. It also potentially introduces enormous legal obstacles to the successful management of common pool resources.

Current Issues Affecting U.S. Policy

As we have seen, environmental issues have taken a distant back seat to economic and geopolitical goals in the formulation of U.S. policy regarding the Caspian. Yet the evolution of U.S. policy is not impervious to international political and economic trends. Regarding the Caspian region, a number of recent developments may affect Washington's outlook in the future:

1. *The partial decline of the Caspian's allure.* This decline is the result of several factors, including initially exaggerated accounts of reserves, unfavorable political and geographic factors complicating the extraction of Caspian energy, and a steep fall in the price of oil. First, there have been mounting criticisms of early, highly optimistic forecasts of oil and gas deposits (criticisms in part owing to disappointments in the exploration of several key geologic structures). Second, operators are facing higher than anticipated costs for preferred export routes owing to difficulties involving terrain and poor existing infrastructure. This problem is compounded by concerns over regional political instability, which cannot be avoided by any foreseeable route. Third, the emergence of an oil glut on international markets and consequent drop in price per barrel for some time called into question the near-term feasibility of exporting Caspian energy. Although oil prices have rebounded following stabilization of the Asian currency crisis, concerns are likely to linger over possible increased Iraqi production and ongoing cooperation problems among OPEC and non-OPEC countries.

2. *The normalization of Iranian politics, reflected in President Khatami's domestic and foreign policies since the late 1990s.* The trend toward normalization is not unchallenged; indeed, there is clearly enormous opposition from the Ayatollah Khameini and other elements of the senior leadership.[42] Nevertheless, this trend suggests that U.S. policy toward Iran may be misplaced. A number of prominent

analysts have cautioned against continuing to isolate Iran, pointing out that this tactic not only misses an important opportunity, but also helps create an anti-American alliance between Teheran and Moscow.[43] Although the administration's response to such arguments has been rather aloof, as of this writing there have been a number of tentative but intriguing indications of increasing flexibility in U.S. policy, which may become more pronounced following the 2000 presidential elections.

3. *Changes in Russian domestic politics and Caspian policy.* The emergence of a pro-extraction Russian policy since mid-1997 (in contrast to previous efforts to block extraction) has reflected a major change in Russian behavior and in the tenor of Russian policy more broadly. Rather than trying to block or completely dominate energy extraction, the prevailing line favors enlarging Russia's share in various consortia arrangements. Although highly competitive and at times aggressive, this policy is no longer bellicose or essentially obstructive.[44] In addition, the poor state of the Russian economy portends a further decline in Moscow's hard power, which also lessens the perceived need to offset Russian influence. Regardless of who succeeds Boris Yeltsin, this combination of domestic trends and external constraints is likely to promote essential stability in Russia's Caspian policy.

In sum, these three developments eliminate much of the rationale for U.S. policy as it has evolved since the mid-1990s. Taken together they imply, objectively, that a lower priority ought to be attached to rapid extraction of Caspian energy. Additionally, they suggest new opportunities for cooperative engagement with Iran and Russia. The combination of reduced urgency of energy extraction and a potential "degeopoliticization" of the region would, in turn, provide greater latitude for addressing long-term issues, including environmental security.

Conclusion

U.S. policies aimed at pursuing geopolitical interests have further polarized the already tense relations among Caspian states. This international competition constitutes a major obstacle to attaining environmental cooperation. Indeed, U.S. attempts to project influence and to achieve full or partial containment of Iran and Russia, respectively, may have insidious consequences by helping to undermine the foreign-policy liberalism promoted by elements within these states. Even proactive efforts by the United States to encourage geopolitical cooperation are unlikely to succeed if they are divorced from environmental cooperation, because the environment is one of the few areas in which perceived national interests are essentially compatible.[45]

At the same time, the burden of success or failure in environmental cooperation cannot be laid entirely at the door of the United States. National identities, regional competition, domestic political institutions, and developmental time horizons are complex and intertwined factors. At best, they are only in part amenable to American influence. Yet although U.S. policy is not the most important factor responsible for the emergence of a given foreign policy on the part of the Caspian states, it nevertheless remains a significant factor. The willingness of the United States to provide or withhold political, technological, managerial, and financial support will go a long way toward making or breaking environmentalism in the Caspian basin. Specifically, in seeking environmental cooperation, U.S. support for the CEP has the potential to be enormously productive.

Advocating such a policy is likely to be a hard sell in Washington because the outcome it foresees would almost inherently diminish U.S. influence in zero-sum terms and would instead promote a relatively nongeopoliticized context. On the other hand, both the stability of the region and its sustainable economic growth would certainly benefit U.S. national interests in the long run—which would also be in keeping with the trend of globalization toward diffusion of political control and dramatically increased flows of information and capital. Indeed, the future prospects of the United States in the Caspian Sea region may ultimately depend on its ability to adopt this perspective.

Notes

1 For a general overview, see A. Mekhtiev and A. Gul, "Ecological Problems of the Caspian Sea and Perspectives on Possible Solutions," in *Scientific, Environmental, and Political Issues in the Circum-Caspian Region*, ed. M. Glantz and I. Zonn (Dordrecht, Holland: Kluwer, 1997), 79–96.

2 A. Shcherbakova and W. Wallace, "The Environmental Legacy of Soviet Peaceful Nuclear Explosions," *CIS Environmental Watch* 4 (summer 1993): 43; see also *Aziyah-Ezh* (Almaty) 9 (15 September 1995), 7, in *Foreign Broadcast Information Service—Former Soviet Union*, 95-185-S, 25 September 1995.

3 A good discussion of fisheries problems can be found in Igor Zonn, *Kaspiiskii memorandum* (Moscow: Russian Academy of Natural Sciences, 1997), 137–68.

4 Henri Dumont, "Ecocide in the Caspian Sea," *Nature* 377 (26 October 1995): 673–75.

5 Gilbert Rowe, "Azerbaijan, Oil, and Sustainable Development in Azerbaijan," *Quarterdeck* 4 (winter 1996), available at <http://www-ocean.tamu.edu/Quarterdeck/QD4.3/rowe-4.3.html>.

6 A prominent discussion is G. Golitsyn, D. Ratkovich, M. Fortus, and A. Frolov, "On the Present-Day Rise in the Caspian Sea Level," *Water Resources* 25 (1998): 131–36.

7 Statement of the Honorable Federico Peña, U.S. secretary of energy, for the Committee on International Relations, U.S. House of Representatives, U.S.

Information Service, 30 April 1998; and see U.S. Department of State, *Caspian Region Energy Development Report* (Washington, D.C.: U.S. Government Printing Office, 15 April 1997).

8 See, for example, the testimony of Robert W. Gee (assistant secretary of energy for policy and international affairs) before the U.S. House of Representatives, International Relations Committee, Subcommittee on Asia and the Pacific, 105th Cong., 2d sess., 12 February 1998, reported by Federal News Service, 12 February 1998.

9 Theodore Streit of the U.S. Agency for International Development, head of the Caspian Environmental Partnership program, interview by author, Almaty, Kazakhstan, June 1999. As part of the partnership, the United States Agency for International Development has granted $425,000 to the Minerals Management Service (a division of the Department of the Interior) to provide environmental and managerial advice to Kazakhstan and Turkmenistan on leasing offshore oil and gas fields. "U.S. to Help Kazaks, Turkmens Develop Offshore Legal Regime," Reuters, 15 October 1998.

10 Section 907 restricts the government's ability to provide direct financial support to Azerbaijan by tying such aid to Azerbaijani concessions in the Nagorno-Karabakh conflict.

11 The Aral Sea program also includes a range of international agreements and protocols dealing with water sharing, water quality, and energy. Interview with Theodore Streit; and see the testimony of Don Pressley, an official with the United States Agency for International Development, before the House International Relations Committee, U.S. Information Service, Washington, D.C., 2 May 1998.

12 NATO, "The Caspian Sea," *Science and Society Newsletter* 50 (first quarter 1998), available at <http://www.nato.int/science/newsletter/980503.htm>. Indeed, at a meeting of the Caspian Environmental Program held in Moscow in May 1999, attended by the author, the head of the Russian Thematic Center for Legal Problems rejected a suggestion to incorporate NATO's scientific findings on the grounds that they would cause political strife.

13 Douglas W. Blum, "The Russian Trade-Off: Environment and Development in the Caspian Sea," *Journal of Environment and Development* 7 (September 1998): 248–77.

14 "Azerbaijan's New Pollution Standards Less Strict Than in Soviet Era," *Pipeline News* 62 (31 May–6 June 1997): 8; also, officials from the State Committee for Environmental Protection, interview by author, Baku, May 1999.

15 Scott Horton and Natik Mamedov, "Azerbaijan's Legal Environment," *CIS Law Notes* (June 1997), available at <http://www.pbwt.com/CIS9706.HTM>.

16 "Ecology of the Caspian Sea Is in Danger," *AzadInform News Bulletin* 35 (5 November 1998); "Discussion on Removal of Possible Oil Floods on Land

and Sea Held at State Ecology Committee," Turan News Agency (8 September 1998). Both available at <harbarlar-1@usc.edu>.

17 "Off-Shore Oil Spill Response Training Exercise to Be Held in the Caspian," AssA-Irada, Azerbaijan International Independent News Agency (1 September 1998); "AIOC Focus on Environmental Excellence," *AzadInform News Bulletin* 45 (20 November 1998). Both available at <harbarlar-1@usc.edu>.

18 For an Iranian perspective, see A. Badakhshan and J. Shayegan, "Iranian Perspective on Environmental Problems in the Caspian Sea Region," in Glantz and Zonn, eds., *Scientific, Environmental, and Political Issues,* 191–209.

19 For a journalistic report, see "Oil-and-Gas Rich Country Swallows Money, Still Needing More," *Christian Science Monitor,* 28 September 1998, A7. Caspian environmental issues have been addressed mainly in the limited independent press. "Caspian Sea Needs Urgent Protection," *Neitralny Turkmenistan,* reprinted in *Turkistan-Newsletter: Business* (13 March 1998), available at <http://www.soros.org/tajik/cenasia/1114.html>.

20 For examples see *Izvestiia,* 12 November 1994; and "SOCAR Starts Preparation of Draft Agreement on Cleaning of Lands Polluted with Oil," *Turan Energy* (17 August 1998), available at <http://www.soros.org/tajik/cenasia/1114.html>.

21 "Highlights from the Global Environment Facility Assembly," *Sustainable Developments* 14 (April 1998), available at <http://www.iisd.ca/sd/gef/sdvol14no2e.html>.

22 Although the initial focus of this program would be Nagorno-Karabakh, the program is also intended to deal with the Caspian Sea region as a whole. "State Committee for Ecology Proposes to Set Up an International Audit in Conflict Zone," AssA-Irada, Azerbaijan International Independent News Agency (11 September 1998), available at <harbarlar-1@usc.edu>.

23 "Soros Foundation Organizes International Ecological Movement to Protect Caspian," AssA-Irada, Azerbaijan International Independent News Agency (28 August 1998), available at <harbarlar-1@usc.edu>.

24 Caspian Environmental Program, *Concept Paper* (Washington, D.C.: World Bank, 3 May 1998).

25 Karen Dokken, "Environmental Conflict and International Integration," in *Conflict and the Environment,* ed. Nils Gleditsch (Dordrecht: Kluwer, 1997), 519–34; Peter Haas, *Saving the Mediterranean: The Politics of International Environmental Cooperation* (New York: Columbia University Press, 1990); Ronald Mitchell, "Sources of Transparency: Information Systems in International Regimes," *International Studies Quarterly* 42 (March 1998): 109–30; Kal Raustiala, "States, NGO's, and International Environmental Institutions," *International Studies Quarterly* 41 (December 1997): 719–40.

26 David Aubrey and Vladimir Mamaev from the United Nations Development Program and the Caspian Environmental Program, interview by author,

Woods Hole, Massachusetts, October 1998; also Jan Kalicki, ombudsman for Energy and Commercial Relations with the New Independent States, interview by author, Providence, Rhode Island, May 1999.

27 For background on the "deal of the century" and the ensuing scramble for oil and gas, see Rosemarie Forsythe, *The Politics of Oil in the Caucasus and Central Asia*, Adelphi Paper 300 (London: IISS, 1996).

28 "Speech by Ambassador Richard Morningstar at the Central Asia Institute of the Paul H. Nitze School of Advanced International Studies," Johns Hopkins University, Washington, D.C., 9 September 1998, in *Turkmenistan Newsletter: Business* 98 (10 September 1998), available at <http://www.soros.org/tajik/cenasia/1114.html>.

29 David Ottaway and Dan Morgan, "Former Top U.S. Aides Seek Caspian Gusher," *Washington Post*, 6 July 1997, A1.

30 For a similar argument, see Amy Myers Jaffe and Robert Manning, "The Myth of the Caspian 'Great Game': The Real Geopolitics of Energy," *Survival* 40 (winter 1998–99): 112–29.

31 President Clinton has reaffirmed that the "state of emergency" declared in 1979 remains in effect. U.S. Newswire, White House, Washington, D.C., 9 November 1998.

32 Such fears are evidenced in North Atlantic Treaty Organization expansion, a process from which Moscow has been essentially excluded.

33 "Ivanov Warns Russia Will Protect Its Interests in Caucasus; Slams Baku-Ceyhan, Trans-Caspian Pipelines," *RFE/RL Newsline* (2 September 1999), available at <http://www.rferl.org/newsline/>.

34 Although repeal has been unsuccessful to date, both the House and Senate have passed legislation allowing numerous exemptions for direct funding. Embassy of the Republic of Azerbaijan, "U.S. Congress Adopts Further Exemptions to Section 907," *Azerbaijan Newsletter*, Washington, D.C., 21 October 1998, 1–2.

35 Examples include "Central Asia: U.S. to Participate in Joint Military Exercise," *RFE/RL Newsline* (29 August 1997); "Shevardnadze Welcomes Assistance from U.S. Navy," *RFE/RL Newsline* (11 September 1998). See also Sonia Winter, "Former Soviet Union: U.S. Senate Stresses Equality for Republics," *RFE/RL Report* (16 July 1997); and "U.S. Calls for Four-way Agreement on Trans-Caspian Pipeline," *RFE/RL Newsline* (20 August 1999). All available at <http://www.rferl.org/newsline/>.

36 At the same time, officials have attempted to avoid alienating Moscow by encouraging Russian involvement in extraction and transportation schemes. Text of speech by Jan Kalicki, ombudsman for Energy and Commercial Relations with the New Independent States, at the "Caspian Pipelines" conference, Washington, D.C., 19 November 1997 (author's personal copy).

37 "U.S. Backs Non-Iranian, 'Eurasian' Corridor West for Caspian Sea Oil," *Washington Post*, 20 November 1997, A37.

38 For a sharply critical assessment of these prospects, see Martha Brill Olcott, "The Caspian's False Promise," *Foreign Policy* 111 (summer 1998): 95–113.

39 U.S. Department of State, *Caspian Region Energy Development Report* (Washington, D.C.: U.S. Government Printing Office, 15 April 1997); "U.S. to Mediate in Conflicts over Caspian Oil," *Financial Times*, 16 September 1998, available at http://www.globalarchive.ft.com>.

40 Rory Cox and Doug Norlen, *The Great Ecological Game: Will Caspian Sea Oil Development Lead to Environmental Disaster?* (Oakland, Calif.: Pacific Environment and Resources Center, January 1999).

41 According to Energy Secretary Bill Richardson, U.S.-based oil firms operating off the coast of Azerbaijan are projected to invest roughly $30 billion in the next twenty years, $5 billion of which will be earmarked for environmental protection. "U.S.A. Planning to Mediate in Turkmenian-Azerbaijan Dispute," ITAR-TASS, 16 September 1998.

42 On the 23 October 1998 election of the third Assembly of Experts, which reflected the entrenched power of conservative clerics in Iran, see "Defining Election in Iran," *Turkistan-Newsletter* (13 November 1998), available at <http://www.soros.org/tajik/cenasia/1114.html>.

43 For example, S. Frederick Starr, "Power Failure: American Policy in the Caspian," *The National Interest* 47 (1997): 20–31; Ian Bremmer, "Oil Politics: America and the Riches of the Caspian Basin," *World Policy Journal* 15 (spring 1998): 27–35.

44 Douglas W. Blum, "Domestic Politics and Russia's Caspian Policy," *Post-Soviet Affairs* 14 (April–June 1998): 137–64.

45 A narrow endorsement of U.S. efforts to spur geopolitical cooperation is given by Michael Croissant, "U.S. Interests in the Caspian Sea Basin," *Comparative Strategy* 16 (October–December 1997): 353–67.

DOMESTIC AND INTERNATIONAL POLITICS

5 Evolution of the Ozone Regime: Local, National, and International Influences

Srini Sitaraman

The 1987 Montreal Protocol on Substances that Deplete the Stratospheric Ozone Layer, which restricts the production and consumption of ozone-depleting substances (ODSs), is considered an exemplary model of international cooperation.[1] However, the development of the Montreal Protocol has puzzled some scholars of international relations. They are particularly perplexed by the behavior of self-interested utility-maximizing states, which banded together to cooperate over an international collective good—the ozone layer—in an anarchical world.[2] How did the cooperating states manage to overcome the free-rider and cheating problems in an international environment that lacks strict governance mechanisms to enforce interstate contracts?[3] Despite collective action problems and the scientific uncertainty surrounding ozone depletion, the Montreal Protocol was ratified and has been strengthened several times. Even countries that did not participate in the original negotiations have since joined the treaty.

This chapter is concerned with the factors that influenced the construction and subsequent revisions and extensions of the Montreal Protocol. To explain the emergence of the ozone regime, previous studies of international cooperation on the ozone layer have emphasized different aspects of domestic and international politics, such as science and cognitive factors, international institutions, and the leadership role of the United States. In this chapter, I argue that both domestic and international factors should be combined to understand the evolution of the Montreal Protocol more fully. I analyze the evolution of the ozone regime through the prism of local, national, and international levels of analysis to assess the independent impact of domestic *and* international factors.

The chapter is divided into five main sections. The first section establishes the theoretical argument and argues why the integration of all three levels of analysis is necessary to understand the development of the ozone treaty. The second section discusses how local politics and growing environmental awareness within the United States galvanized public opinion and influenced international environmental policy. The third section shows how the movement of science from the confines of academia into the policy arena enabled the development of national and international consensus on the dangers posed to humankind by ozone-layer depletion. The fourth section focuses on international institutions and the role they played in facilitating the Montreal Protocol. The last section explains how interactions among the three levels—local, national, and international—influenced U.S. foreign environmental policy and the related development of the ozone regime. Moreover, it will elucidate why the ozone treaty and its subsequent extensions are considered to be milestones in the development of international environmental institutions.

Local Actors, the State, and the International System: Combining Domestic and International Levels of Analysis

What is the appropriate unit of analysis to uncover the causes of international cooperation? Do these causes reside in the fundamental nature of human beings? Or does the answer lie in the domestic political and social structures with which human beings interact? If not, do the underlying causes of international events lie in systemic factors such as the structure of interstate relations? The issue of levels of analysis—or images—has been of interest in the discipline of international relations even before international relations became a formal academic discipline.[4] However, to date no authoritative answer exists as to which level or image is the determinative causal unit for international cooperation and conflict.[5] For a short time, it seemed to some scholars that international-level (or third-image) explanations, which attribute conflictual and cooperative behavior to the structural features of the international system, such as anarchy, had adequately addressed the issue of levels of analysis.[6] As Waltz suggested, because all states are functionally similar and because all states desire to maximize their security, one could conveniently ignore domestic politics (second image) and the vagaries of individual human behavior (first image), and instead focus on the international level.[7]

State behavior at the international or "systemic" level is characterized by competition for power and resources under conditions of anarchy, which means that no supranational organization exists to regulate state behavior and mediate collective action problems. In other words, according to structural realists, the world of international politics is purely competitive, without much allowance for cooperative behavior. However, the revival of interest in cognitive studies and domestic politics shows that analyses that rely exclusively on international or structural factors have not provided wholly convincing answers.[8] Therefore, scholarly attention has turned recently toward domestic politics to improve our understanding of the mechanisms that generate international cooperation.[9] And some scholars have sought to develop an integrated understanding of interstate relations, combining domestic and international politics.[10]

According to Robert Putnam, domestic politics and international relations are hopelessly entangled. Therefore, any explanation of an international event cannot be made without taking the domestic and international contexts into consideration. In order to accommodate both domestic and international factors simultaneously, Putnam has developed the concept of two-level games.[11] A two-level game attempts to capture the strategic interaction between the chief of government (COG) and his or her rivals, nested within a second set of negotiations between the COG and domestic constituents. Negotiations between COGs and their domestic constituents indicate that international deals must receive support at the domestic level, especially from legislative bodies.

In this chapter, I extend the conceptual logic of two-level games to three levels of analysis—local, national, and international. The first level of analysis captures the interaction among the different societal actors; the second level focuses on the dynamics between the societal actors and the national government; and the third level concentrates on international negotiations among the different national governments and the influence of international institutions.

An integrated approach to understanding the evolution of the ozone regime requires tracing the causal influence of scientific knowledge, epistemic actors, and institutional structures that propelled the ozone depletion hypothesis from the realm of science to international public policy. At the local level (Level I), scientists had to convince themselves and their colleagues about the validity of their claims. This process involved generation of evidence to establish authoritatively that ODSs were primarily responsible for the destruction of the ozone layer. Hence, atmospheric scientists were involved in exchanging ideas, repeated testing of the ozone depletion theory, and publication of their findings in major scientific journals. These research findings were subsequently published in non-technical magazines and newspapers, which enabled the popularization of the ozone problem.

The context of scientific research changed when the U.S. government entered the ozone debate by forming expert panels to examine the ozone depletion theory and its public policy significance. Research indicating that chlorofluorocarbons (CFCs) were harming the stratospheric ozone layer entered the national level (Level II) of the policy process when it moved from the confines of academia to the national political arena. In other words, ozone research became a political process because of its public policy implications. If the claims of the CFC-ozone theory were correct, the primary chemical culprits—CFCs found in common household items such as aerosol sprays, refrigerators, coolants, and packaging materials—had to be regulated. Industry groups with vested interests in limiting CFC regulation began to question the validity of the ozone depletion theory, whereas environmental groups began a campaign to accelerate the regulatory process.

The United States government could not embark on an active regulation program because the environmentalists exaggerated the costs and consequences of ozone depletion, whereas chemical industry groups downplayed the effect of CFC emissions. In such a politically charged setting, U.S. policymakers had to assure themselves that they could develop a public consensus favoring regulatory policies. Therefore, many of the public policy endeavors in the United States centered on consensus development, which was pursued through a series of congressional hearings based on major scientific studies conducted under the aegis of the National Academy of Sciences (NAS). Nonetheless, the global dimension of the ozone depletion problem complicated the domestic regulatory process in the United States. Any independent domestic regulation by the United States was unlikely to stop depletion of the ozone layer because other countries could increase their CFC emissions and accelerate the rate of depletion. Hence, any permanent and lasting solution to the ozone depletion problem required international policy coordination.

Development of an ozone protection treaty required the internationalization of the problem (Level III) through international institutions such as the United Nations (UN) and the Organization for Economic Cooperation and Development (OECD). Later, a new institution—the Ozone Secretariat under a United Nations Environmental Program (UNEP) framework—was created exclusively to facilitate international policy coordination over ozone-depleting substances. Simultaneously, transnational collaboration developed among international organizations (IOs), nongovernmental organizations (NGOs), and national governmental agencies (NGAs). The efforts of these organizations focused on exchange of ideas, sponsorship of international scientific cooperation, and joint research programs and information sharing, all leading to the development of international scientific consensus. Active diplomatic initiatives of the United States were instrumental in the negotiation of the Montreal Protocol.

Initially, the evolution of the ozone regime moved rather explicitly from local to national to international levels. However, in the later stages of its development, especially after 1978, the lines separating the different levels gradually disappeared. The movement was haphazard, and the progress made in international negotiations significantly slowed down between the late 1970s and early 1980s. However, domestic political developments and active U.S. diplomatic initiatives accelerated the international negotiations, resulting in negotiation of the Vienna Convention in 1985 and the Montreal Protocol in 1987.

Level I, the Local Level:
Origins of the Science of Ozone Depletion

In 1961, the United States began work on a supersonic transport airplane (SST). The airplane was never developed commercially owing to considerable economic and technical difficulties. What is more, there were serious concerns that a fleet of supersonic planes flying at altitudes of sixty thousand feet might modify or permanently damage the upper atmosphere by emitting ozone-depleting chemicals.[12] This concern prompted the SST project committee to launch an investigation into the possible effects of SST emissions on stratospheric ozone. Subsequently, in 1971 the U.S. Department of Transportation (DOT), with the assistance of the NAS, established the Climatic Impact Assessment Program (CIAP) to develop a comprehensive report on ozone depletion.[13] A panel of experts was created to perform a four-year study and publish a comprehensive report.[14]

Both the CIAP and the NAS studies suggested that nitrogen, sulfur, and carbon compounds released by supersonic planes could reduce ozone levels in the upper atmosphere.[15] In addition, the reports indicated that reduction in the amount of ozone could also affect surface temperatures and rainfall patterns. These conclusions echoed the testimonies provided during 1971 congressional hearings,[16] and they reinforced the conclusions reached by two other NAS studies published earlier.[17] While working on an independent project for the National Aeronautics and Space Administration (NASA), Ralph Cicerone and Richard Stolarski of the University of Michigan found that chlorine compounds ejected from space rocket boosters could harm the ozone layer.[18] Although the NAS panel concluded that it would be difficult to estimate the impact of SST effluents on climate change, it indicated that the effects of ozone-layer depletion on human health could be estimated.[19] The NAS report indicated that the destruction of the ozone layer would lead to a rise in UV-B radiation, which had the potential to increase skin cancer rates and also produce vision defects among humans. Earlier, James McDonald of the University of Arizona had suggested that ozone depletion could increase instances of skin cancer, but his theory was not taken very seriously.[20]

Meanwhile, Sherwood Rowland and Mario Molina were working independently on a different aspect of the ozone depletion problem. They had reason to believe that CFCs widely used as aerosol spray propellants and refrigerants could be destroying the ozone layer.[21] Rowland and Molina argued that because the rate of worldwide CFC consumption exceeded at least a million tons a year, the ozone layer was depleting rapidly, and this process could continue for a long time because of fluorocarbon accumulation in the upper atmosphere. Rowland and Molina contended that CFCs were resistant to molecular breakdown and so linger in the upper atmosphere for a long time, slowly destroying the ozone layer. Most of the chemicals that escape into the upper atmosphere break down either by interacting with other chemicals or by being washed out by rainfall. Rowland and Molina found that the real culprits were chlorine atoms found in fluorocarbon compounds, which react with oxygen molecules and disrupt the formation of the ozone layer.[22]

Initially, the Rowland-Molina theory did not receive much attention, except from DuPont Chemicals, which objected to Rowland and Molina's using its brand name—freon—to refer to chlorofluorocarbons. Although the CFC-ozone theory was hotly debated at American Chemical Society (ACS) meetings, it was generally considered to be "off the wall."[23] However, it gradually gained recognition among some atmospheric scientists. Six months after the publication of the Rowland-Molina theory, the U.S. Congress held its first hearing to consider the health and environmental effects of ozone depletion.[24] A Harvard research group also confirmed that the CFCs used in aerosol sprays and as refrigerants were indeed capable of destroying the ozone layer.[25] Simultaneously, the ozone depletion theory began to receive extensive media coverage, and demands for a ban on fluorocarbons began to grow.

The Rowland-Molina theory marked a radical shift in the ozone debate because it changed the focus from the issue of nitrogen and chlorine emissions from aircraft and space vehicles to an issue of widespread chlorine emissions from ordinary household activities. Effluents from the SST could be regulated easily, whereas control of fluorocarbon emissions from millions of individual spray propellants and refrigeration units was a difficult task. This task was particularly challenging because the evidence linking CFC discharge to ozone-layer destruction was insufficient to embark on a massive regulation program. However, at the same time, the federal government could not remain inactive and continue to dismiss the CFC-ozone theory as mere scientific speculation. Environmental groups and pro-environment politicians were demanding immediate action, such as a ban on fluorocarbon production. On the other hand, industry groups such as the Manufacturing Chemists Association (MCA) and DuPont were equally vociferous in discrediting the Rowland-Molina theory. They argued that it would be foolish to hastily ban CFC production and consumption based on a speculative and untested theory because doing so would impose undue economic costs.[26] Because the scientific evidence was not indisputable, Congress decided that further research was necessary before any policy decision could be made.

Level II, the National Level: Scientific Uncertainty and Ozone Politics

The ozone crisis became a major policy issue a few months after the publication of the Rowland-Molina theory, when it began to receive widespread media coverage. Seventy articles on the ozone issue were published in the *New York Times* between 1974 and 1975, with more than forty-four news items appearing in 1975 alone.[27] Because of the extensive media attention, many concerned citizens and environmental groups began to lobby policymakers, urging them to ban fluorocarbon production. The federal government commissioned the NAS to produce a series of comprehensive reports to examine the nature and extent of ozone depletion. The NAS conducted eleven major studies between 1971 and 1984, examining the different dimensions, issues, and the problems associated with the ozone depletion theory.[28] Later, the policy implications were examined during congressional hearings that initiated proceedings to regulate fluorocarbon emissions. The first major hearing on the CFC-ozone theory was held in December 1974, seven months after the Rowland-Molina paper was published.[29]

Preliminary investigations were started by a federal task force referred to as the Inadvertent Modification of the Stratosphere (IMOS). The IMOS task force was composed of fifteen different federal agencies,[30] and it unequivocally reinforced Rowland and Molina's conclusions. In addition, it indicated that decreasing ozone concentrations would produce adverse health effects such as increased instances of fatal and nonfatal melanoma.[31] Hence, the IMOS panel suggested that the fluorocarbon industry should be regulated unless new scientific evidence were to refute the results of the Rowland-Molina theory. Nevertheless, the IMOS panel indicated that finding alternatives to CFCs would require a long period. Hence, it cautioned that any restrictions imposed on CFC production would affect more than one million jobs and have impacts on the economy because the refrigeration and the fluorocarbon industry was a $7.2 billion business.[32] Overall, the IMOS study made three main policy suggestions: (1) reorganize federal regulatory agencies so that a single agency would have complete jurisdiction over the entire fluorocarbon industry; (2) continue funding more research; and (3) encourage international cooperation because the United States could not solve the ozone problem by itself. Moreover, the IMOS report suggested that the federal government should await the results from improved scientific research before it considered any policy action.

After the initial study, the IMOS task force was disbanded and the responsibility of producing reports on the ozone problem was transferred to the NAS, which released a major report on the CFC-ozone theory in 1976. Although the report did not make any specific policy proposals, it strengthened the conclusions reached by the IMOS task force.[33] It stated that even if the fluorocarbon release rates started declining, there would be a "doubling in the expected ozone reduction, to the value of 10 to 15 percent."[34] The IMOS group concluded that the natural and modeling uncertainties prevented it from announcing with absolute certainty that fluorocarbon emissions were the main cause of ozone loss. It emphasized the need for further refinements in modeling techniques, technological innovations, and improvements in understanding the atmospheric chemistry of chlorine compounds in order to generate accurate predictions.

Acknowledgment by the NAS and other atmospheric scientists that they could not declare with absolute certainty that fluorocarbons were the primary cause for ozone depletion became the rallying point for industry groups. Although there was increasing general consensus that man-made CFCs were responsible for ozone loss, the scientists were reluctant to assert with absolute certainty that they had completely understood the chemistry of fluorocarbons in the upper atmosphere. The lack of complete certainty provided the fluorocarbon industry with the needed ammunition to discredit the ozone depletion theory,[35] and DuPont led a campaign to challenge it.[36] Even atmospheric scientists who subscribed to the Rowland-Molina theory were unwilling to suggest any policy prescriptions, especially when industry groups and other atmospheric scientists were against banning or regulating fluorocarbon use.[37]

DuPont asserted that additional experimental data and further study were absolutely necessary before any regulation policy was contemplated.[38] DuPont's position was supported by the chemical industry and by allies in academia. Many scientists recognized that modeling uncertainties associated with CFC-ozone theory were unavoidable, and they were not convinced that the extant models closely approximated the actual situation. Nevertheless, DuPont announced that if new evidence established with certainty that fluorocarbons were the primary cause of ozone loss, it would stop manufacturing the offending compounds.

Some of the leading opponents of the ozone-CFC theory, such as Fred Singer, contended that the scientific evidence was too inconclusive to warrant draconian measures such as banning CFC production and consumption.[39] Singer argued that the environmental bureaucracy and the scientific community shut down his dissenting voice because they were eager to demonstrate their social worth and fulfill their narrow self-interested goals. Natural causes, he claimed—such as periodic fluctuations in the surface temperature of the sun, volcanic eruptions, and natural methane release—also contribute to ozone depletion.[40] Richard Scorer, an atmospheric scientist from the United Kingdom, dismissed the ozone depletion theory as "utter nonsense."[41] He argued that for millions of years the ozone layer had survived innumerable natural perturbations and so was capable of withstanding the effects of a "little more chlorine from the fluorocarbons."[42] Similarly, James Lovelock, another U.K.-based atmospheric scientist, contended that natural halocarbon cycles reduce the importance of man-made chemicals in disrupting the atmospheric balance.[43] Overall, adversaries of the Rowland-Molina theory asserted that it was difficult to separate the impact of man-made fluoro-carbons on the ozone layer because they coalesce with naturally occurring chlorine, nitrogen, and other radicals. They further argued that even if the impact of anthropogenic emissions were separated analytically from natural chemical effects, the results would not clearly establish that human intervention was the primary cause of ozone depletion.

The counterclaims of dissenting scientists and the fluorocarbon industry were largely based on their disagreements over the methodology and modeling techniques utilized in measuring ozone loss. Differences regarding the basic structure, assumption, and type of the ozone depletion model (i.e., whether the model was one, two, or three dimensional) and regarding the method used to calculate the rate of ozone loss were the primary causes of controversy. Ozone depletion models produced widely fluctuating estimates not only because of modeling difficulties, but also because of measurement and data problems. Most models of ozone loss have to be calibrated with atmospheric data to determine the actual rate of ozone destruction. Ozone depletion rates are measured using the ground-based Dobson spectrophotometer and the balloon-borne spectrophotometer. After 1975, ozone depletion rates were also measured from the NASA weather satellites. All these instruments seek to calculate the average oxygen (O_3) content in the stratosphere. This process becomes difficult because of periodic fluctuations in O_3 content from seasonal changes and other natural causes. Moreover, in the 1970s, scientists lacked strong evidence to claim that CFCs reached the upper atmosphere unaltered. If the chemical structure of CFCs changed during transportation, it might not have the predicted impact on the ozone layer.

Scientific uncertainty and the lobbying efforts of the chemical industry affected the credibility of ozone science, leading some policymakers to believe that the ozone problem did not require urgent solutions. Public interest in the ozone issue dwindled, and media attention declined. From 1978 to 1983, only twenty-seven major articles were published in the New York Times on ozone-related issues.[44] From 1980 to 1984, the ozone issue practically disappeared from the public radar.[45] A small group of atmospheric scientists who had devoted many of their resources on ozone protection faced the daunting task of sustaining active government involvement. Moreover, the economic realities—the high cost of the CFC substitutes—compelled lawmakers in the United States not to introduce any strong regulatory measures. The fluorocarbon industry argued that CFC use should not be banned until cheap substitutes were developed and scientific uncertainty surrounding the CFC-ozone theory was settled.

Meanwhile, the Reagan administration appointed Anne Gorsuch Burford as chief administrator of the Environmental Protection Agency (EPA). She did not share the general scientific consensus that fluorocarbons were the primary cause of ozone depletion.[46] Hence, during her tenure, the EPA started to delay and even cancel environmental policies that specifically dealt with the ozone issue. This trend led the fluorocarbon industry to suspend its research and development efforts.[47] When the CFC-ozone crisis had erupted, the fluorocarbon industry identified several possible substitutes that met the toxicological standards set by the EPA. DuPont invested $2.5 million annually between 1974 and 1980 to develop several CFC substitutes.[48] However, when Burford assumed office, the major CFC manufacturers, especially DuPont, stopped the search for alternatives.[49]

Furthermore, various ozone depletion estimates released in the early 1980s revised projections of ozone depletion rates from a high of 16.5 percent, predicted in 1979, to 5–9 percent in 1981.[50] Later, the estimate was lowered further to 3 percent.[51] Lack of initiative at the executive and bureaucratic level and these downward revisions of ozone depletion rates signaled to the fluorocarbon manufacturers that the fears of ozone depletion were highly exaggerated.[52] Hazardous effects of UV-B radiation were downplayed, and the causal links between skin cancer and ozone depletion were questioned.[53] Ozone issue fatigue seemed to have set in, and sincere efforts were not made to seek international cooperation.

Environmental policymakers were unwilling to limit domestic production and consumption of CFCs because of political pressure from the chemical industry groups. The U.S.-based DuPont had a near monopoly in the production and sales of materials containing CFCs. It produced more than 50 percent of U.S. domestic output and 25 percent of world output.[54] It also had industrial operations all over the world and exported to some major markets in Europe and Asia. Therefore, policymakers realized that CFC phaseout within the United States was unlikely to have a significant impact on the overall ozone depletion process.

Moreover, serious political obstacles prevented American policymakers from pursuing strong control policies. First, they had to convince the domestic producers to limit their production, even though competitors in Europe continued to produce and export the same commodity. Second, they realized that even if they completely stopped all domestic production, it would have no impact on ozone depletion because European Community (EC) members as well as Japan, Canada, and Australia consumed 41 percent of the world CFC output.[55] Without an international agreement, the EC manufacturers could simply increase their share of production. The net effect of U.S. domestic regulation would produce only a minor downturn in ozone depletion rates. Therefore, the United States realized that it could effectively reduce CFC emissions only by encouraging the limitation of the *global* release rates, which required moving the ozone issue to an international forum.[56]

Level III, the International Level: Ozone Depletion and International Environmental Institutions

The 1972 Stockholm Conference on the Human Environment is commonly acknowledged as a major watershed event in the development of international environmental institutions. It was instrumental in the establishment of the United Nations Environment Program (UNEP), and it laid the groundwork for an international framework for identification and control of pollutants that have broad international significance.[57] Soon after its creation, UNEP recognized that ozone depletion was a major threat to Earth's atmosphere. It sponsored an international technical conference in 1975, which issued a call for global monitoring of fluorocarbon emissions.[58] The following year, the United States requested UNEP's participation and assistance in organizing an international conference on the ozone layer. In March 1977, UNEP organized an international meeting that was attended by advanced industrialized countries such as Australia, Canada, Japan, Russia, and the thirty-three member nations of the EC.[59] The participants drafted the "World Plan of Action on the Ozone Layer," which recognized that the ozone layer was a global resource, and suggested that UNEP should coordinate international research and monitoring efforts to reduce ozone depletion.[60] In addition, suggestions for possible harmonization of fluorocarbon production and regulation were also discussed. Further follow-up meetings were held at Bonn and Munich in 1978. The Munich meeting was significant because all the concerned parties and organizations recognized the coordinating role of UNEP in the area of scientific research on the ozone layer.[61] Furthermore, there was agreement among them that fluorocarbon emissions should be internationally regulated because domestic regulation would not solve the problem.

Selection of UNEP as the main facilitator of international negotiations on the ozone problem was surprising because of its weak organizational and financial strength. Moreover, its being located in Nairobi isolated it from the growing CFC-ozone controversy in North America and Europe. Hence, some countries suggested that interstate negotiations for reducing fluorocarbon emissions should be conducted under the aegis of the OECD because it had the necessary financial and organizational strength, as well as the necessary infrastructure to conduct major international negotiations. However, some EC countries doubted the ability of the OECD to function as an unbiased and independent negotiator.[62] Hence, the selection of UNEP, whose executive director, Mustafa Tolba, subsequently played an active role in sustaining international interest on the ozone issue, even when early negotiations did not produce any concrete results.

Early international negotiations did not produce any results because most industrialized countries were wary of negotiating an international treaty on a major industrial chemical when the scientific results were inconclusive. Britain, in particular, vociferously contested the need for any international regulation of fluorocarbons.[63] The EC countries also realized that the United States was actively internationalizing the ozone problem to spread the costs of regulation. Although they were facing pressure from local environmental groups, the EC nations were unwilling to negotiate a multilateral treaty that limited fluorocarbon production and use by industrialized states alone. The developing countries were equally against joining an international treaty because they felt that they had not contributed to the destruction of the ozone layer and so should not be asked to share the costs of international regulation. As a result, international negotiations did not proceed beyond general recognition that ozone depletion needed to be prevented.[64] From 1976 to 1983, international negotiations were largely limited to preparing reports that summarized the state of ozone research. Meanwhile, after President Reagan appointed a new EPA director, the United States started advocating a cautious wait-and-see approach toward international negotiations. Therefore, between the Oslo summit in 1979 and the Bonn meeting in 1983, no major attempt was made to negotiate a CFC-reduction agreement.

Domestic Politics and Changes in the U.S. Negotiating Position

When William Ruckelshaus became the chief administrator of the EPA, he moved the management of the stratospheric pollution issues from the Office of Toxic Substances to the Office of Air and Radiation.[65] Immediately after the change in jurisdiction, the Office of Air and Radiation announced that it would support the position of the Nordic Annex group,[66] which called for deep cuts in CFC emissions and a worldwide ban on aerosol production and use.[67] The year before the 1985 Vienna Convention, the United States, Canada, Austria, Switzerland, and other Nordic Annex countries met informally at Toronto and floated four proposals.[68] The first two proposals called for a complete ban or an 80 percent reduction in nonessential aerosol use and exports. In the third proposal, this "Toronto group" suggested that all countries should aim to reduce CFC emissions by 20 percent within four years, starting in 1984.[69] Last, they supported a 70 percent reduction in aerosol use and a production cap on all aerosol products.

The new U.S. position, which changed from supporting a limited ban and gradual reduction to a complete ban, shocked the EC countries.[70] They were opposed to the Nordic Annex position and were relying on the support of the United States to stall the Nordic initiative. They were not willing to go beyond a 30 percent reduction in aerosol production from 1970 levels, with no expansion in fluorocarbon production.[71] However, the Toronto group dismissed the EC proposal as disingenuous because, it claimed, the EC states had already agreed among themselves (i.e., within the European Community) to limit aerosol production by 30 percent and that their producers were already operating under reduced capacity.[72] The EC group in its turn contended that the Toronto group's suggestion for reductions was excessive.[73]

The consequences of deadlock between the EC and the Toronto group can be seen in the framework Vienna Convention. No significant control mechanisms were introduced. Instead, a list of controlled chemicals was appended to Annex 1 of the convention.[74] The important provisions of the Vienna Convention called for increased cooperation on legal and scientific issues; development of domestic regulatory measures; monitoring; and information exchange among the competent international bodies. The Vienna Convention was a carefully worded document. Although it recognized that ozone depletion required international cooperation, the preamble declared that countries have sovereign rights to exploit resources within their territory according to local laws as long as they did not harm the environment outside the "limits of their national jurisdiction."[75] The benign language of the treaty also symbolized the fear of international commitments among the participating countries. Nevertheless, the Vienna Convention was a useful first step toward developing a framework for the later Montreal Protocol negotiations.

Hole in the Sky: Renewal of the CFC-Ozone Debate

Not long before the Vienna negotiations, Joe Farman, leader of the British Antarctic Survey team, discovered a large hole in the ozone layer over the Antarctic.[76] Farman and his collaborators published the results from their study in the May 1985 issue of *Nature*, three months after the Vienna Convention.[77] Farman's article immediately created a furor among American atmospheric scientists. Nonetheless, there was some skepticism about the validity of data coming from a relatively unknown research group. Dr. Ralph Cicerone, a leading atmospheric scientist, apparently remarked, "have you ever heard of the British Antarctic Survey?"[78] Most American scientists did not have much faith in Farman's data because the *Nimbus-7* satellite, which was monitoring Antarctic ozone levels, did not detect extensive ozone loss over Antarctica.

After the British team's results were published, NASA scientists reexamined their assumptions, discovering that they had programmed their computers to reject automatically any data received from the satellite below 180 Dobsons.[79] Scientists at NASA thought that such low readings of ozone concentrations over Antarctica could occur only because of natural fluctuations or data transmission errors and thus had not incorporated the low Dobson readings into their computer models. Reexamination of NASA computer banks showed that the results of the British Antarctica survey were indeed correct.[80] In January 1986, using the rediscovered data, NASA and the EPA jointly released a major study. Six months later, NASA released another report in collaboration with UNEP. More than 150 scientists from all over the world endorsed the NASA-UNEP report. Sherry Rowland, proponent of the Rowland-Molina thesis, said, "now we've got a hole in our atmosphere that you could see from Mars . . . it is harder to label [it] as just a computer hypothesis."[81]

This new discovery propelled EPA officials to address the ozone crisis aggressively.[82] The EPA launched its own stratospheric ozone protection plan and later solicited the help of UNEP in organizing an international workshop. The U.S. Congress began holding public hearings to determine the need for domestic legislation. The new director of the EPA, Lee Thomas, announced that active government intervention was required to prevent ozone depletion.[83] Sensing that the momentum was shifting in favor of an international regulatory treaty, fluorocarbon manufacturers claimed that substitutes could be produced. DuPont publicly announced that it was willing to support a gradual reduction of fluorocarbon production and use. The McDonald's fast-food chain announced that it would suspend the use of packaging materials that contained CFCs. Overall, the U.S. fluorocarbon industry expressed its willingness to support the U.S. position in pushing for an accelerated global CFC phaseout.[84]

Visible Threats: Falling Skies Shadow the Montreal Protocol
After publication of the British Antarctica Survey and the NASA-UNEP scientific reports, UNEP reinvigorated the international negotiating process. However, for some time, continued disagreements between the United States and the EC prevented negotiators from even discussing the possibility of an international treaty. Even after the discovery of the Antarctic ozone hole, the EC was adamant that the empirical data supporting the CFC-ozone theory was still uncertain. In response, the U.S. State Department mounted a careful and coordinated plan in which U.S. embassies around the world were asked to contact their host nations and explain the U.S. negotiating position.[85] The obvious strategy was to build

consensus among all countries before the ozone protection negotiations started. Initially, like-minded governments were contacted. Later, diplomatic efforts were extended to countries that were unsympathetic to the U.S. position.

At home, the United States developed an interagency consensus-building process, which involved all branches of the U.S. government and the major science and environmental agencies. Even the fluorocarbon producers were included to forge a strong and unified U.S. position. These connections were largely made to prevent interagency politics from affecting the three basic policy goals of the United States.[86] The first objective was to develop a proposal for a complete worldwide ban on all ozone-depleting substances. Second, the United States wanted to develop and incorporate into the main treaty text a long-term schedule for CFC phaseout. The third goal was to negotiate an international treaty that would include periodic assessments, an arrangement to remove and add new chemicals to the list of ozone-depleting substances, and provisions to change emission targets and accelerate phaseout schedules.[87] These three basic policy objectives became the main building blocks of the Montreal Protocol.

Official protocol negotiations for an international agreement to limit CFC production and consumption began in Geneva in December 1986. The Geneva meetings did not produce any results because the EC was opposed to the U.S. position of a 95 percent cut in CFC emissions and an immediate freeze on fluorocarbon production.[88] EC nations, particularly France and the United Kingdom, argued that the U.S. position was excessive and nonnegotiable. France was especially opposed to export controls because it was one of the largest exporters of CFC products in Europe, and it did not want to jeopardize its domestic industry. When the second round of meetings began in Venice in June 1987, the Nordic countries and Canada abandoned their individual positions and began actively to support the U.S. position. There was also heavy domestic pressure from environmental groups on the West German government to negotiate an international CFC treaty, but the Germans could not do much because of the split among the EC countries.

The early stages of the Montreal negotiations seemed to be doomed. The United States continued to hold its position, and the EC continued to assert that it would not agree to any cuts greater than 30 percent. When it became evident that the Montreal negotiations were going to end without any agreement, the Americans decided to revise their position. The United States and the Toronto group backed down from their original proposal of a 95 percent cut, suggesting instead a 50 percent cut in CFC production. The EC nations relented, and the Montreal Protocol was initially signed by forty-six states in September 1987. The language of the Montreal Protocol was precise and it clearly identified a range of controlled substances. It also included the establishment of a noncompliance committee to examine periodically whether the participating countries were meeting their targets. In addition, the United States ensured that a clause calling for a periodic review was included in the treaty.

Provisions of the Evolving Montreal Protocol

Negotiation of the Montreal Protocol is considered to be a momentous event in the history of international environmental cooperation. Unlike other treaties, the Montreal Protocol is not immutable; it continuously evolves in response to developments in scientific knowledge, building new control measures to regulate ozone-depleting substances. Regular annual meetings of parties are held to review progress and development of the protocol, to adjust emission targets, to enlarge the list of ozone-depleting substances, and to develop proposals to assist countries that are unable to achieve their ODS reduction goals. Since the treaty was negotiated in 1987, eleven Meetings of the Parties to the protocol, twenty-two meetings of the Implementation Committee under the Noncompliance Procedure, and more than twenty Open-Ended Working Group meetings have been held. Furthermore, three major amendments to the Montreal Protocol—London, 1990; Copenhagen, 1992; and Montreal, 1997—have been introduced. The London and the Copenhagen amendments were responsible for expanding the list of ozone-depleting substances not included in the protocol. More than 170 countries have ratified the Vienna Convention and the Montreal Protocol,[89] and more than 100 countries have ratified the London and the Copenhagen amendments.[90]

A new institution—the Ozone Secretariat—facilitated negotiations of the London, Copenhagen, and Montreal amendments. It was established in accordance with Article VII of the Vienna Convention and Article XII of the Montreal Protocol to facilitate compliance with treaty measures.[91] The secretariat is responsible for arranging Conferences of the Parties, Meetings of the Parties and their committees, Scientific Assessment Panels, and the working groups. In addition, the secretariat is responsible for organizing expert panels to evaluate new scientific evidence and generate comprehensive reports prior to each Meeting of the Parties. The assessment panels play a pivotal role in determining the parameters and the policy prerogatives of the ozone regime by ensuring that regulations keep pace with scientific advancements. For example, negotiation of the 1997 Montreal amendment, which enabled the inclusion of methyl bromide as an ozone-depleting substance, was achieved largely because of the efforts of the assessment panels. With amendments, the protocol regulates the consumption and production of ninety-eight different ozone-depleting substances.[92]

Parties to the Montreal Protocol were separated into Article V and non-Article V groups to accommodate the concerns of developing countries. Developing countries, which belong to the Article V group, were given ten more years than developed countries to reduce consumption and production of ODSs. The non–Article V group, which consists of advanced industrialized nations, started to reduce emissions of ODSs as soon as the Montreal Protocol came into force in 1989.[93] These countries produced and consumed large quantities of ozone-depleting substances, so they were expected to participate in an accelerated ODS phaseout program. The developing countries argued that they would not be able to follow the accelerated ODS reduction schedules.[94]

The ozone treaty verifies compliance by examining the annual production and consumption data on ODSs that all the ratifying countries are required to submit to the Ozone Secretariat. Analysis of the data reveals whether a country is compliant. If a state fails to report production and consumption data, it is given three months to formally explain the situation to the Ozone Secretariat. If there is no response from the noncompliant country, administrative initiatives are pursued to understand why it is having difficulty meeting the control measures. If the initial efforts fail, the matter is referred to the Implementation Committee. No system of sanctions is built into the treaty. All ratifying states are expected to comply with the treaty measures voluntarily. Chronic violators are not sanctioned; instead, they are provided assistance to meet their goals.

A separate institution—the Multilateral Fund—was established to provide financial and technical assistance to Article V developing nations, thus helping them achieve compliance with the control measures.[95] The Executive Committee of the Montreal Protocol, in cooperation with the World Bank and the United Nations Development Program (UNDP), administers the Multilateral Fund. As of 1999, the Multilateral Fund has disbursed more than U.S.$900 million dollars for special projects and incremental costs that developing countries have incurred while phasing out ODSs. Parties to the protocol have also agreed to establish an import-export licensing scheme to prevent illegal trafficking of ozone-depleting substances.[96] Every country is expected to develop a system for validation and approval of imports for all controlled substances. The licensing system is to be accompanied by a system for reporting and cross-checking export-import information. All these measures are expected to result in complete phaseout of all listed ODSs by 2020.

Because of the ozone regime, global CFC consumption decreased to 146,000 tons in 1997, from a high of 1.1 million tons in 1986. In 1986, the industrialized countries alone consumed about 1 million tons of CFCs, but by 1997 their consumption had decreased to 23,000 tons. Production of ODSs by non–Article V countries decreased by more than 95 percent in the 1990s.[97] It is estimated that without the Montreal Protocol, global CFC consumption would have increased to 3 million tons by the year 2010, which would have resulted in a 50 percent reduction in the ozone layer.

Conclusion

This chapter set out to address the following question: What factors influenced the evolution of the Montreal Protocol? The preceding description of events shows that evolution of the Montreal ozone treaty and of its subsequent revisions and extensions has to be understood by combining the insights from local, national, and international levels of analysis. Different factors at each level influenced the development of the ozone regime. Scientific findings, the active involvement of the atmospheric scientists in ozone politics, efforts of international organizations such as UNEP, and the leadership role of the United States coalesced at critical historical junctures to facilitate the negotiation of the Montreal Protocol.

The main focus here has been the institutional process of consensus building, which involved the mitigation of scientific uncertainty associated with the CFC-ozone theory and the harmful effects of ozone depletion on health. Although the community of atmospheric scientists and policymakers eventually shared a set of common causal beliefs about the relationship between fluorocarbon emissions and ozone-layer depletion, there were widespread disagreements regarding the rate of depletion, the impact of particular chemical elements, and proposed solutions to mitigate the problem. These disagreements stemmed not only from differences regarding the methodology employed to measure the rates of ozone depletion, but also from the variations in the institutional goals and strategies among the different national and international groups involved in ozone research.

When atmospheric scientists first discovered that anthropogenic fluorocarbon emissions could deplete the ozone layer, their efforts focused largely on the generation of new evidence to map systematically the causal links between fluorocarbons and the ozone layer. However, the context of the scientific research changed when the U.S. government decided to intervene actively in the scientific debate to investigate the public policy implications of the ozone depletion theory. Once the ozone issue entered the pubic policy domain, it became a divisive and hotly contested political issue. Those groups skeptical of the Rowland-Molina theory, particularly the fluorocarbon industry, sought to discredit its scientific foundations, which only emboldened atmospheric scientists to defend their claims more aggressively. Hence, the entire public policy debate revolved around the validity of scientific claims and whether those claims were strong and significant enough to pursue active regulation of CFC products.

The Montreal Protocol was negotiated, despite disagreements and divisions among the cooperating countries, because the eventual scientific consensus mitigated some of the uncertainty associated with ozone depletion. Various governmental agencies were involved not only in active atmospheric research, but also simultaneously in developing a broad policy consensus that consistently emphasized that fluorocarbons were the primary cause of ozone depletion. This process of consensus building was achieved by coherent and authoritative articulation of contested scientific claims through powerful national and international scientific institutions. Articulation of the ozone depletion theory by groups of highly regarded scientists convinced policymakers and influenced public opinion, enabling the development of a broad international policy consensus. Scientific consensus-building activities of the national scientific organizations influenced the direction of U.S. foreign environmental policy and the diplomatic initiatives of the U.S. negotiators, which eventually resulted in the negotiation of the Montreal Protocol and its subsequent extensions and amendments.

Notes

1 Throughout this essay, I also refer to the Montreal Protocol as the ozone treaty, the protocol, or the ozone regime.

2 See Mancur Olson, *The Logic of Collective Action* (Cambridge, Mass.: Harvard University Press, 1965).

3 See Robert O. Keohane, *International Institutions and State Power* (Boulder, Colo.: Westview, 1989).

4 Kenneth N. Waltz, *Man, the State, and War* (New York: Columbia University Press, 1959); J. David Singer, "The Levels of Analysis Problem," *World Politics* 14 (October 1961): 77–92.

5 Robert D. Putnam, "Diplomacy and Domestic Politics: The Logic of Two-Level Games," *International Organization* 42 (summer 1988): 427–60.

6 See Kenneth N. Waltz, *A Theory of International Politics* (Reading, Mass.: Addison-Wesley, 1979).

7 See Kenneth N. Waltz, "Political Structures," in *Neorealism and Its Critics,* ed. Robert Keohane (New York: Columbia University Press, 1986).

8 For example, see John G. Ikenberry, "The Intertwining of Domestic and International Politics," *Polity* 29 (winter 1996): 293–98; John Kurt Jacobsen, "Are All Politics Domestic? Perspectives on the Integration of Comparative Politics and International Theories," *Comparative Politics* 29 (October 1996): 93–115.

9 Peter M. Haas, "Introduction: Epistemic Communities and International Policy Coordination," in *Knowledge, Power, and International Policy Coordination,* ed. Peter M. Haas (Columbia: University of South Carolina Press, 1992); Karen T. Liftin, *Ozone Discourses: Science and Environment in Global Environmental Cooperation* (New York: Columbia University Press, 1994).

10 Andrew Moravcsik, "Introduction: Integrating International and Domestic Theories of International Bargaining," in *Double-Edged Diplomacy: International Bargaining and Domestic Politics,* ed. Peter B. Evans, Harold K. Jacobson, and Robert D. Putnam (Berkley: University of California Press, 1993), 3–42.

11 See Putnam, "Diplomacy and Domestic Politics."

12 John Gribbin, *The Hole in the Sky: Man's Threat to the Ozone Layer* (New York: Bantam, 1988), 24.

13 See J. Mormino, D. Sola, and C. Patten, *Climatic Impact Assessment Program (CIAP): Development and Accomplishments, 1971–1975, Final Report* (Washington, D.C.: Department of Transportation, 1975).

14 National Academy of Sciences (NAS), *Environmental Impact of Stratospheric Flight: Biological and Climatic Effects of Aircraft Emissions in the Stratosphere* (Washington, D.C.: National Academy Press, 1975).

15 The CIAP and NAS published independent reports that concentrated on different aspects of the SST project. However, both studies point out that SST effluents would lead to ozone depletion.

16 House Committee on Appropriations, *Civil Supersonic Aircraft Development (SST), Continuing Appropriations, FY71,* 92d Cong., 1st sess., 1–4 March 1971, H181–2, subdoc. no. Y.ap6/1:Ai7/4.

17 See National Academy of Sciences (NAS) Division of Physical Sciences, *Summary Statement of the Ad Hoc Panel on (NO$_x$) and the Ozone Layer* (Washington, D.C.: National Academy Press, 1971); National Academy of Sciences (NAS) Environmental Studies Board, Ad Hoc Panel on the Biological Impacts of Ultraviolet Radiation, *Biological Impacts of Increased Intensities of Solar Ultraviolet Radiation: A Report* (Washington, D.C.: National Academy Press, 1973).

18 See Richard S. Stolarski and R. J. Cicerone, "Stratospheric Chlorine: A Possible Sink for Ozone," *Canadian Journal of Chemistry* 52 (September 1974): 1610–15.

19 National Research Council, Climate Impact Committee, *Environmental Impact of Stratospheric Flight: Biological and Climatic Effects of Aircraft Emissions in the Stratosphere* (Washington, D.C.: National Academy Press, 1975), 9.

20 House Committee on Appropriations, *Civil Supersonic Aircraft Development (SST),* 299–342.

21 Mario Molina and Sherwood Rowland, "Stratospheric Sink in Chlorofluoromethanes: Chlorine Atom Catalyses Destruction of Ozone," *Nature* 249 (June 1974): 810–12.

22 Rowland and Molina estimated that a single chlorine atom is capable of destroying 100,000 molecules of ozone.

23 Sharon Roan, *Ozone Crisis: The 15-Year Evolution of a Sudden Global Emergency* (New York: John Wiley and Sons, 1989), 27.

24 House Committee on Interstate and Foreign Commerce, *Fluorocarbons—Impact on Health and Environment: Hearings before the Subcommittee on Public Health and Environment,* 93rd Cong., 2d sess., 11 and 12 December 1974.

25 See Steven C. Wofsy, Michael B. McElroy, and Nien Dak Sze, "Freon Consumption: Implications for Atmospheric Ozone," *Science* 187 (14 February 1975): 535–37.

26 Roan, *Ozone Crisis,* 38.

27 Based on the author's count of news items published on the ozone issue from 1974 to 1988 in the *New York Times.*

28 Also based on the author's count.

29 House Committee on Interstate and Foreign Commerce, *Fluorocarbons.*

30 The IMOS report was produced jointly by major federal agencies such as the Department of Agriculture, the Department of Commerce, the Consumer Safety Commission, etc. See United States Federal Task Force on Inadvertent Modification of the Stratosphere, *Fluorocarbons and the Environment: Report of the Federal Task Force on Inadvertent Modification of the Stratosphere (IMOS)* (Washington, D.C.: Council on Environmental Quality, U.S. Government Printing Office, 1975).

31 U.S. Federal Task Force, *Report of the Federal Task Force*, 17.

32 Ibid., 5.

33 National Research Council (NRC), *Halocarbons: Effects on Stratospheric Ozone* (Washington, D.C.: National Academy Press, 1976).

34 The NAS report was based on 1973 CFC emission rates. See NRC, *Halocarbons* (1976), 20.

35 "Is Earth's Ozone Layer Endangered by Industry?" *The Economist* (17 November 1979), 103–4.

36 DuPont, "You Want the Ozone Question One Way or Other. So Does DuPont," *Science* 190, no. 4209 (3 October 1975): 8–9.

37 Frederik Pohl and James P. Hogan, "Ozone Politics: They Call This Science?" *Omni* 15, no. 8 (15 June 1993): 34–40.

38 DuPont, "You Want the Ozone Question," 9.

39 Ironically, Fred Singer, an atmospheric and space physicist, designed the ozone-monitoring instrument for early versions of U.S. weather satellites. He was also the deputy assistant administrator of the EPA in 1971.

40 S. Fred Singer, "My Adventures in the Ozone Layer," *National Review* 41, no. 12 (June 1989): 34–38; S. Fred Singer and Candence Crandall, "Assessing the Threat to the Ozone," *Consumers' Research Magazine* (July 1987): 1–14.

41 Quoted in Walter Sullivan, "Scientist Doubts Spray Cans Imperil Ozone Layer," *New York Times*, 8 July 1987, 12.

42 Ibid.

43 William K. Hoskins, "Of Aerosols and the Ozone Layer," letter to the editor, *New York Times*, 3 July 1975, 30.

44 Based on the author's count of *New York Times* stories.

45 The *New York Times* published only eight major stories on the ozone issue from 1981 to 1985.

46 Kathlyn Gay, *Ozone* (New York: Franklin Watts, 1989), 88.

47 Peter M. Haas, "Banning Chlorofluorocarbons: Epistemic Community Efforts to Protect Stratospheric Ozone," in *Knowledge, Power, and International Policy Coordination*, ed. Peter M. Haas (Columbia: University of South Carolina Press, 1992), 195.

48 Arjun Makhijani and Kevin R. Gurney, *Mending the Ozone Hole: Science, Technology, and Policy* (Cambridge, Mass.: MIT Press, 1995), 267.

49 The DuPont press statement—issued in 1987, when it restarted its R&D efforts—indicated that the company had stopped the search for alternatives

in the early 1980s because it believed that the ozone threat was not as severe as initially predicted. See DuPont press release cited in Makhijani and Gurney, *Mending the Ozone Hole*, 268.

50 National Research Council (NRC), *Causes and Effects of Stratospheric Ozone Reduction: An Update* (Washington, D.C.: National Academy Press, 1982), 20.

51 NRC, *Causes and Effects of Stratospheric Ozone Reduction: An Update* (Washington, D.C.: National Academy Press, 1983), 101.

52 Donald R. Strobach, "New CFC Data Cheers Industry," *Contractor* 1 (15 August 1983): 1.

53 A U.S. Interior Department official proposed a "personal protection plan," which called for increased use of sunblock to prevent the harmful effects of UV radiation, especially during the hot summer months. See Cass Peterson, "Administration Ozone Policy May Favor Sunglasses, Hats," *Washington Post,* 29 May 1987.

54 Haas, "Banning Chlorofluorocarbons," 197.

55 Ibid., 199.

56 Arlen J. Large, "The Spread of International Controls," *Wall Street Journal,* 22 November 1976, 20.

57 Lynton K. Caldwell, *International Environmental Policy: Emergence and Dimensions* (Durham, N.C.: Duke University Press, 1984), 45, 54.

58 Richard Elliot Benedick, *Ozone Diplomacy* (Cambridge, Mass.: Harvard University Press, 1998), 40.

59 Thomas B. Stoel Jr., "Fluorocarbons: Mobilizing Concern and Action," in *Environmental Protection: International Dimension,* ed. David A. Kay and Harold K. Jacobson (Totowa, N.J.: Allanheld, Osum, 1983), 57.

60 See Asit K. Biswas, ed., *The Ozone Layer* (New York: Pergamon, 1979).

61 Stoel, "Fluorocarbons," 58.

62 Ibid.

63 Benedick, *Ozone Diplomacy,* 38.

64 Dick Kirschten, "EPA's Ozone Standard Faces a Hazy Future," *National Journal* (10 December 1978): 2015–19.

65 The Office of Toxic Substances, which controlled stratospheric pollution issues and fluorocarbon regulation, was not convinced that ozone depletion was a serious problem. Therefore, it did not show any urgency in pursuing domestic or international regulatory solutions. The Office of Air and Radiation, on the other hand, considered ozone depletion to be a major environmental problem that required immediate global attention.

66 Litfin, *Ozone Discourses: Science and Politics in Global Environmental Cooperation* (New York: Columbia University Press, 1994), 72–73.

67 "U.S. Delegation Supports Global CFC Ban in Face of Opposition," *Contractor* 31 (January 1984): 16–18; Roan, *Ozone Crisis,* 114.

68 Edward Parsons, "Protecting the Ozone Layer," in *Institutions for the Earth: Sources of Effective International Environmental Protection,* ed. Peter M. Haas,

Robert O. Keohane, and Marc A. Levy (Cambridge, Mass.: MIT Press, 1993), 38.

69 Litfin, *Ozone Discourses*, 75.

70 Stoel, "Fluorocarbons," 65.

71 Parsons, "Protecting the Ozone Layer," 38.

72 Litfin, *Ozone Discourses*, 74.

73 The EC was particularly against the Toronto group's multi-options approach to international regulation because of the possibility of enforcement failure. Benedick, *Ozone Diplomacy*, 35.

74 United Nations, Treaty Series, *Vienna Convention for the Protection of the Ozone Layer* (1985), available at <http://www.unep.ch/ozone/vienna_t.htm>. This treaty can also be found in United Nations Environment Program (UNEP), Ozone Secretariat, *Handbook for the International Treaties for the Protection of the Ozone Layer: The Vienna Convention (1985), the Montreal Protocol (1987)*, 4th ed. (Nairobi, Kenya: UNEP, 1996).

75 Vienna Convention, preamble, May 1985.

76 Gribbin, *The Hole in the Sky*, 109.

77 J.C. Farman., B. G. Gardiner, and J. D. Shanklin, "Large Losses of Total Ozone in Antarctica Reveal CLO_x/NO_x Interaction," *Nature* 315 (16 May 1985): 207–10.

78 Cited in Edward Edelson, "The Man Who Knew Too Much," *Popular Science* 234 (January 1989), 65.

79 A Dobson is the atmospheric measurement unit for ozone levels.

80 Gribbin, *The Hole in the Sky*, 112.

81 Rowland's interview with the *New York Times* cited in Roan, *Ozone Crisis*, 144.

82 Stanley Wellbon, "Putting a Freeze on Freon: EPA Warns of Destruction to Ozone Blanket Around the Earth," *U.S. News and World Report* 101 (November 1986): 72.

83 Janet Raloff, "EPA Estimates Major Long-Term Ozone Risks," *Science News* 130 (November 1986): 308.

84 Marc Reisch and Pamela Zurer, "CFC Production: DuPont Seeks Total Phaseout," *Chemical and Engineering News* (April 1988): 4–5.

85 Benedick, *Ozone Diplomacy*, 55–67.

86 Ibid., 53.

87 See House Committee on Energy and Commerce, *Ozone Layer Depletions: Hearing Before the Subcommittee on Health and Environment*, 100th Cong., 1st sess., 9 March 1987, 119–29.

88 Benedick, *Ozone Diplomacy*, 53.

89 According to the Ozone Secretariat, 73 countries had ratified the Vienna Convention and 172 countries had ratified the Montreal Protocol as of 15 November 1999.

90 The exact ratification status of the amendments as of 15 November 1999 is as follows: London (136 countries), Copenhagen (101), and Montreal (29).

91 United Nations, Treaty Series, *The 1987 Montreal Protocol on Substances that Deplete the Ozone Layer*, 4 June 1998, available at <http://www.unep.org/mont_t.htm#6>. This treaty can also be found in United Nations Environment Program (UNEP), Ozone Secretariat, *Handbook for the International Treaties for the Protection of the Ozone Layer: The Vienna Convention (1985), the Montreal Protocol (1987)*, 4th ed. (Nairobi, Kenya: UNEP, 1996).

92 Each annex to the Montreal Protocol lists ozone-depleting substances that are to be regulated. Each is divided into two or three groups with each group containing a set of closely related ozone-depleting chemicals.

93 Currently, 110 countries are categorized as Article V countries. This categorization is temporary and is subject to periodic review. A country's status is determined through petition to the executive committee of the Montreal Protocol.

94 The base year for controlling the production and consumption of ODSs for non-Article V countries is 1986 for Annex A (Groups I and II), 1989 for Annex B (Groups I, II, and III) and Annex C (Group I), and 1991 for Annex E (methyl bromide) categories. The base year for Article V countries is based on the average production during 1995–97 for ODSs found in Annex A (Groups I and II). Average production in the years 1998–2000 is the base year for ODSs listed in Annex B (Groups I, II, and III) and Annex C (Group I) of the protocol. The base year for calculating methyl bromide reduction targets for Article V countries is 2015. However, both developing and industrialized countries were expected to phase out Annex C (Group II: HBFCs) ozone-depleting substances completely by 1996.

95 United Nations Multilateral Fund Secretariat, *The Secretariat of the Multilateral Fund for the Implementation of the Montreal Protocol* (Montreal: Secretariat of the Multilateral Fund for the Implementation of the Montreal Protocol, 1991). United Nations Environment Program, "General Information," available at <http://www.unmfs.org.general.htm>.

96 UNEP and Stockholm Environment Institute (SEI), *Regulations to Control Ozone-Depleting Substances: A Guidebook* (Stockholm: UNEP OzonAction Program, 1996), available at <http://www.unepie.org.ozoneaction.html>.

97 Production of ODSs listed in Annex A (Groups I and II) and Annex B (Groups I, II, and III) have decreased by more than 95 percent. However, production of ODSs listed in Annex C, particularly HCFCs, have increased by 140 percent during the past decade, and methyl bromide (Annex E) production has declined by only 9.5 percent.

6 U.S. Foreign Policy and the Ocean Environment: A Case of Executive Branch Dominance

John Barkdull

Scholarly attention to U.S. foreign policy has not been as sustained or as central to the environmental research agenda as in security and economic studies. Studies of international environmental politics include discussions of U.S. views and interests, but focused analysis of foreign environmental policy is scarce. One way to begin to fill this gap in our knowledge is to approach foreign environmental policy in terms of the role of the presidency. Doing so makes sense because U.S. foreign policy analysis generally assumes that the president is the predominant actor because of constitutional allocations of authority and institutional practices, especially since World War II. Presidential dominance is most evident in security affairs. Whether the president dominates international economic policy remains a debated question. The degree of presidential dominance in foreign environmental policy remains largely unexplored. Further, the process of foreign environmental policymaking within the executive branch has received little attention. Given presidential dominance, it remains to determine whether the locus of policy formulation is in the White House or in the executive agencies. Assessing the role of the presidency in foreign environmental policy affords purchase on two pertinent questions: What accounts for U.S. initiatives to secure international environmental treaties? What accounts for U.S. preferences regarding the specific content of a given treaty? An additional issue, which bears on the U.S. role in furthering or hindering international environmental policy, is the degree to which treaty negotiation outcomes correspond to U.S. preferences.

President Richard Nixon's administration saw some of the most significant advances in U.S. environmental law and policy. This chapter focuses on the Nixon administration's sponsorship of the ocean dumping treaty of 1972. The study is exploratory in nature, using a single case to illustrate some tendencies in the making of U.S. foreign environmental policy. Information comes from public documents, such as the annual reports of the Council on Environmental Quality, Nixon's presidential papers, congressional hearings, and contemporary news reports. In addition, the study relies on archival research in the Nixon Materials at the National Archives in College Park, Maryland.

The key document outlines the administration's then secret negotiating position entering treaty talks. Comparing this document to the outcomes of treaty negotiations shows the extent and the limits of U.S. influence in international environmental negotiations. The ocean dumping case also illustrates the domestic origins of international agreements. It shows the effects of security and commercial concerns on U.S. foreign environmental policy when an issue reaches international negotiations. Last, contrary to critics, this case indicates that the Nixon administration pursued an ambitious environmental agenda. Foreign policy is the president's domain. If the president did seek and obtain effective environmental agreements, these agreements must be credited primarily to the administration rather than to Congress or domestic pressures.

The Nixon Administration and Foreign Environmental Policy

Richard Nixon's reputation has risen and fallen perhaps more than any other American politician's. His journey from landslide victory in 1972 to resignation from the presidency in August 1974 exemplifies his meteoric career. Recently, scholars have sought to assess the Nixon record in more measured terms than was possible during the Vietnam War and Watergate. A few have spoken against the generally negative assessments of the Nixon administration's environmental record. Critics have found Nixon to be so pro-industry that environmental accomplishments during his term are discounted or attributed to other actors. Michael A. Genovese considers Nixon's record "mixed" at best and attributes the significant accomplishments of the time to congressional leadership.[1] James Brooks Flippen argues that Nixon's land-use policy failed to address urban sprawl adequately owing to shifts in attitudes both inside and outside the White House.[2] He also asserts in regard to wilderness protection that "a closer inspection of [Nixon's] record reveals a president whose commitment to the environment was tenuous at best."[3] Even stronger criticism of the Nixon environmental record occurred during Nixon's term. A representative text is the League of Conservation Voters report that appeared in 1972 with the subtitle *The Politics of Devastation.*[4] Thirteen essays offer varying but negative appraisals of the Nixon record. Several authors noted some improvement and allowed that things could have been worse, but all agreed that Nixon's policy fell well short of true commitment to environmental protection.

Others have found Nixon's presidency to be more environmentally progressive. One important example of this reassessment is Joan Hoff's assertion that Nixon's domestic policy successes are more important than what she finds to be a mediocre foreign policy record.[5] Hoff identifies five areas in which the Nixon administration initiated significant domestic policy change: welfare, civil rights, economic policy, executive branch reorganization—and the environment. Relying on archival research, interviews, and other sources, she found that John Ehrlichman, assisted by Egil ("Bud") Krogh, John Whitaker, and Chris DeMuth, "substantially influenced both Nixon's ideas and the content of his environmental legislation by making it into a crisis issue."[6] Contrary to the proposition that Congress led, dragging a reluctant president behind, Hoff notes, "The fact remains that Congress turned down more of the president's environmental legislation than it passed."[7] She complains that environmental activists still will not give Nixon credit for his accomplishments, despite his solid environmental record.

Similarly, Charles S. Warren observes that although Nixon did not make the environment a priority, "tremendous progress was made during the administration in attempting to clean up the air and water and in raising the public's consciousness with regard to the issue of environmental protection."[8] Nixon administration officials have also written in defense of their environmental record. John C. Whitaker's book, which details his activities as John Ehrlichman's chief assistant for environmental and resource issues, is the most important instance.[9] Whitaker reiterates his case in a response to Warren's article.[10] In addition, Russell Train has argued in favor of the administration's efforts.[11]

The Missing Dimension

Except for Russell Train's account of Nixon's environmental policy, these studies tend to ignore the international dimension, without which a comprehensive appraisal of the Nixon administration's environmental policy is impossible. Hoff, for instance, explicitly casts Nixon's environmental policy as an aspect of a domestic record she feels deserves more credit. The League of Conservation Voters text makes only passing references to international problems. Observers writing during and soon after Nixon's tenure generally did not note the administration's activities in international environmental negotiations. Even John Whitaker failed to observe the international environmental initiatives under way while he toiled on the domestic side. Consequently, critics and defenders overlook an important part of any overall assessment of Nixon's environmental record.

This neglect has occurred despite the emphasis laid on the international dimension in the annual reports of the Council on Environmental Quality (CEQ). These reports show that the administration was involved in wide-ranging international negotiations on the environment. The importance of this dimension for assessing Nixon's record lies in presidential dominance of foreign policy. Congress could not and did not force the president into international negotiations. Members of the administration took the initiative. Perhaps internationalizing environmental issues ensured the greatest possible presidential control over the policy outcomes. Indeed, in the ocean dumping case, a treaty was hardly needed to protect U.S. interests. Perhaps the result was to blunt more far-reaching proposals emanating from Congress. Nonetheless, in the end, more countries became involved in protecting more of the ocean environment than would have occurred had the United States not sought an agreement. The ocean dumping case is one of many of the Nixon administration's international initiatives. Generally, throughout his presidency, Nixon's environmental policies were formulated with regard to the global context.

The international environmental subjects addressed during Nixon's term included such matters as marine pollution, marine mammals, seabed resources, population growth, cooperation with Canada to protect the Great Lakes, water resources on the U.S.-Mexico border, endangered species, and environmental monitoring. In pursuit of environmental policy, the United States acted bilaterally and through international organizations. Environmental cooperation even became a part of Nixon's détente strategy with the Soviet Union. Nixon's first chair of the CEQ, Russell Train, asserts, "While environmental initiatives by President Nixon on the international front tended to be obscured by other more dramatic foreign policy accomplishments, during his administration the United States provided the principal leadership for both bilateral and multilateral international efforts in the field of environmental cooperation."[12]

Public documents outline Nixon's international environmental policy. The annual CEQ reports, beginning in 1970 and continuing beyond Nixon's resignation, outline the administration's extensive international activities to protect the environment.[13] The president's Message to Congress to introduce the CEQ report indicated a global orientation: "Our physical nature, our mental health, our culture and institutions, our opportunities for challenge and fulfillment, our very survival—all of these are directly related to and affected by the environment in which we live. They depend upon the continued healthy functioning of the natural systems of the Earth."[14] The message addressed the issues already noted, the cross-border nature of environmental problems and the need to understand the environment as an interdependent whole. "On the international front," concluded the president's message, "the level of environmental concern and action has been rapidly rising. Many of our most pressing environmental problems know no political boundaries. Environmental monitoring and pollution of the seas are examples of major needs that require international cooperation, and that also provide an opportunity for the world's nations to work together for their common benefit."[15] The same point appeared in the president's report to Congress on U.S. foreign policy for the 1970s, in which he said, "a narrow calculation of national interest is inadequate. Of greater import [than conflicts of interest] is our shared and transcendent interest in the livability of our common home, the earth."[16]

Naturally, CEQ reports and presidential statements will adopt a generally positive approach to reporting an administration's accomplishments. In a president's report, blame for inaction will fall on Congress or other actors. Minor gains will be trumpeted, and negative trends will not receive emphasis. Nonetheless, the CEQ reports in particular do inform us of a wide range of international environmental initiatives and actions during the Nixon years. Most assessments of Nixon's environmental legacy neglect this extensive record.

The following international environmental accomplishments can be attributed to the Nixon administration, according to Russell Train's summary:

- The delegation of authority to the CEQ and the "active engagement of the responsible environmental officials in international matters gave tremendous stimulus worldwide to the establishment of high-level agencies responsible for environmental policy and management."
- The United States took the lead in preparing for the 1972 United Nations Conference on the Human Environment held in Stockholm, "shaping the agenda as well as final actions."
- The Great Lakes Water Quality agreement signed in 1972 "remains an active instrument in protecting the lakes."
- Both in Congress and in international forums, Nixon pressed for controls on dumping of wastes in the ocean, leading to the Ocean Dumping Convention of 1972 (this chapter's focus).
- Nixon's call for a whaling moratorium placed the issue "firmly on the international agenda, and the moratorium was finally approved twelve years later in 1982."
- Nixon's proposal for international efforts to protect endangered species resulted in the 1973 Convention on International Trade in Endangered Species of Fauna and Flora.
- The administration pushed the Organization for Economic Cooperation and Development (OECD) to accept "polluter pays," to "frame their environmental protection measures in a way that avoids creating non-tariff trade barriers," and to seek harmonization in environmental regulations.
- At Nixon's behest, the North Atlantic Treaty Organization (NATO) created the Committee on the Challenges of Modern Society (CCMS) to add a "new non-military dimension" to the alliance. The CCMS dealt with a variety of pollution and environmental management issues.
- Operating through the Intergovernmental Maritime Consultative Organization (now the International Maritime Organization), several advances in marine pollution protection resulted from Nixon administration actions, including international regulations to reduce intentional oil pollution, to control nonoil pollutants, and to ensure compensation for victims of marine pollution.
- Nixon's suggestion for a World Heritage Trust resulted in the 1972 World Heritage Convention to protect "areas of such unique worldwide value that they should be treated as part of the heritage of all mankind and accorded special recognition."
- U.S. bilateral negotiations fostered the upsurge in environmental awareness that had largely occurred first in the United States. One by-product was a

bilateral treaty on migratory birds. The U.S.-Soviet agreements, negotiated during Nixon's term, have been reactivated since the end of the Cold War, with Russia supplanting the Soviet Union.

Train concludes:

It seems to me that the record . . . speaks for itself—an extraordinary environmental record in almost every respect and one that is certainly without parallel in any administration that has followed. At the same time, it is a record that received little more than grudging recognition at the time, although internationally the United States was recognized and accepted as the world leader in environmental protection programs. That recognition was based both upon the leadership roles that the U.S. played in international environmental matters but, even more impor- tantly, on the credibility afforded by our domestic environmental policy and action.[17]

Train's assessment raises questions regarding the U.S. foreign environmental policy process. His central assertion is that the Nixon environmental record is unmatched, but his secondary theme is that this record is largely owing to CEQ leadership during his time as chair of the council. Is his assumption true, or did other players make significant contributions to policy? Especially, what role did the president play? How did the interagency review process affect the positions the administration adopted on international environmental concerns? How far did final positions deviate from CEQ preferences? How did Nixon and his top advisors view the environment as a political issue? Not all of these questions are answerable on all international issues with available documents, but public and archived documents shed light on several questions and issues.

In regard to the theoretical questions posed in chapter 2 of this volume, the ocean dumping case can help us to gain insight into which factors are most important in the making of U.S. foreign environmental policy. Do systemic forces more or less impose policy choices on the United States? If domestic politics matters, do societal influences matter most, or does policy initiative originate with policymakers themselves? At each level, which matters most: power, interests, or ideas? The ocean dumping case suggests that although the initiative to make an environmental issue part of the foreign policy agenda might reside with policy entrepreneurs close to or in the White House, the content of U.S. policy owes much to the interagency review process.

Ocean Dumping: Domestic and International Dimensions

Nixon administration policy originated in a CEQ study leading to "a presidential proposal on limiting ocean dumping that later became law, and ultimately led to an international convention to control ocean dumping."[18] The CEQ conducted the study in response to a presidential directive contained in Nixon's 15 April 1970 message to Congress on pollution in the Great Lakes and other dumping. The problem the Ocean Dumping Convention intended to solve was the unregulated deposition of hazardous materials into the sea. The CEQ estimated that in 1968, forty-eight million tons of waste were deposited in U.S. waters alone, including dredge spoils, industrial wastes, sewage sludge, debris, munitions, and solid waste. CEQ Chair Train, testifying before Congress, outlined the administration's policy on ocean dumping:

- Dumping of undigested sewage sludge, solid wastes, chemical warfare materials, and explosives should stop as soon as possible.
- Dumping of "digested or other stabilized sludge" and contaminated dredge spoils should be phased out.
- Dumping of unpolluted dredge spoils, construction debris, and similar nontoxic waste should be regulated to prevent damage to estuarine and marine areas.

Although wastes dumped in U.S. waters all originated in the United States, the international aspects of ocean dumping were not overlooked. The State Department's position paper on ocean protection asserted "that existing threats to the health and productivity of the oceans are both real and grave." It identified the threats as overexploitation, pollution, and simplification of complex ecosystems. "Existing institutions," the paper stated, "have not yet been able to prevent pollution or overfishing," and time was short to deal with the interdependent challenges to oceans, atmosphere, and land. Lost ocean productivity and rising populations would represent "imminent disaster" for developing nations. The report called for "conservation and rational use of the ocean environment," stronger international organizations, international monitoring and data collection, regulations to eliminate or limit discharge of hazardous substances into the seas, and new training and education centers to assist developing countries.[19]

The administration bill to enact ocean dumping regulations into U.S. law (House Resolution 4723) stated, "Unregulated dumping of material into the oceans, coastal, and other waters endangers human health, welfare, and amenities, and the marine environment, ecological systems, and economic potentialities."[20] To limit dumping, the United States would regulate transport of wastes from the United States and any dumping within U.S. waters "by any person from any source." "Material" referred to dredge spoil; solid waste; garbage; sewage sludge; munitions; chemical, biological, and radiological warfare agents; radioactive materials; discarded equipment; rock, sand, cellar dirt; and industrial wastes. The administration bill contained a provision on international cooperation; it instructed the secretary of state, in consultation with the administrator of the Environmental Protection Agency (EPA), to "seek effective international action and cooperation to ensure protection of the marine environment," working through the United Nations or other appropriate venues. This provision was needed because, as the State Department's communication to the House Committee on Merchant and Marine Fisheries stated, without international action, protection of marine areas beyond twelve miles would violate international law.[21]

Train described the connection between effective domestic law and international action:

> A completely effective system for the control of ocean dumping would involve regulation of at least all harmful materials, wherever they may be generated, and wherever and by whomever they may be dumped. . . . If the United States is in fact to exercise leadership in this critical area, if it is to persuade other nations to control their ocean disposal of wastes, then it is essential that the United States first put its own house in order. In my opinion, prompt and favorable action by Congress to establish effective regulation of ocean dumping is a prerequisite to action by other nations.[22]

Another important international aspect of the issue was that the U.S. military was responsible for a major part of the most controversial ocean dumping. The first significant congressional attention to ocean dumping resulted from the army's plan in 1969 to dispose of 1,100 train cars of poisonous gas off the New Jersey coast. Nerve gas disposal became the subject of congressional hearings in 1969 and 1970.[23] Regarding the military's plans to dump toxic wastes off the coast of California, Representative Paul Rogers of Florida said, "Now they are supposed to dump them five to 10 miles off, but if it is good and foggy they say they do it quickly and they even had a problem there where they could not get them to sink so they used rifles to sink the containers and even had one blow up and blow part of the ship out, too, I understand." Pursuant to Nixon's order, the practice of barging chemicals out to sea had stopped, but, reported Representative Rogers, "They are now taking it in trucks and just dumping it into the sewerage system and it goes right into the bay."[24] Other instances were discussed in the hearings as well.

U.S. Legislation and International Treaty Provisions

In his February 1971 message on the environment, President Nixon proposed legislation, coupled with international negotiations, to regulate all ocean dumping. The administration's bill would (1) require permits to transport for purposes of dumping all materials into the oceans, Great Lakes, and estuaries, and (2) allow the EPA administrator to designate safe sites and ban dumping of specific materials. The bill's statement of policy and purpose cautiously declared that the United States found the unregulated dumping of wastes to constitute a threat. Thus, as previously noted, the purpose of the act would be to regulate the transportation of material from the United States for dumping and the dumping of material by any person from any source in U.S. waters. The administration bill vested virtually all authority in the administrator of the EPA, acting in consultation with other agencies.

Members of Congress offered legislation varying from the administration's approach. Several bills wanted the ocean dumping legislation to cover all the navigable waters of the United States, including inland freshwater. The administration, speaking through EPA administrator William Ruckelshaus, argued that such a law would create overlap with existing legislation covering inland waters. Legislators pressed for establishing designated protected areas within two years, whereas the administration wanted to retain discretion. Some bills would have given states priority over federal law if state standards were more stringent. In light of the controversy over dumping nerve gas off the Florida coast, members of Congress argued for a prohibition on using the seas for disposing of military wastes of all kinds. The secretary of the army asserted that the latter provision "could be construed as an attempt to preclude operation of U.S. nuclear powered warships, including the strategic deterrent Fleet Ballistic Missile Submarine force. Such a result would be untenable to the security of the United States."[25] The Atomic Energy Commission opposed both prohibiting ocean disposals of nuclear wastes and giving the EPA control over such disposal; on this issue, the administration bill gave the EPA only rights of consultation. Disagreements on these issues were resolved largely in favor of the administration's position.

Regardless of other differences, members of Congress agreed with the administration that domestic action should complement international action to reduce and control dumping of wastes in the ocean.[26] Although the administration sought to retain discretion over dumping permits and regulation, both the president and many active members of Congress agreed on one desirable goal: an international ban on the dumping of all hazardous wastes in the sea. Nixon administration officials had sought such a commitment from NATO allies, acting through NATO's Committee on the Challenges of Modern Society. But other nations, including Britain, France, and Canada, opposed the idea, reportedly because of the costs and the belief that the oceans remained the best place to dispose of wastes.[27] Perhaps because of this rebuff, the administration bill represented a less-ambitious approach.

Prior to the London Conference on the Dumping of Waste at Sea (30 October to 13 November 1972), the Congress passed the Marine Protection, Research, and Sanctuaries Act (Public Law 92-532). The act was very similar to the administration's bill, except it included a ban on dumping radiological, chemical, or biological warfare agents. Outfalls from nuclear power plants permitted by the Atomic Energy Commission were excluded from the bill's coverage. It also suggested designating dumping sites "wherever feasible beyond the edge of the Continental shelf," required consultation with state and local authorities, and gave the Corps of Engineers authority over dredging. The act contained a title on research and gave the secretary of commerce authority to create marine sanctuaries. The latter required the secretary of state to negotiate with other governments to protect sanctuaries beyond U.S. territorial waters. Last, the bill gave citizens the right to seek injunctions against violations of the act, but a House provision to pay "finder's fees" to citizens reporting violations was deleted in conference.[28]

The Ocean Dumping Convention signed later at London was almost entirely consistent with U.S. law. House Resolution 5450 would bring U.S. rules into conformity with the treaty and required only minor changes to existing statutes. It added to national jurisdiction over vessels operating in foreign waters, included provisions regarding oil intended for dumping, provided that domestic regulations be consistent with international rules, and amended the act to give the EPA administrator authority to issue bans on a wider range of substances.

The convention was, according to Martha Gorman, "far more specific than any previous agreement regarding the substances considered harmful to the marine environment."[29] Sixty-three of the eighty participant countries meeting at London in October 1970 signed the treaty, thus declaring the vital importance of protecting the marine environment. They pledged to act individually and collectively to regulate dumping of prohibited and regulated substances in the ocean, which are listed in two annexes to the treaty. Annex I prohibits dumping in the sea any organohalogen compounds (including DDT and other pesticides), mercury, cadmium, persistent plastics, oil taken on board for the purpose of dumping, high-level radioactive wastes deemed unsuitable for dumping by the International Atomic Energy Agency, and biological and chemical weapons. Substances rendered rapidly harmless by natural processes are excluded, as well as sewage sludge and dredge spoils that might contain prohibited substances. Annex II lists the following substances and materials as requiring special care: arsenic, lead, copper, zinc, organosilicon compounds, cyanides, fluorides, and pesticides not covered in Annex I. Other substances subject to regulation included beryllium, chromium, nickel, vanadium, containers, scrap metal, bulky wastes, and low- and medium-level radioactive wastes not covered in Annex I. A third annex details the criteria for considering additions to the lists. The treaty makes exceptions for emergency situations and for military vessels (although governments are urged to bring military ships into compliance). It calls for monitoring and reporting of permitted ocean dumping. Enforcement falls to the states. Finally, the treaty contains a pledge to limit marine pollution from other non-dumping sources.

The U.S. report to Congress on the conference outlines some areas of disagreement between the United States and other delegations.[30] The United States sought sufficient jurisdiction to regulate ocean dumping while avoiding issues relating to the Law of the Sea negotiations. According to the report, a group of developing states as well as Canada, New Zealand, Iceland, Australia, and Spain (the "group of 34") pressed for increased coastal authority over ships and other sources of ocean disposal. "The package as proposed by the group of 34 was not acceptable to most of the developed nations since it was slanted in favor of broad coastal control and was opposed by the Western Europeans, the United States, Japan, and the Soviet Union." Ultimately, the participants forwarded a vague compromise that largely left the controversial issues for the Law of the Sea negotiations. The group of 34 tended to interpret this "saving clause"—which declared the precedence of the Law of the Sea negotiations—to mean they could promote wider coastal authority, but those opposed to wider authority interpreted the clause otherwise.

Three proposals for military vessels and aircraft were forwarded. The first granted sovereign immunity but required military craft to comply with the treaty. The second required each state to adopt standards consistent with the convention for noncommercial government vessels and aircraft. The third, on which the United States insisted, exempted military vessels and aircraft from the provisions of the treaty but required governments to adopt rules to achieve the objectives of the treaty. The aim was to remove any suggestion that foreign governments would have regulatory powers over U.S. military assets. Interestingly, the report stated that "Debate on this issue was among the least heated of any of the substantive issues in the Convention," but the delegation's report does not detail disagreements on other matters. The vehemence of the U.S. insistence on this point, reflected in other documents, indicates more conflict than the report admits. A State Department telegram now in the Nixon Materials at the National Archives discusses British and Japanese "difficulties" with the emergency clause allowing dumping of wastes when human life is at threat. In addition, some countries discussed with the U.S. delegation their doubts about the wording of Annex I. Britain and Japan expressed concern about Canada's "use of vague language in justifying their pollution claim," which was seen as a way to extend coastal state authority over a wider area of the oceans.[31]

The U.S. Negotiating Position

The U.S. delegation to London observed that "The regulation of ocean dumping offers at best the management of approximately 10% of the pollutants entering the world's ocean," but that the treaty represented a gain in international environmental protection. The delegation's report noted that more steps would have to be taken to gain more comprehensive mitigation of ocean pollution. Nonetheless, it claimed that the Dumping Convention "is the first time a large number of governments on a world-wide basis have agreed to control their daily actions for the benefit of the environment."[32] Although the Nixon administration was no doubt responding to both the general rise in environmental consciousness and specific concerns with military and civilian ocean pollution, it also showed considerable initiative in taking to the international community what might have been a domestic matter. How committed was the administration to this policy course? Was the administration dragged along by events, or did it lead? Internal documents can shed some light on the matter.

From the beginning, the ocean dumping initiative was entangled in domestic politics. A 17 November 1970 *New York Times* article claimed that Senator Edmund Muskie had "outmaneuvered" Nixon by introducing Nixon's bill himself. Muskie's intent was not to change the substance of the legislation but to counter Nixon administration attempts to manipulate the legislative process. The administration wanted the bill sent to the Senate Commerce and House Merchant Marine and Fisheries (MMF) committees, but Muskie wanted it directed to Public Works. In the event, the various ocean dumping bills did go to the Commerce Department and MMF committees. John Whitaker remarked in response to the *New York Times* article, "In perspective, this story [was] on p. 28 of the *Times* and the Ocean Dumping Report of the CEQ was front page and wire service—so Muskie doesn't have an initiative."[33] This incident speaks against the claim that Nixon habitually took credit for Muskie's actions.

U.S. success in achieving international commitment to an ocean dumping agreement did not escape high-level White House attention. John Whitaker, speaking by phone from Stockholm in June 1972, informed John Ehrlichman that "In spite of the attempts of the Chinese and the Swedes to politicize the Stockholm conference, there will be some significant accomplishments [led] by the United States." These accomplishments would include the moratorium on whale hunting, information exchange, an environment fund, the World Heritage Trust, and a new United Nations agency for environmental research. In addition, the U.S. would achieve "An ocean dumping prevention agreement whereby countries would agree to stop dumping certain pollutants—oil, toxic material, etc— modeled after the president's legislation to the same effect in the U.S."[34]

Still, the U.S. position was not reached without internal dissension. The general counsel of the Commerce Department, William N. Letson, wrote to John Whitaker to express the department's dissatisfaction with the U.S. proposal. The memo noted that Commerce had been part of drafting a convention in 1971, but by March 1972 a new version had been formulated without Commerce's participation. The general counsel objected to the draft's broad scope, possible encroachment on Congress's prerogatives, lack of clarity regarding the permitting process, inclusion of sources of pollution beyond dumping, the extension of international law to territorial waters, and interference with regional agreements on ocean dumping. "It is our view," the memo concluded, "that execution and implementation of the Convention, as presently drafted, would have serious consequences as a matter of both domestic and international law and policy."[35] At drafting sessions and in a memo written in anticipation of a working group meeting scheduled to be held in London, Letson reiterated his complaints and urged Commerce Department representation. He expressed "dismay" that the London meeting would include "all of the most vigorously obstructive LDCs [less-developed countries]," and he feared that the domestic impact of the proposed treaty would not be fully considered.[36] Letson's complaints possibly had some effect because the U.S. delegation to London included Raymond Peck from the Department of Commerce Office of the General Counsel. Similarly, as noted, congressional hearings showed the Atomic Energy Commission (AEC) to be concerned with losing jurisdiction over nuclear disposal, the Department of Defense (DOD) with freedom of action for military ships and aircraft, and the Corps of Engineers with loss of control to the EPA over dredging permits. The AEC, if it tried, did not secure a place among the delegation, but a representative from the Corps of Engineers joined officials from the DOD, State Department, the CEQ, the Coast Guard, and the EPA.

On 2 November 1972, a State Department official sent the National Security Council Secretariat a copy of the Draft Ocean Dumping Convention and the delegation's position paper. The position paper was a paragraph-by-paragraph discussion of the convention, indicating what changes the United States intended to seek, what fallback positions it would adopt if necessary, and on what points the United States would not yield. Comparing the U.S. "bottom line" to the actual outcome tells us what U.S. policy actually was by the time the treaty reached the final negotiating stage.

The position paper responded to the "Draft Articles of a Convention for the Prevention of Marine Pollution by Dumping" resulting from the Inter-Governmental Meeting on Ocean Dumping at Reykjavik, Iceland, in April 1972, and to the report of a later meeting at London in May 1972. According to the paper, "The objective of the U.S. is to see that present sources of marine-based pollution are completely regulated by the combination of the Ocean Dumping Convention, the Law of the Sea Treaty, and the 1973 IMCO Convention on the Prevention of Pollution from Ships."[37] Although the United States did not sign the Law of the Sea treaty until the 1990s, the Nixon administration had achieved agreement on pollution from ships in the 1973 International Convention for the Prevention of Pollution from Ships (MARPOL) treaty. Of course, the focus on marine sources of pollution left out the vast amount of land-based pollution of the sea, recently accounting for almost 80 percent of marine pollution.[38]

One significant aim of the U.S. delegation's negotiating position was to ensure that nothing in the ocean dumping convention would encourage encroachments on freedom of the seas, which meant striving to narrow the wording of various paragraphs in the negotiating text so as to limit the rights of coastal states. As noted, U.S. negotiators perceived Canada and some developing states as seeking to expand their coastal jurisdiction using the environment as pretense. For instance, on exempting military assets from the treaty, consider the following two paragraphs added to the position paper "at the insistence of DOD," although "not all agencies agree that they are factually correct":

Those delegates who forcefully maintain that a military exemption clause is unequivocally unacceptable are, for the most part, representatives of a number of less developed nations that admittedly have no intention whatever of signing, acceding or otherwise ratifying any ocean dumping convention irrespective of its provisions. Indeed, it is quite incongruous to witness the obstructionist tactics of these LDC representatives who have privately admitted that their countries will not sign any ocean dumping convention primarily because they feel they must pollute to become developed and will countenance no restrictions upon that right to develop. Consequently, under no circumstances should the U.S. [government] be pressured into accepting anything less than a military exemption, especially since the pressure originates from LDCs which themselves will not participate in the ultimate agreement.

On the other hand, we have discerned considerable support for a military exemption provision in conversations with delegates of a number of developed countries at the London meeting, at the Stockholm Conference on the Human Environment and at the U.N. Seabeds Committee in Geneva. . . . Since it is with these countries that any agreement is likely to be reached, there is no requirement for a fallback position on this issue.[39]

In regard to a later draft treaty provision, the entire delegation supported the following: "The U.S. seeks the early establishment of an Ocean Dumping Convention with all major dumping nations included as signatories. However, the achievement of this objective should not override the national security interests in preserving the freedom of mobility and secrecy of movement of U.S. military vessels and aircraft through and over the world's oceans." As noted, the U.S. position on military exemption was accepted, although with perhaps more controversy than the delegation report to Congress indicated.

By the same token, a change not sought in the U.S. position paper—and perhaps intended to bring aboard the LDCs to which DOD had made reference— made its way into the final document. In the earlier version of the preamble, a paragraph asserted the "responsibility [of governments] to ensure that activities within their jurisdiction or control do not cause damage to the environment of other States or of areas beyond the limit of national jurisdiction." In the final version, the following phrase preceded the one just quoted: "Recognizing that States have, in accordance with the Charter of the United Nations and the principles of international law, the sovereign right to exploit their own resources pursuant to their own environmental policies."[40] The addition guaranteed that the Dumping Convention would not interfere with the sovereign right to economic development.

In further limiting the scope of the treaty, the United States insisted on exempting pollution arising from seabed mining. Article III, Paragraph 1, of the draft convention defined "dumping" without mentioning seabed mining. The

U.S. position paper stated that the United States had "no fallback position" (that is, would accept no less) to language that "will effectively exclude dumping generated by seabeds resource activity." The exemption is in the convention. Similarly, the United States insisted on retaining language that would exempt incidental discharges from the normal operation of ships and airplanes and "placement of matter for a purpose other than mere disposal," such as building gravel pads for oil exploration purposes. Again, "there is no fallback to the last two positions," and they were both included in the convention.

Article IV of the draft convention mandated that "each party shall prohibit the dumping of any matter in the sea except as this Convention may allow." The U.S. position paper said, "The United States must insist that the first sentences to this Article be modified or understood so that the requirement to prohibit dumping will not be asserted to be a blanket authorization to adopt novel jurisdictional bases apart from the constraints of international law." The United States achieved inclusion of the phrase "In accordance with the provisions of this Convention," to reinforce the proposition that the Ocean Dumping Convention did not create new rights of coastal jurisdiction.

The United States also insisted on an "emergency clause," which would allow ocean dumping in the event of threats to human life or property. The convention does contain such a clause, but had the delegation not been able to achieve the specific text it sought, it was to cable Washington for further instructions. The U.S. position went beyond providing authorization to respond to immediate threats, including situations "where safety of life may be only threatened at two or three removes." The convention language, which the United States interpreted this way, allows emergency dumping "if there is every probability that the damage consequent upon such dumping will be less than would otherwise occur,"[41] a fairly lenient grant to make judgment calls.

The United States sought to limit the effects of regional agreements on nonparty states. Although the convention encourages regional agreements to regulate ocean dumping, it calls on other states merely to "act consistently with the objectives and provisions of such regional agreements" and to cooperate with parties to regional agreements in developing "harmonized procedures."[42] This stipulation represents a considerable retreat from the draft convention's mandate that "more stringent criteria or prohibitions required under a regional agreement shall be respected by all parties to the present Convention if dumping within that region." The position paper states, "The United States cannot agree to any formulation which appears to apply the requirements of regional agreements as a matter of law to non-parties outside the territorial seas or contiguous zone of parties. There is no fallback to this position."

Likewise, the United States sought clear language to limit the scope of the treaty to deliberate disposal of wastes in the sea. The reason: "The U.S. cannot accept any formula that provides for a new juridical basis for preventing dumping." The United States would seek a comprehensive regulatory scheme but resist any significant changes to existing allocations of authority that might expand the reach of coastal states or limit the freedom of movement of ships and planes. Presumably, even if such changes were to improve environmental protection significantly, the United States would not accept them because of the higher value it placed on free movement of ships and aircraft.

Regarding liability for damages from ocean dumping, the U.S. position was to defer specific rules for later, unspecified discussion. Draft Article X asserted, "the parties recognize that in accordance with the principles of international law States bear responsibility for damage to the environment" of other states or commons areas. The draft said the parties "undertake to develop procedures for assessment of liability and for the settlement of disputes." Instead of accepting responsibility for damages, the United States proposed language calling on the parties to "promote the development of procedures." The United States based this change on a number of unsettled questions regarding liability, such as whether the existence of a national regulatory scheme relieves the state of liability and whether the complaining state must also have an adequate regulatory scheme. The U.S. position was incorporated in the convention.

The United States insisted on stringent procedures for changing the content of the convention. The United States sought to have Article XIV "rewritten so as to make it clear that the amendment of the Annexes is subject to ratification but that no conference is required. The Article must contain the last sentence of paragraph (a) (i). There is no fallback to this position." The sentence in question stated that an amendment would come into force for all parties except those that "make a declaration that they do not accept the amendment."[43] Thus, any state could opt out of any additions to the list of prohibited or regulated substances. The United States supported language to ensure that amendments to the annexes would be based on "scientific criteria."

Interestingly, the United States achieved the least change in regard to the listing and handling of hazardous substances in the annexes. It sought and achieved recognition that no established definition of high-level radioactive wastes existed, and it achieved broadening of the provisions for rapidly degraded materials. Yet, regarding Annex III, which detailed the criteria for classifying substances, the conference rejected language to assess toxicity "under field conditions," retaining the simpler "toxicity." It also rejected the U.S. proposal to consider "rate of accumulation" of materials in "biological materials or sediments." The convention refers only to "accumulation and biotransformation. On the characteristics of the dumping site, the United States suggested adding consideration of "migratory pathways or routes for migratory species."[44] This addition did not appear in the convention. In sum, the final provisions of the Ocean Dumping Convention reflected U.S. positions. In all cases in which the position paper indicated "no fallback position," the United States prevailed. For the most part, these nonnegotiable items related to U.S. insistence on retaining maximum freedom of the seas for military and commercial vessels. The United States also resisted encroachments on normal commercial activity, such as oil exploration and anticipated seabed mining. The U.S. position was to limit the scope of the treaty only to routine dumping of garbage, chemicals, sludge, and other materials when transported from land solely for the purpose of disposal. Primary regulatory authority over such operations would reside with the country that was the point of origin of the materials to be dumped, by way of requiring a permit to carry the waste away from land. This position would leave virtually all control over U.S. ocean dumping in U.S. hands. On the high seas, flag-state authority would remain supreme. Coastal states could enforce regulations only within their own territorial seas and contiguous zone, and regional agreements would not have legal force over nonparties. Military craft would have complete exemption from the provisions of the treaty, except where states pledged to regulate their own ships and airplanes. The result was an international treaty to cover a category of pollution that had before been subject to virtually no regulation. Yet, the treaty left intact existing jurisdictional arrangements, and it was narrowly written to foreclose expanding its scope to other sources and kinds of ocean pollution. The treaty had this character in large part owing to U.S. influence.

Conclusion: Lessons from the U.S. Environmental Policy Process

What does the ocean dumping case tell us about environmental policymaking in the Nixon administration? Again, conclusions can be only tentative in an exploratory study. Still, certain observations suggest themselves. First, internationalizing the issue seems to have originated entirely in the executive branch, not in Congress. Congress spurred interest in the topic by raising the hue and cry about the military's dumping of chemical weapons and other hazardous materials in the ocean, but regulating dumping off the U.S. coast would not in itself require an international treaty. Nonetheless, probably because of Russell Train's influence, the likely passage of U.S. legislation became an opportunity to initiate international negotiations to regulate ocean dumping.

Second, the interagency review process ensured that ambitious environmental proposals would become diluted in light of other U.S. interests. The military in particular successfully resisted all encroachments on its freedom of action. The Commerce Department's vehement objections to being excluded may also have affected the U.S. position, although further research is required to establish this point one way or the other. Regardless, it is clear that making ocean dumping a matter of international concern brought a different cast of players into the process than would have participated had the problem been treated as a domestic issue. Absent the treaty negotiations, the State Department and the Department of Defense in particular would have had little role to play (aside from the matter of military ocean disposals). It is not evident whether Train and others who wanted the matter raised in international negotiations considered the effects of including such players as the DOD on environmental protection.

Last, the entire negotiating process took place with very little direct White House involvement, although, as we have seen, it did not escape the notice of the White House advisors with the most environmental interest, namely John Ehrlichman and John Whitaker. Train wrote to Nixon to report the successful conclusion of the London conference, and in that memo he called the president's attention to several things. He noted that both U.S. legislation and the Dumping Convention came about because of Nixon's "personal initiative."[45] Yet, beyond the incorporation of the call for international ocean dumping regulation in the president's messages to Congress, Nixon and his inner circle of foreign policy advisors appear to have had little to do with the treaty process. Thus, Train's assertion that Nixon "had little personal interest in or enthusiasm for the environmental program his administration pursued so vigorously and effectively"[46] finds no disconfirmation from the ocean dumping case.

Although the ocean dumping case does not indicate Nixon himself was the "environmental president," it does add to the evidence that his was an environmental presidency. Indeed, broadening our vision to encompass the international dimension lends considerable weight to the positive assessments of the Nixon environmental record. Certainly, Nixon can be faulted for retreating considerably on his domestic environmental agenda late in his administration. Yet that tells only part of the story. Nixon did not thwart those in his administration who pursued international environmental policy. What is more, his willingness to include international environmental initiatives in speeches and messages to Congress offered sufficient authority for activists in the administration to carry on a fairly progressive and ambitious foreign environmental policy.

Alternatively, we cannot overlook the efforts the administration made to narrow and limit the scope of the ocean dumping treaty it had sponsored. Research conducted so far does not clearly speak to whether the United States was in front of the rest of the world. If the negotiating draft was acceptable to a substantial number of other nations, then it would appear that the administration reduced the level of environmental protection the treaty might have afforded. If instead the narrowing resulted from intra-administration second thoughts, then the United States might have been the international leader, albeit a less-ambitious one than it had been earlier in the process. Further research on ocean dumping and other issues would help to assess Train's claim that the United States was the acknowledged leader on international environmental issues.

Adding a single case to the empirical evidence can only be indicative. Research on the Nixon administration and its activities regarding marine oil pollution points in the same direction as the ocean dumping case, but attention to such contentious issues as pesticides and water use on the borders might lead to different conclusions. Again, public official documents and archival documents can help make judgments regarding the administration's commitment to the global environment, but compiling and publishing the implications of such evidence remains to be done. Now, although we have added a piece of evidence to show (with qualifications) that Nixon's environmental record deserves the more positive reading it has received lately, more definitive judgments await further inquiry. Still, adding the international dimension is indicative because a president is under no compulsion to negotiate treaties, certainly not treaties that the Senate will ratify. Nixon's administration sought and obtained such a treaty to deal with ocean dumping.

The contemporary relevance of the case includes several major points. Environmental advocates need to think carefully about whether to push an issue to the global level. They tend to favor global agreements to deal with transnational issues and to extend environmental protection as widely as possible, but internationalizing environmental issues brings into the process many actors with different interests, such as the U.S. military. Because the United States has been an international leader in environmental negotiations, the U.S. foreign policy process, including who participates, becomes crucial for determining global policies. Sometimes, stronger environmental policy might well emerge if an issue remains domestic.

The ocean dumping case also shows the strength of U.S. influence. On every important point and on most minor points, the United States prevailed in altering the draft convention toward its own position. U.S. hegemony might have declined somewhat since 1972, but the case shows how important it is to include foreign policy when examining such questions as the formation and change of international regimes. The ocean dumping case could be an instance of a two-level game. It shows that analysis of the two-level game must include domestic bargaining before treaty negotiations begin, including the interagency review process. That is, a comprehensive two-level game model would include interest formation as well as the problem of achieving both international agreement and domestic ratification.

The ocean dumping case raises questions about what has changed since 1972. When the Nixon administration negotiated the ocean dumping treaty, the nation-state was clearly the predominant international actor. Since then, a dense network of environmental NGOs has arisen, and more scientific knowledge is available to strengthen the hand of epistemic communities in formulating environmental policies. Globalization of the world economy has made rules governing trade and investment more crucial for enhancing environmental protection than had previously been the case. The end of the Cold War has allowed priorities to shift away from military security toward other kinds of security, including environmental. These broad trends raise in another way the question of whether environmental activists should concentrate their energy on the U.S. government or turn elsewhere to achieve their goals.

Last, the ocean dumping case can shed light on theoretical questions. This case suggests that understanding foreign environmental policy requires attention to two distinct processes: the initiation of policy and the content of policy. The evidence tentatively suggests that domestic politics drew attention to the ocean dumping problem. Certainly, international attention to the fate of the oceans was rising, but Congress's concern with military hazardous waste disposal gave rise to U.S. ocean dumping legislation. This largely domestic concern then offered policy entrepreneurs such as Russell Train the opportunity to broaden the agenda to include other kinds of dumping and to make the problem a matter of foreign policy. Once made part of the president's foreign policy agenda, ocean dumping became a concern for the foreign policy agencies of the U.S. government. As we have seen, the DOD's wishes, as well as commercial concerns, then entered into the U.S. position at the treaty negotiations. To understand the content of U.S. policy (and, by the same token, of the treaty), requires attention to the interagency review process and the influence of various bureaucratic actors.

Interestingly, the explanation for U.S. policy in both instances is best characterized as state-centric. The international system did not impose an ocean dumping treaty on the United States. To the contrary, without U.S. action, the world probably would not have noticed the need for one. The United States did not enhance its relative position by negotiating an ocean dumping treaty (although its security concerns did override environmental concerns, when the two were in perceived conflict). No compelling collective action problem stood in the way of achieving collective and individual interests: to control dumping in U.S. waters required only U.S. domestic legislation. Nothing suggests that an epistemic community concerned with ocean waste disposal had arisen to influence U.S. policy. Similarly, no evidence of concern on the part of U.S. elites presents itself, nor of public demand for an ocean dumping treaty (although public demand to halt offshore domestic dumping might have motivated Congress).

This leaves state-centric theory as the best way to account for both the presence of ocean dumping on the U.S. foreign policy agenda and for the content of U.S. policy. Although further research is required, it appears that the desire to leave a lasting legacy motivated policy entrepreneurs in the Nixon administration to seize on growing environmental consciousness in the United States. They took this opportunity to encourage U.S. leadership in developing new international environmental agreements to protect the global environment, even if the target was not, properly speaking, part of the global commons. Hence, a cognitive change—rising recognition of the widespread, multifaceted environmental threat— led to administration initiatives to bring about both new international law and new domestic legislation in the United States and in other countries. Once launched, the treaty process engaged the organizational routines (interagency review) and the parochial interests of the executive branch agencies. The result was a considerable dilution of the ocean dumping treaty. Thus, two distinct state-centric processes—policy initiation and policy formulation—can work at cross-purposes. To understand U.S. policy at various stages and the subsequent impact on negotiation outcomes, then, requires attention to both. In both instances, the state-centric approach seems to offer more insight than either systemic or societal approaches to U.S. foreign environmental policy.

Notes

1 Michael A. Genovese, *The Nixon Presidency: Power and Politics in Turbulent Times* (New York: Greenwood, 1990), see 90–95.

2 James Brooks Flippen, "Containing the Urban Sprawl: The Nixon Administration's Land Use Policy," *Presidential Studies Quarterly* 26, no. 1 (winter 1996): 197–207.

3 James Brooks Flippen, "The Nixon Administration, Timber, and the Call of the Wild," *Environmental History Review* (summer 1995): 37–54, quote at 37.

4 James Rathlesberger, ed., *Nixon and the Environment: The Politics of Devastation,* a Village Voice Book (New York: Taurus Communications, 1972).

5 Joan Hoff, *Nixon Reconsidered* (New York: Basic Books, 1994).

6 Ibid., 21.

7 Ibid., 25.

8 Charles S. Warren, "The Nixon Environmental Record: A Mixed Picture," in *Richard M. Nixon: Politician, President, Administrator,* ed. Leon Friedman and William F. Levantrosser (New York: Greenwood, 1991): 191–99.

9 John C. Whitaker, *Striking a Balance: Environmental and Natural Resources Policy in the Nixon-Ford Years* (Washington, D.C.: American Enterprise Institute, 1976).

10 John C. Whitaker, "Discussant: John C. Whitaker," in Friedman and Levantrosser, eds., *Richard M. Nixon,* 200–203.

11 Russell Train, "The Environmental Record of the Nixon Administration," *Presidential Studies Quarterly* 26, no. 1 (winter 1996): 185–96.

12 Ibid., 185.

13 Council on Environmental Quality, *Environmental Quality* (Washington, D.C.: CEQ, 1970).

14 Ibid., vi.

15 Ibid., xiv.

16 Richard M. Nixon, cited in Train, "Environmental Record."

17 Train, "Environmental Record," 192–95.

18 Council on Environmental Quality, *Ocean Dumping* (Washington, D.C.: Government Printing Office, 1970). Quote from Whitaker, *Striking a Balance,* 51.

19 U.S. Congress, House Committee on Merchant Marine and Fisheries, *Ocean Dumping of Waste Materials,* 92d Cong., 1st sess., 5 April 1971, 115–17, serial no. 92-2.

20 House Committee on Merchant and Marine Fisheries, *Ocean Dumping,* 63.

21 Ibid., 113.

22 Ibid., 170.

23 U.S. Congress, House Committee on Foreign Affairs, *International Implications of Dumping Poisonous Gas and Waste into Oceans*, 91st Cong., 1st sess., 8 May 1969 (no serial no.); U.S. Congress, House Committee on Merchant Marine and Fisheries, *Ocean Disposal of Unserviceable Chemical Munitions*, 91st Cong., 2d sess., 3 August 1970, serial no. 91-31; U.S. Congress, Senate Committee on Commerce, *Dumping of Nerve Gas Rockets in the Ocean*, 91st Cong., 2d sess., 5 August 1970, serial no. 91-76.

24 House Committee on Merchant Marine and Fisheries, *Ocean Dumping*, (1971), 171.

25 Ibid., 90.

26 House Committee on Merchant Marine and Fisheries, *Ocean Dumping*, (1971), 161.

27 Alfred Friendly, "U.S. Plan Fails at NATO Conference—Ban on Ocean Dumping Is Rejected," *Washington Post*, 20 April 1971, reprinted in U.S. Congress, Senate Committee on Commerce, *Ocean Waste Disposal*, 92d Cong., 1st sess., 21 April 1971, 198, serial no. 92-11.

28 U.S. Congress, House of Representatives, *Marine Protection, Research, and Sanctuaries Act of 1972*, 92d Cong., 2d sess., 9 October 1971, H. Rept. 92-1546.

29 Martha Gorman, *Environmental Hazards: Marine Pollution* (Santa Barbara: ABC-CLIO, 1993), 74.

30 Russell E. Train, "The Report of the U.S. Delegation to the Intergovernmental Conference on the Convention on the Dumping of Wastes at Sea, Held at London, October 30–November 13, 1972, Which Produced the Convention on the Prevention of Marine Pollution by Dumping of Wastes and Other Matter," reprinted in U.S. Congress, House Committee on Merchant Marine and Fisheries, *Ocean Dumping*, 93rd Cong., 1st sess., 5 June 1973, serial no. 93-14, 16–26.

31 U.S. Embassy, London, to Secretary of State, "Ocean Dumping Conference, Oct. 30 Discussions," folder "International Agreements," Box 139, John Whitaker files, White House Central Files, Nixon Presidential Materials Staff, College Park, Maryland.

32 Ibid.

33 John Whitaker to Ken Cole, 18 November 1970, "Ocean Dumping," Box 35 (HE), White House Central Files, Subject Files, Nixon Presidential Materials Staff.

34 John Whitaker to John Ehrlichman, 13 June 1972, "Talking Points for John Ehrlichman," folder "Council on Environmental Quality," Box 126, John Whitaker files, White House Central Files, Nixon Presidential Materials Staff.

35 William N. Letson to John Whitaker, 10 April 1972, "United States Position on Convention for the Prevention of Pollution of the Sea by Dumping,"

folder "Council on Environmental Quality," Box 126, John Whitaker files, White House Central Files, Nixon Presidential Materials Staff.

36 William N. Letson to John Whitaker, 24 May 1972, "United States Position on Convention for the Prevention of Pollution of the Sea by Dumping," folder "International Agreements," Box 139, John Whitaker files, White House Central Files, Nixon Presidential Materials Staff.

37 Department of State to NSC Secretariat, 2 November 1972, "Ocean Dumping Convention," folder "[Ex]HE 9-4 (Water)," Box 36, HE, White House Central Files, Nixon Presidential Materials Staff.

38 Peter Weber, *Abandoned Seas: Reversing the Decline of the Oceans*, Worldwatch Paper 116 (Washington, D.C.: Worldwatch Institute, November 1993).

39 Department of State to NSC Secretariat, 2 November 1972, "Ocean Dumping Convention."

40 Preamble to the Convention on the Prevention of Marine Pollution by Dumping of Wastes and Other Matter, reprinted in U.S. House of Representatives, Committee on Merchant Marine and Fisheries, *Ocean Dumping*, 93rd Cong., 1st sess., 5 June 1973, serial no. 93-14, 26–39, quote on 26.

41 Ibid., Article V, *Ocean Dumping*, 28.

42 Ibid., Article VIII, *Ocean Dumping*, 29.

43 United States Embassy, London, to the Secretary of State, "Ocean Dumping Conference, Oct. 30 Discussions," folder "International Agreements," Box 139, John Whitaker files, White House Central Files, Nixon Presidential Materials Staff.

44 Preamble to the Convention on the Prevention of Marine Pollution, Committee on Merchant Marine and Fisheries, *Ocean Dumping*, 33.

45 Russell E. Train to Richard M. Nixon, 20 November 1972, "Ocean Dumping Convention," folder "[Ex]HE 9-4," Box 36 HE, White House Central Files, Nixon Presidential Materials Staff.

46 Train, "Environmental Record," 196.

7 Business Conflict and U.S. International Environmental Policy: Ozone, Climate, and Biodiversity

Robert Falkner

Corporations play a central role in U.S. foreign environmental policy.[1] Large multinational firms in particular possess extensive economic and technological power that shapes outcomes in international environmental policy-making. This chapter analyzes the extent to which corporate power affects the making of foreign environmental policy. It suggests that business is in a privileged position because of its central role in making economic and technological choices that set parameters for international environmental action. Corporate power, in this sense, constrains state autonomy and the influence of environmental interest groups. However, because of the fragmentation of the business community and the potential for business conflict, corporations cannot fully determine U.S. foreign environmental policy.

Contending Perspectives on U.S. Foreign Environmental Policy

The United States is of crucial importance in the pursuit of global environmental sustainability. As the politically and economically most powerful state, it has the potential to be a major driving force in reaching international agreement on environmental protection. Indeed, since the 1970s, the global spread of environmentalism owes much to American influence in world politics. The United States pioneered domestic environmental programs that were adopted elsewhere in the industrialized world, and the U.S. environmental movement has played a leading role in global environmentalism. The U.S. government also provided the necessary political clout to achieve important international environmental accords, most notably the Montreal Protocol to protect the stratospheric ozone layer (see chapter 5 of this volume).

But at the same time, American power can be a serious stumbling block in international environmental politics. As the biggest economy of the world, with a myriad of transnational economic links that permeate the global economy, the United States can also act as a de facto veto power in environmental politics, just as in many other global policy areas. In recent years, it has done so repeatedly, slowing progress toward international agreement in important areas of global environmental concern, such as climate change and biodiversity/biosafety.

One of the main concerns in the study of U.S. foreign environmental policy has been to account for this striking policy variation. A popular misconception sees the fluctuating fortunes of environmental concerns on the U.S. foreign policy agenda as a reflection of changing ideological orientations at the heart of the U.S. state, the presidency. Thus, for example, the antiregulatory and pro-business stance of the Reagan and Bush administrations have been cited as the cause for major anti-environmental policy reversals during the 1980s and early 1990s.[2] But, at closer look, the correlation between presidential ideology and environmental policy is much weaker than it would seem. The Reagan administration ultimately failed to roll back environmental regulation domestically, and it supported, in the form of the Montreal Protocol (1987), one of the most far-reaching international environmental agreements. In contrast, the Clinton administration, which took office in 1992 with a decidedly pro-environmental policy program, has failed to deliver many of its promises and has continued to obstruct progress at the international level in areas such as climate change and biosafety.

One of the main reasons why U.S. foreign environmental policy does not simply reflect the political ideology of the administration is a complex system of foreign policymaking that involves not only the presidency and Congress, but also a myriad of interest groups that lobby both the executive office and the legislature. Analysts of U.S. foreign policy have emphasized the important influence of congressional politics and domestic pressure groups. The same pluralist pattern of policymaking extends to foreign environmental policy.[3] According to the pluralist understanding of foreign policymaking, changes in foreign policy reflect shifts in the relative influence of domestic interest groups and bureaucratic units within the institutional setup. In this perspective, the corporate sector is but one interest group competing with, for example, environmental pressure groups and scientific communities.

Pluralist explanations have come under attack from mainly two directions: state-centric realists, on the one hand, and radical ecologists and neo-Marxists, on the other, have produced contrasting accounts of the autonomy of the state in the conduct of foreign policy. Although both approaches acknowledge the relevance of lobbying activities by a variety of domestic interest groups, including business, they differ from pluralism (and from each other) in their assessment of the influence of lobbying on policy choices. State-centric realists maintain that despite attempts of business and other interest groups to influence foreign policy, the U.S. state remains autonomous in making policy choices, and that therefore the locus of explanation lies with the state and shifting alliances among state actors.[4] In contrast, radical ecologists and neo-Marxists claim that the pervasive influence of American business has led to a situation in which U.S. foreign policy has been undermined, if not entirely captured, by corporate interests.[5] This chapter argues that both influential perspectives fail to account for the role of business in U.S. foreign environmental policy. The former view tends to underestimate the power of business by adopting a too narrowly conceived notion of the political role of firms that neglects structural aspects of corporate power. Corporate decisions on investment and technological development set important parameters for states in their choice of policy options. The latter perspective tends to overstate the dominance of the corporate sector by failing to account for conflicting business interests and the fragmentation of the business community with regard to international environmental protection. Business conflict can give rise to competing alliances between sectoral business interests and state actors, thus making it impossible to determine a priori the outcome of the lobbying and foreign policymaking process.

This chapter suggests that by focusing on the role of business in the context of a neopluralist framework, we can advance our understanding of U.S. foreign environmental policy and of international environmental politics in general. It argues that the analysis needs to go beyond the conventional perspective on domestic interest-group politics as a battle between environmentalists and business interests. Business is in a privileged position in the establishment of international environmental policy owing to its central role in making economic and technological choices that affect environmental sustainability. The economic and technological power of firms acts as a constraining force on state autonomy and on the influence of other domestic interest groups. It sets parameters for the regulatory choices available to states. But divisions within the business community prevent business from determining outcomes in foreign environmental policy. The state derives a significant degree of autonomy from business conflict through the creation of political alliances between sectoral business interests and state actors.

This chapter first reviews recent contributions to the study of business influence in the making of foreign policy, especially research in international political economy that is centered around the *business conflict model*. The subsequent sections discuss the relevance of business conflict to the study of foreign environmental policy and consider three cases of U.S. foreign environmental policy: ozone-layer protection, climate change, and biodiversity/biosafety.

The Business Conflict Model and International Environmental Politics

International relations scholarship has recently seen a growing interest in the role of corporations, which reflects both changes in the theoretical orientation of the discipline and a renewed interest in empirical aspects of foreign policymaking. Efforts to "bring the firm back in"[6] are part of a wider return of the transnationalist research agenda and a renewed focus on the domestic sources of foreign policy, signifying the declining dominance of structural realism.[7] Similarly, studies in international political economy (IPE) have seen a shift away from the structuralist emphasis on markets and global capitalism toward a concern for corporations as national and international actors.[8] Furthermore, the study of foreign policy-making, and of U.S. foreign policy in particular, has produced a wealth of empirical insights into the role of the corporate sector in areas as diverse as superpower relations during the Cold War, trade policy, foreign investment, international debt, and Third World policy.[9]

Although the renewed interest in corporations is fuelled by a variety of theoretical approaches, many of the recent firm-centered studies share a concern with the diverging interests and political strategies of corporations in international relations. The focus on the rifts and cleavages among business groups has been at the heart of an approach that has recently been dubbed the "business conflict school."[10] This approach dispenses with the notion that business is a monolithic interest group or represents a uniform capitalist class interest. Instead, the analytical focus is on the nondeterministic nature of corporate influence in foreign policy and the conditions in which corporate power manages to shape policy outcomes. The fragmentation of the business community and the ability of sectoral or individual corporate interests to form alliances with state actors are seen as central determinants of corporate influence in foreign policy.

This concern with business conflict stands in contrast with the early research literature on the rise of multinational corporations (MNCs) and with contemporary studies of globalization, both of which tend to view the corporate sector as a homogenous political group. Globalization is seen to create conditions in which the territorially defined logic of the Westphalian states system is being sidelined by a global logic of economic production and exchange. In this view, globalization has given rise to a new type of actor—the global firm—whose interests are in conflict primarily with the territorially defined nation-state. Multinational firms and states are engaged in a tug of war, pulling on opposite ends of the rope, and the lines of conflict are drawn primarily between the world of politics and the world of economics. For many, the rise of MNCs even signals the end of the nation-state and the decline of a state-based system of governance.[11]

This notion of a fundamental conflict between MNCs and states has also informed the study of environmental politics.[12] Many environmental scholars consider the growth in international trade and production a serious threat to the environment. Work on the role of multinationals has highlighted the ways in which transnational industries are circumventing and undermining national environmental standards by relocating high-polluting manufacturing facilities to developing countries with lax environmental laws. It is through international environmental regulation that states try to control the economic forces of the world economy, with the economy and ecology being locked into a fundamental conflict. The successful creation of international environmental rules is thus seen as an indication of the ability of the states system to overcome corporate resistance. The implicit assumption in this perspective is that firms possess a uniform set of preferences in environmental politics. As more recent work on business conflict demonstrates, however, business does not constitute a monolithic interest group in important areas such as trade and investment, and the conflicts and tensions within the business community are important, if not crucial, factors in determining state policy. If anything, globalization is likely to increase the potential for business conflict. Furthermore, globalization does not simply create "global" firms that shed the characteristics of their national origins; instead, MNCs remain embedded within specific national and regional contexts.[13] Although acting across national boundaries and dealing with a multitude of governments, global firms continue to rely on close political links with home governments. Globalization does not simply empower global firms at the cost of governments and should not be seen as leading to the demise of the states system. On the contrary, under conditions of economic globalization in a fragmented international political system, MNCs will seek the support of their home country governments to influence international markets and regulatory structures for their commercial benefit. The "new diplomacy" of global firms involves close relations and political alliances with states in the pursuit of comparative advantage in a global market.[14]

There is no reason to suggest that international environmental politics is an exception. Insofar as international environmental regulation affects corporate interests and market structures—and collective-action problems can be overcome—we can expect conflicting business groups to seek to influence foreign environmental policy in pursuit of commercial goals. Recent developments in environmental protection have only served to reinforce the "new environmental diplomacy" of firms.

This new environmental diplomacy emerged during the 1980s, a time when national environmental policies had been firmly established in the industrialized world and a number of industrial accidents (e.g., Bhopal 1984, Chernobyl 1986) further strengthened the resolve of the environmental movement and regulatory agencies. In response to these developments, large corporations began to reconsider their strategies for dealing with the ecological challenge.[15] Rather than simply continuing to obstruct environmental policies as they did during the 1970s, a growing number of firms began to accept the need for incorporating environmental goals into corporate strategy.

Proactive corporate environmental practices emerged for a number of reasons: such practices serve, at a minimal level, to deflect environmentalists' criticisms by presenting a "green corporate image." For some companies, environmental management helps to reduce the costs of compliance with environmental laws. More innovative firms even go as far as making pollution prevention an integral part of corporate strategy, with the aim of reducing consumption of energy and natural resources in order to boost both environmental performance and profitability. In these cases, "win-win" solutions have emerged that allow firms to improve their competitiveness vis-à-vis other firms through environmental leadership.

As a consequence, regulatory policies at the national or international level no longer pose a uniform threat to corporate interests. Innovative firms can drastically reduce the costs of regulation and in some cases even develop business opportunities out of environmental regulation, whereas others remain hostile to raising environmental standards. Environmental regulation can benefit individual firms or industries by creating barriers to entry into existing markets, by favoring environmental leaders in a given market, by increasing demand for environmentally friendly products, and by restricting overall output and thus raising prices.[16] But because environmental markets and win-win opportunities arising from environmental protection are to a large extent dependent on market interventions by regulatory bodies, relations with states remain central to firms' environmental strategies. The political economy of environmental regulation is thus closely built around the political strategies of and alliances between states and firms.

Building on the insight of the business conflict school, we can develop a better understanding of the forces that shape the formation of foreign environmental policy. Without falling prey to economic determinism, the business conflict model highlights the privileged position that business occupies in the domestic context of foreign policymaking, but it emphasizes the need to locate dominant business interests among a diversity of corporate interests and to explain their relative power and influence against the backdrop of actual or potential business conflict.

The potential diversity of corporate interests stems from the fact that international environmental regulation can have differential effects on individual firms or sectors. In many cases, regulation increases costs of production and reduces profitability unless the costs can be passed on to consumers. But in some cases, regulation can also improve the competitiveness of certain firms within their sector or of one industry relative to another. In determining the structure of business interests, we thus need to consider the positive and negative externalities of regulation.

Lines of conflict among firms or industries may be drawn in several ways:

1. As suggested by studies of international trade policy,[17] a basic dividing line exists between *national* and *global* firms. The former are more likely to advocate protectionism in economic crises than the latter, which tend to favor open-trade rules. In environmental politics, a similar distinction can be made between national firms that usually consider international regulation just as damaging as national regulation and global firms that may prefer internationally harmonized rules in order to create a global level playing field.

2. Within the group of global firms, conflict may arise, however, between *market leaders* and *laggards* over the creation and design of international environmental regulation if it affects the competitiveness of firms or market structures. Technologically advanced market leaders are more likely than other firms to advocate stringent international environmental standards.

3. A further distinction can be drawn between *producers* of environmentally damaging goods and their industrial *users*. In certain cases, the policy preferences of producers and users diverge, reflecting the distribution of costs and benefits from the conversion to environmentally less-damaging products.

Business and U.S. Foreign Environmental Policy: Three Cases

Three cases of corporate influence in U.S. foreign environmental policy are examined next. In the first case—ozone-layer protection—the United States adopted an active pro-environmental policy that led to the creation of a successful international regime; the other two cases—climate change and biodiversity/biosafety—are characterized by a more defensive, pro-business stance that has held up the establishment of strong international regimes. As is argued below, the variation in policy and outcome cannot be explained by simple reference to weak versus strong business influence. U.S. leadership in environmental politics does not mean that business influence has been successfully contained. In fact, business has played a key role in all three cases. But the important point that emerges from the analysis is that the nature of business competition and patterns of business conflict have a crucial impact on the formation of U.S. foreign policy.

Case 1: Stratospheric Ozone Depletion

The case of international ozone-layer protection has been widely cited as an example of successful environmental action by international society. The U.S. government in particular has been credited for displaying leadership functions in bringing about international consensus on the need to reduce and eventually phase out ozone-depleting substances (ODSs) such as chlorofluorocarbons (CFCs).[18] Analysts of U.S. policy have emphasized the important role played by domestic interest groups, including the major American CFC producers. Particular emphasis has been given to international competition between CFC-producing firms and to the way in which the major CFC-producing countries have sought to boost the competitiveness of their national industries while phasing out ODSs.[19]

In this view, foreign environmental policy aims at reconciling the often conflicting goals of environmental protection, on the one hand, and economic growth and industrial competitiveness, on the other. States will choose policies that under ideal conditions promote both goals at the same time. But tradeoffs are often required, and it is at this point that domestic interest groups can shift the balance toward one of the two policy goals. However, as the business conflict model reminds us, the business community may itself be divided about the proper balance between environmental and economic considerations. As a closer analysis of the steps taken to protect the ozone layer reveals, U.S. policy has evolved in direct response to the changing patterns of business conflict among the American CFC producer and user industries. We thus need to look not only at international competition between CFC producers, but also at interest formation and conflict within the U.S. business community.

The ozone controversy joined the environmental agenda shortly after the first scientific hypothesis of a link between ozone-layer depletion and CFC emissions was published in 1974. The U.S. CFC industry soon found itself engulfed in a heated public debate over the need for precautionary action. Responding to widespread concern by scientists and the public, the U.S. government was among the first to consider restricting CFC emissions.[20] The focus at this point was firmly on the use of CFCs as propellants in aerosol products, which accounted for approximately half of U.S. CFC consumption. The CFC producers and the aerosol industry strongly denied the need for precautionary action and insisted that any regulation be based on full scientific proof of the CFC–ozone loss hypothesis.

Soon after the first signs of consumer disquiet showed, industry opposition to the CFC-ozone theory began to crumble. In 1975, S. C. Johnson, one of the leading U.S. aerosol manufacturers, announced a complete phaseout of CFC propellants in its product range, and shortly afterward other firms followed suit. As a consequence, almost the entire U.S. aerosol market switched to non-CFC technologies within only three years and before a national CFC ban came into effect.[21] Despite their insistence that there was no scientific justification for precautionary action, the CFC producers failed to keep the antiregulatory business front united and lost the largest segment of the CFC market.

U.S. regulatory agencies soon seized the opportunity and announced further restrictions on CFCs in other industrial uses. At this point, CFC producers made a concerted effort to build a united business front against further CFC regulations by mobilizing the diverse group of CFC user industries that had kept a low profile during the CFC aerosol debate. In 1980, the Alliance for Responsible CFC Policy was formed, representing some five hundred companies. The alliance, led by the CFC producers, mounted a massive lobbying campaign against new Environmental Protection Agency (EPA) regulatory proposals. The alliance insisted that there was no scientific basis for further unilateral restrictions, but argued at the same time for the need to seek international consensus on CFC controls. Industry complaints fell on fertile ground during the first few years of the Reagan administration, which was keen to drive through a business friendly program of deregulation.[22] Squeezed from two sides, by both the new presidential team and Congress, the EPA had to shelve its ambitious regulations and signaled that it would not cause further damage to the competitiveness of U.S. industry while other nations abstained from drastic CFC regulations.[23]

Faced with strong domestic resistance to unilateral action, the pro-environmental forces within the U.S. government shifted their focus to the international arena and began pushing for an international accord on CFCs. U.S. industry had given its support to an international agreement in principle, although it hoped that international negotiations would prove to be too cumbersome to achieve a result—except for the prevention of unilateral U.S. regulations. The alliance as a whole remained skeptical of U.S. efforts to negotiate an international ozone treaty, but differences among the CFC industries soon began to reemerge.

This time, it was the large CFC-producing chemical firms that were more likely to go along with the U.S. regulatory strategy. Unlike most of the user industries, the CFC producers were faced with a strategic choice: their overriding concern was to avoid further competitive disadvantages as a result of unilateral restrictions. But because companies such as DuPont and Allied Chemical were competing with European and Japanese firms in a global market, they were more likely to settle with an internationally harmonized CFC regime as a second-best strategy, as long as their competitors were equally affected. In contrast, the majority of the U.S. user industries operated within national markets and had little to gain from an international agreement. They remained hostile to any form of CFC regulation, be it national or international.

The first signs of the breakup of the united business front emerged shortly after the signing of the 1985 Vienna Convention, which provided the framework for future regulations but failed to specify concrete CFC restrictions. In the summer of 1986, DuPont, the world's largest CFC producer, signaled a more cooperative approach by announcing that it accepted the need for international restrictions on the growth of CFC production and consumption. This move was warmly welcomed by the EPA and pro-environment members of Congress, but aroused suspicions among the user industries, which feared that they would have to bear the costs of CFC reductions. Crucially for the evolution of U.S. policy, however, the producer companies dominated the alliance's lobbying campaign and were able to establish a closer quid pro quo relationship with the EPA and the State Department. In the negotiations leading to the Montreal Protocol in 1987, the alliance supported the international agreement in principle, but insisted that economic and technological considerations be taken into account in the design of the international ozone regime.

As the subsequent revisions of the protocol demonstrate, the American CFC producers succeeded in gaining the support of the U.S. government in their effort to shape the international regime according to their own commercial interests. After Du Pont and the alliance announced their support of an eventual phaseout of CFCs in 1988, the U.S. government worked more closely with the CFC producers to coordinate the national CFC reduction plan and to promote

U.S. commercial interests in international ozone negotiations. Crucially for the CFC producers who had invested in new production facilities for substitute chemicals such as hydrochlorofluorocarbons (HCFCs), the United States argued in international negotiations that a "realistic" phaseout schedule for these so-called transitional substances should be adopted so as to not undermine the phaseout of CFCs.[24]

In sum, U.S. leadership in ozone politics did not reflect weak business influence, but was based on the concurrence of particular commercial interests and pro-environmental policies. Business fragmentation initially weakened corporate influence in U.S. ozone policy, but in the 1980s the major CFC-producing firms were able to unite the CFC industry behind a coordinated lobbying attempt to influence U.S. policy. They led the business community into supporting the international ozone regime and helped to strengthen the U.S. position in international negotiations. Conversely, the U.S. government promoted the commercial interests of American CFC producers in the evolution of the international CFC phaseout regime.

Case 2: Climate Change

Whereas the United States provided political leadership at crucial junctures in the creation and evolution of the ozone regime, it has emerged as one of the most important opponents of drastic international action to combat greenhouse gases. Within only a few years, between the 1987 Montreal Protocol and the 1992 Framework Convention on Climate Change, the worldwide reputation of the United States in global environmental protection was profoundly undermined by U.S. obstinacy in international climate negotiations.

There are several reasons for this change in policy. The onset of the economic recession in the early 1990s as well as ideological objections to binding international agreements led the Bush administration to adopt a cautious approach in international environmental negotiations. The scientific evidence of climate change was considered to be less conclusive than the evidence of CFC-induced depletion of the ozone layer. And as the world's biggest per capita consumer of fossil fuel energy, the United States faced particularly costly measures to reduce greenhouse gases. The U.S. administration's position was further compounded by stiff domestic opposition from business and Congress against international reductions of greenhouse gas emissions.

The lobbying efforts by the U.S. fossil fuel industries (coal, oil, and gas) as well as by a wide range of energy-intensive manufacturing firms (e.g., chemical manufacturers, car manufacturers) have had a powerful impact on the international negotiation position of the United States. Although there is widespread consensus among analysts that business interests influence U.S. climate policy, the analytically interesting point is to establish the extent of that influence. Climate change provides an easy case for those who argue that U.S. foreign environmental policy is effectively determined by the corporate sector. Analysts working within the neo-Marxist tradition, for example, have interpreted climate change policy as a classic case of capitalist "capture" of the state by powerful corporate interests whose structural power is based on "the centrality of fossil energy in twentieth-century capital accumulation."[25] But this structuralist explanation fails to account for the evolution in U.S. climate change policy between the Bush and Clinton administrations, and is ultimately insensitive to the friction and conflict that (potentially) exists in the business sector with regard to international climate policy.[26]

The Clinton administration in fact made some progress, although limited in scope, in edging the United States toward an international commitment to introduce carbon dioxide (CO_2)–reduction measures.[27] This progress is in contrast to the efforts of the Bush administration to avoid altogether any binding international commitments on climate change. Under President Bush, the United States used its diplomatic clout to water down the Framework Convention on Climate Change (FCCC) signed at the 1992 Earth Summit, but it did sign up to the voluntary agreement subsequently ratified by the U.S. Senate. President Clinton—after campaigning in 1992 in support of the FCCC and, upon taking office, declaring that the United States would aim to stabilize its greenhouse gas emissions at 1990 levels by 2000—soon introduced legislative measures to limit domestic CO_2 emissions. In 1996, the Clinton administration accepted the need for a binding international agreement on the reduction of CO_2 emissions and eventually signed the 1997 Kyoto Protocol that obliges the United States to reduce its greenhouse gas emissions by 7 percent below 1990 levels by 2012.

Despite the U.S. agreement to the Kyoto Protocol, however, environmentalists at home and governments abroad continued to criticize the U.S. position for having resisted larger emissions cutbacks. The cautious approach in international negotiations reflected the tight constraints domestic opposition had imposed on the U.S. government. These constraints manifested themselves when the Clinton administration had to retreat from its proposed energy tax when it met with determined resistance from the business lobby, leading Congress to refuse legislative authorization in 1993. As a consequence, the U.S. negotiating position was the most defensive among industrialized countries; U.S. diplomats had to admit at the 1995 Berlin climate change conference that the president's greenhouse gas–reduction pledge would not be fulfilled.[28]

But despite these setbacks, the targets signed up to in 1997 were stricter than most representatives of the corporate sector had wanted. U.S. business is therefore not omnipotent in its attempt to prevent climate change politics from damaging corporate interests. Other interest groups—primarily environmental nongovernmental organizations (NGOs), but also pro-environmental actors within the state—influence U.S. foreign environmental policy sufficiently to move the agenda forward. To be sure, business opposition has so far been powerful enough to prevent *stringent* U.S. commitments to reduce greenhouse gas emissions. But in order to determine the nature and extent of business influence, it is instructive to look at the potential for fragmentation and conflict among the business community.

Given the diversity of industry groups whose interests are, directly or indirectly, affected by international climate change politics, it should not be surprising to find some degree of disunity among the business community. The arguably most powerful business grouping actively involved in climate change negotiations is the fossil fuel energy industries. This group is represented most notably by the Global Climate Coalition (GCC) that has earned itself a reputation for being the most outspoken and resourceful industry lobby against international regulation. The GCC does not, however, represent all major energy and manufacturing industries. Cracks in the energy lobby first emerged when British Petroleum (BP) left the GCC in order to take a more moderate and cooperative stance on climate change. Furthermore, some of the large U.S. manufacturing firms have distanced themselves from the energy producers and have formed a separate lobbying group, the International Climate Change Partnership (ICCP). The ICCP grew out of the Alliance for Responsible CFC Policy and aims to continue the cooperative style of business lobbying that proved so successful in the creation of the ozone regime.[29]

Although differences between industrial groupings have arisen primarily over political strategy and tactics, the potential for a more fundamental rift has emerged with the creation of a loosely organized group of corporations that have actively supported international controls on CO_2 emissions. This group comprises large international insurance companies who have been hit recently by a growing number of insurance claims resulting from natural catastrophes that they perceive to be linked to changes in climate. A number of insurance firms have advocated more tangible efforts to curb greenhouse gas emissions and have supported the 1997 Kyoto agreement. Given its central role in directing portfolio investment and in underwriting commercial projects, the insurance industry possesses considerable power vis-à-vis the energy and manufacturing industries as well as state actors. It could therefore become an important ally of pro-environmental forces.[30]

Although there is considerable scope for business conflict over climate change policy, and although some analysts have expressed the hope that the fragmentation of the business community with regard to this issue may form the basis for new pro-environmental political alliances,[31] business conflict has for several reasons not had a significant impact on international climate policies so far.

First, unlike the CFC producers, which supplied ozone friendly alternatives, the major fossil fuel energy producers are unlikely to benefit from international regulation. Their best political strategy by far is to block any progress in reducing CO_2 emissions. Some oil companies, such as Shell and BP, have begun to invest in solar energy in an attempt to hedge their bets, but for most of these large multinational firms renewable energy cannot provide a commercially attractive alternative to their established fossil fuel business.

Second, renewable energy firms that would potentially benefit from CO_2 reductions have not yet formed a powerful business lobby in favor of international greenhouse gas restrictions, in part because the industry is not significant enough in terms of size and market share, and therefore does not possess sufficient economic clout. Another reason is that the dominant fossil fuel energy firms themselves are providing a growing proportion of investment in renewable energy sources such as solar energy, thus reducing the potential for business conflict between competing industrial sectors.

Third, the fossil fuel energy producers and their main industrial users are, on the whole, pulling in the same direction. The users include powerful sectors such as the chemical and automobile industries and are primarily worried about the cost effects of regulatory action against climate change. Unlike some of the CFC user industries, which experienced cost savings from switching to non-CFC technologies (e.g., aerosols, solvents), the main energy users can expect only higher energy costs in the absence of sufficient alternative energy sources.

Fourth, for most insurance companies that support international action against climate change, the costs of changes to the earth's climate remain uncertain and may not justify concerted political intervention in favor of regulatory measures, so the industry has failed to flex its muscles in international negotiations. Furthermore, the biggest source of power for the industry lies in its role as investor in industrial holdings, and there is little evidence as yet that it has shifted its portfolio investments out of the highly profitable fossil fuel energy sector.

Given that the powerful and well-organized fossil fuel lobby faces comparatively weak and dispersed countervailing forces within the business community, the overall impact of the business lobby has been to obstruct progress in combating climate change. The Clinton administration found itself severely limited in its attempt to commit the United States to more drastic targets for greenhouse gas reductions. But the potential for business conflict in climate politics nevertheless exists, and the U.S. state may in the future be able to develop a stronger alliance with pro-environmental business interests in order to overcome domestic resistance against international environmental action.

Case 3: Biodiversity and Biosafety

Industry has also been a powerful force in the formation of a U.S. biodiversity/ biosafety policy, limiting the scope for American participation in international policymaking. The United States acted as a major obstacle in the creation of the Convention on Biological Diversity (CBD) in 1992. It also played a crucial role in the failure at the February 1999 Cartagena Conference to negotiate a protocol on the safety of trade in biotechnological products and adoption of the Cartagena Protocol on Biosafety in January 2000.[32]

In a sense, this cautious approach reflects the underlying political economy of U.S. and international biotechnology regulation.[33] The United States has the largest and most advanced biotechnology sector in the world. Both business and government hail biotechnology as a key innovative sector in modern industrial society with the potential to inject long-term growth into the economy. Accordingly, the U.S. government has made it one of its economic priorities to promote the development and commercial application of biotechnological innovation through national competitiveness strategies, research funding, and a favorable regulatory environment.

From the outset of international negotiations on biodiversity/safety, the U.S. government has paid close attention to the impact of any international agreement on the competitive position of its biotechnology industry. U.S. firms were skeptical of international biodiversity/safety norms, and the Bush administration itself held a number of reservations about the legal implications of a binding international agreement, fearing that such an agreement would undermine its own efforts to roll back antibusiness regulation.[34] It eventually refused to sign the CBD at the United Nations Conference on Environment and Development (UNCED) in 1992.

U.S. industry was originally content with this position, but soon a few firms began to reconsider their stance in light of the overwhelming support the CBD received worldwide. The biotech industry was primarily concerned with the impact of the convention on intellectual property rights and free trade, but did not object to the principle of biodiversity protection in general. In fact, some firms had already begun to initiate bilateral projects with developing countries to support biodiversity conservation and to safeguard access to the genetic material in the Southern Hemisphere.[35] What worried these international research-intensive pharmaceutical firms was the prospect of a worldwide backlash against American intransigence that could eventually threaten U.S. commercial access to the genetic pool held by developing countries.[36]

Following the election of President Clinton in 1992, three U.S. firms (Merck, Shaman Pharmaceuticals, and Genentech) and three NGOs (World Resources Institute, World Wildlife Fund, and Energy Studies Institute) formed a private initiative, with the encouragement of Vice President Al Gore, to study the obstacles to signing the CBD. The group concluded that the United States could accede to the convention while protecting intellectual property rights, but it would need to add an interpretative statement to safeguard corporate interests. At the same time, these global firms managed to achieve industry consensus within the Pharmaceutical Manufacturers Association on ratification of the CBD when the administration made a commitment to defend intellectual property rights more vigorously. In their draft interpretative statement to the president, the group also stressed that there was no need for a protocol on the procedures for the safe transfer, handling, and use of genetically modified organisms (GMOs) resulting from biotechnology.[37]

As a consequence of these efforts by global pharmaceutical firms and NGOs, most of the remaining firms concerned came out in support of the Clinton administration's decision to sign the CBD.[38] Industry had negotiated with the administration that a unilateral "interpretation" to the CBD would be submitted. That interpretation would prevent the international agreement from infringing patent rights or commercial opportunities for research and innovation.

Ironically, it is Congress that has persisted in its opposition to the biodiversity convention. Clinton failed to secure Senate ratification of the treaty. Since the first Conference of Parties in 1994, the United States was confined to the role of an "observer." The administration continued to express its willingness to push for full U.S. participation in the biodiversity regime and supported international biodiversity programs (e.g., the International Coral Reef Initiative), but could not overcome Republican opposition to Senate ratification of the convention.[39]

Despite this setback, the United States was able to participate in the drafting and negotiation of the first protocol to the convention, the Cartegena Protocol on Biosafety. The biotech industry achieved its goal of influencing international negotiations without risking direct infringement of its commercial interests. This time, industry was keen to participate in the international negotiations and stood behind the U.S. administration's official support for an international treaty on trade in biotechnological products. Given the reservations Congress has held about binding international treaties, industry hoped it could gain maximum leverage on international negotiations without risking a strong U.S. commitment to intrusive international biosafety standards.

The parties to the CBD decided to conclude negotiations on a biosafety protocol by early 1999 and convened a final negotiating round in February 1999 in Cartagena, Colombia. Despite being only an "observer" at the conference, the United States played a key role in steering the group of GMO-exporting countries, the so-called Miami Group (Argentina, Australia, Canada, Chile, the United States, Uruguay), which opposed the more stringent control proposals put forward by the European Union and most developing countries. Agreement was reached on a number of important points, but insurmountable differences remained concerning the degree to which the biosafety protocol would interfere with international trade. European participants at the Cartagena conference complained that the U.S. biotechnology industry had lobbied hard—and successfully—against the more stringent regulatory proposals, particularly during the end phase of negotiations.[40] The conference concluded without a final agreement, but the parties pledged to reconvene within the next fifteen months to try again to reach an agreement.

After the collapse of the Cartagena conference, two important developments changed the domestic context of U.S. policy on biosafety. First, the environmental movement stepped up its campaign against the use of biotechnology in agriculture and food production, causing the Food and Drug Administration (FDA) to hold high-profile public consultations on its approval of genetically modified crops. Second, a growing number of agricultural producers and exporters began to question the commercial benefits of agribiotechnology, causing a widening rift between the interests of farmers and the biotechnology industry.[41] At the same time, both the U.S. administration and biotechnology industry began to signal at the international level that they were in support of an international biosafety standard. Facing continuing opposition in Europe and growing public concern at home, the U.S. biotechnology industry was now ready to acknowledge the need for international harmonization of trade-related biosafety rules. In the final biosafety talks in January 2000, the U.S. government played an active part in reaching a compromise that led to the adoption of the Cartagena Protocol, which was widely welcomed by environmentalists and industry representatives.[42]

In sum, U.S. policy on biodiversity and biosafety has been constrained by a powerful business front against binding international commitments that would infringe on the commercial rights and opportunities of its thriving biotechnology industry. Leading international biotechnology firms, however, have supported U.S. participation in international negotiations with a view to influencing international norm setting. Thus, U.S. policy has evolved from President Bush's refusal to sign the CBD to Clinton's support for international biosafety standards, largely in line with the evolution of corporate strategy, but it continues to reflect corporate concerns about intrusive international standards that threaten to harm U.S. biotechnology interests.

Conclusion

In the past two decades, U.S. foreign environmental policy has undergone profound changes. The United States has moved from the position of political leader on ozone-layer protection during the 1980s to the role of footdragger on climate change and biodiversity/safety in the 1990s. Even the pro-environmental Clinton presidency was unable to restore American leadership in global environmental protection and has repeatedly put business interests above environmental concerns. However, the decline of environmental issues on the foreign policy agenda does not necessarily indicate a shift in the balance of power between business and environmentalists in favor of the former. Business has been a potent force in the making of U.S. policy throughout the period under consideration in this essay. Rather, as the above analysis suggests, it is at the microlevel of business competition and conflict that we can find important clues to the changing direction of U.S. foreign policy in environmental affairs.

Business plays a central role in the formation of U.S. foreign environmental policy. It is argued in this chapter that the analysis of U.S. policy needs to be firmly placed in a political-economic context. Business, of course, is not the sole influencing factor in the making of U.S. foreign policy, but it does occupy a privileged position among the variety of interest groups involved in the process because of its command over "technological power." Also, through its key role in giving direction to investment and technological innovation, business is able to set parameters for the regulatory options available to policymakers. Based on technological power and lobbying clout, American firms have been able to exert considerable influence over the formation of U.S. foreign environmental policy.

In the case of ozone-layer protection, the producers of CFCs were able to assume a central role in U.S. foreign policy because of their key role in technological innovation to reduce CFC emissions (i.e., developing CFC substitutes). Given their willingness to cooperate with the administration in creating an international ozone regime, the CFC producers could muster the support of state actors in their attempt to shape the emerging ozone regime to their own commercial benefit. In climate change politics, the fossil fuel industry has been able to create a powerful business front against strong U.S. commitments to reduce greenhouse gas emissions, based on its key role in energy production and industrial manufacturing. Fossil fuel energy firms are also heavily engaged in developing alternative energy forms (e.g., solar energy). They play a crucial part in the technological conversion away from fossil fuels, thus setting the pace for political change. Similarly, the biotech industry's central role in technological and economic innovation has provided it with considerable leverage over the U.S. biodiversity/safety policy to redirect the administration's approach to international biosafety issues.

In many cases, corporate power serves to constrain state actors in their choice of regulatory instruments and in international negotiations. The corporate sector can set parameters for international environmental action that states find difficult to ignore. Given the centrality of corporate decisions for technological change and global sustainable development, states are not fully autonomous in environmental policymaking. U.S. foreign environmental policy often represents a bargain between the state and corporate interests in the pursuit of both environmental sustainability and corporate profitability and competitiveness.

At the same time, however, corporations are not in control of U.S. foreign environmental policy. They cannot fully determine policy choices or completely eliminate state autonomy. Other actors, especially environmental and consumer groups, can significantly affect the political environment within which both states and corporations formulate their environmental strategies. Most importantly, however, the business community is far from united in its attempt to influence U.S. foreign environmental policy. The fragmentation of the corporate sector and the emergence of divergent, often conflicting business interests in environmental politics have given rise to a new political economy of environmental protection. In this new political economy, some corporations or industries may support a proactive U.S. role in establishing international environmental standards, whereas others will continue to oppose such policies. Wherever the potential for business conflict arises, political alliances between state actors and powerful corporate interests will play an important role in shaping U.S. foreign environmental policy.

The notion of "business conflict" thus provides important insights into the scope for state autonomy in environmental policymaking. Pro-environmental state actors can derive limited autonomy from business conflict if sufficiently powerful corporate interests support international environmental standards. The convergence of environmental concerns and particular commercial interests creates conditions in which U.S. leadership in international environmental politics becomes possible. State autonomy is, however, severely limited if powerful business groups succeed in creating a united front against international environmental action.

The analytical focus on business conflict and alliances between state actors and corporate interests goes some way in explaining the variation in U.S. foreign environmental policy in the last two decades of the twentieth century. To be sure, other factors, most notably the strength of the environmental movement and the role of Congress, also influence the scope for an active U.S. role in global environmental affairs. There is no reason to assume that the United States cannot reestablish itself as a global environmental leader, but, as this analysis suggests, such a development will crucially depend on the emergence of a powerful alliance between pro-environmental U.S. business interests and sympathetic state actors.

Notes

1 I thank Andrew Hurrell and Andrew Walter for helpful comments on an earlier draft of this chapter and the German Historical Institute in Washington, D.C., for financial support in carrying out research in the United States.

2 In the early 1980s, President Reagan introduced a comprehensive regulatory overhaul that weakened the influence of the Environmental Protection Agency (EPA) in foreign policymaking. Similarly, President Bush adopted an increasingly obstructionist position in the run-up to the United Nations Conference on Environment and Development (UNCED) in order to emphasize his pro-business credentials during the 1992 presidential campaign. See David Vogel, *Fluctuating Fortunes: The Political Power of Business in America* (New York: Basic Books, 1988); and "Bush's New World Order Takes Back Seat at Summit," *Wall Street Journal*, 15 June 1992, 14.

3 See Robert Paarlberg, "Earth in Abeyance: Explaining Weak Leadership in U.S. International Environmental Policy," in *Eagle Adrift: American Foreign Policy at the End of the Century*, ed. Robert J. Lieber (New York: Longman, 1997), 135–60; and Barbara J. Bramble and Gareth Porter, "Non-Governmental Organizations and the Making of U.S. International Environmental Policy," in *The International Politics of the Environment: Actors, Interests, and Institutions*, ed. Andrew Hurrell and Benedict Kingsbury (Oxford: Clarendon, 1992), 313–53.

4 See Stephen Hopgood, *American Foreign Environmental Policy and the Power of the State* (Oxford: Oxford University Press, 1998).

5 The Ecologist, *Whose Common Future? Reclaiming the Commons* (Philadelphia: New Society, 1993); Peter Newell and Matthew Paterson, "A Climate for Business: Global Warming, the State and Capital," *Review of International Political Economy* 5 (1998): 679–703.

6 Lorraine Eden, "Bringing the Firm Back In: Multinationals in International Political Economy," *Millennium* 20 (1991): 197–224.

7 See Thomas Risse-Kappen, ed., *Bringing Transnational Relations Back In: Non-State Actors, Domestic Structures, and International Institutions* (Cambridge: Cambridge University Press, 1995); and David Skidmore and Valerie M. Hudson, eds., *The Limits of State Autonomy: Societal Groups and Foreign Policy Formulation* (Boulder, Colo.: Westview, 1993).

8 This shift in emphasis is evident in, for example, the influential writings of Susan Strange, who provided a structuralist foundation for IPE in her *States and Markets* (London: Pinter, 1988) but shifted the focus in her later work to the state-firm relationship. See John Stopford, Susan Strange, and John S. Henley, *Rival States, Rival Firms: Competition for World Market Shares* (Cambridge: Cambridge University Press, 1991).

9 Ronald W. Cox, ed., *Business and the State in International Relations* (Boulder, Colo.: Westview, 1996), brings together a representative selection of studies in these areas.

10 David Skidmore, "The Business of International Politics," *Mershon International Studies Review* 39 (1995): 246.

11 See Kenichi Ohmae, *The End of the Nation State: The Rise of Regional Economics* (London: HarperCollins, 1995); and Susan Strange, *The Retreat of the State: The Diffusion of Power in the World Economy* (Cambridge: Cambridge University Press, 1996).

12 See Jane H. Ives, ed., *The Export of Hazard: Transnational Corporations and Environmental Control Issues* (London: Routledge and Kegan, 1985); and Pratap Chatterjee and Matthias Finger, *The Earth Brokers: Power, Politics, and World Development* (London: Routledge, 1994).

13 Louis W. Pauly and Simon Reich, "National Structures and Multinational Corporate Behavior: Enduring Differences in the Age of Globalization," *International Organization* 51 (1997): 1–30.

14 See Susan Strange, "States, Firms, and Diplomacy," *International Affairs* 68 (1992): 1–15; and Paul Hirst and Grahame Thompson, *Globalization in Question: The International Economy and the Possibilities of Governance* (Cambridge: Polity, 1996).

15 Bruce Piasecki, *Corporate Environmental Strategy: The Avalanche of Change Since Bhopal* (New York: John Wiley and Sons, 1995).

16 Scott Barrett, "Environmental Regulation for Competitive Advantage," *Business Strategy Review* 2 (1991): 1–15.

17 Helen V. Milner, *Resisting Protectionism: Global Industries and the Politics of International Trade* (Princeton: Princeton University Press, 1988).

18 See Richard E. Benedick, *Ozone Diplomacy: New Directions in Safeguarding the Planet* (Cambridge, Mass.: Harvard University Press, 1996); and Patrick Széll, "Negotiations on the Ozone Layer," in *International Environmental Negotiation*, ed. Gunnar Sjöstedt (Newbury Park, Calif.: Sage, 1993), 31–47.

19 See Benedick, *Ozone Diplomacy;* Edward A. Parson, "Protecting the Ozone Layer," in *Institutions for the Earth: Sources of Effective International Environmental Protection,* ed. Peter M. Haas, Robert O. Keohane, and Marc A. Levy (Cambridge, Mass.: MIT Press, 1993), 27–73; and Kenneth A. Oye and James H. Maxwell, "Self-Interest and Environmental Management," in *Local Commons and Global Interdependence: Heterogeneity and Cooperation in Two Domains,* ed. Robert O. Keohane and Elinore Ostrom (Newbury Park, Calif.: Sage, 1995), 191–221.

20 For an overview of the ozone controversy during the 1970s, see Sharon Roan, *Ozone Crisis: The 15-Year Evolution of a Sudden Global Emergency* (New York: John Wiley and Sons, 1989).

21 ICF, Inc., *An Analysis of the Economic Effects of Regulatory and Non-regulatory Events Related to the Abandonment of Chlorofluorocarbons as Aerosol Propellants in the United States from 1970 to 1980* (Washington, D.C.: ICF, 1986); and "Fluorocarbons Canned," *Chemical Week* (25 June 1975): 18.

22 Vogel, *Fluctuating Fortunes,* 247–49.

23 In the early 1980s, the European CFC industry was subject to only modest CFC restrictions that included a 30 percent reduction of CFC use in aerosols and a production cap. See Markus Jachtenfuchs, "The European Community and the Protection of the Ozone Layer," *Journal of Common Market Studies* 28 (1990): 261–77.

24 On the revisions of the Montreal Protocol and the issue of an HCFC phaseout, see Karen Litfin, *Ozone Discourses: Science and Politics in Global Environmental Cooperation* (New York: Columbia University Press, 1994).

25 Newell and Paterson, "A Climate for Business," 680.

26 To be sure, Newell and Paterson mention the potential for business conflict in climate change policy but fail to consider the consequences of this admission for their quasi-deterministic approach (ibid.).

27 See Paul G. Harris, *Understanding America's Climate Change Policy: Realpolitik, Pluralism, and Ethical Norms* (Oxford: Oxford Centre for the Environment, Ethics, and Society, 1998), 18–29.

28 Paarlberg, "Earth in Abeyance," 140.

29 BP has since been joined by Shell, Amoco, Ford, GM, and Southern Electric in an effort to strike a more cooperative chord with the Kyoto Protocol; see Simon Retallack, "An Interview with the Global Climate Coalition," *The Ecologist* 29 (1999), 124.

30 See Jeremy Leggett, ed., *Climate Change and the Financial Sector: The Emerging Threat, the Solar Solution* (Munich: Gerling Akademie, 1996).

31 Newell and Paterson, "A Climate for Business."

32 Robert Falkner, "Regulating Biotech Trade: The Cartagena Protocol on Biosafety," *International Affairs* 76, no. 2 (2000): 299–313.

33 On the international differences in biotechnology regulation, see Jacqueline Senker and Ronald van Vliet, eds., *Biotechnology and Competitive Advan-*

tage: Europe's Firms and the U.S. Challenge (Cheltenham: Edward Elgar, 1998).

34 See Kal Raustiala, "Domestic Institutions and International Regulatory Cooperation: Comparative Responses to the Convention on Biological Diversity," *World Politics* 49 (1997): 482–509.

35 For example, in September 1991, Merck & Co. signed a contract with Costa Rica's INBio, a scientific organization with the mission to maintain the country's biodiversity. Merck was granted the right to screen a specified number of biological samples for commercial applications, and INBio and the Costa Rican government were guaranteed royalty payments for any commercial development resulting from this research.

36 In 1995, India used the threat of blocking U.S. access to biological and genetic material to push for U.S. ratification of the CBD (*New York Times*, 23 April 1995, A13).

37 Abby Munson, "Should a Biosafety Protocol Be Negotiated as Part of the Biodiversity Convention?" *Global Environmental Change* 5 (1995): 7–26.

38 See U.S. Senate, Committee on Foreign Relations, *Hearing on the Convention on Biological Diversity*, 103rd Congress, 2d sess., 12 April 1994.

39 Paarlberg, "Earth in Abeyance," 139–40.

40 EU negotiation team member, interview by the author, 4 March 1999.

41 Cf. Robert Falkner, "International Trade Conflicts over Agricultural Biotechnology," in *The International Politics of Biotechnology: Investigating Global Future*, ed. Alan Russell and John Vogler (Manchester: Manchester University Press, 2000).

42 Cf. Falkner, "Regulating Biotech Trade."

8 Multilateral Development Banks, Environmental Impact Assessments, and Nongovernmental Organizations in U.S. Foreign Policy

Morten Bøås

State politics, international treaties, and intergovernmental organizations are the formal focal points of international relations, and they have become increasingly important in addressing environmental issues on the global, regional, national, and subnational levels. Among these intergovernmental organizations are the multilateral development banks (MDBs). The MDBs are jointly owned by developed and developing member countries, but their main resources come from the paid-in capital and the callable capital contributions of the developed member countries. The main objective of the MDBs is to facilitate loans and grants to the developing member countries. In the MDBs, the principal influence on environmental policies and practices is from member states who elect the MDB president and appoint or elect the executive directors (EDs) who vote on each loan and policy proposed by management. However, often the driving force behind all these apparently state-led activities has been popular pressure expressed through nongovernmental organization (NGO) activity.

Concerning the United States, this chapter argues that one of the prime movers behind government initiatives are U.S. NGOs, whose leaders have brought to the attention of government administrators and legislators the failure of MDBs to pursue sound environmental practices in their loan operations. This chapter shows that the NGO community, through its ability to gain access to formal decision makers, is a force that has to be taken into consideration in analyses of international environmental policy. However, increased NGO involvement does not necessarily equal improved environmental policies. Rather, this chapter highlights that access to formal decision makers and decision-making processes has a doubled-edged nature, and it is therefore not always self-evident whose interests—the environment's, the NGOs', or the formal decision makers'—are actually served.

Even though the strength and influence of the NGOs are not equal, and their role in various forums and institutional settings differ, the NGO community emerged during the 1990s as an important actor in international relations. The NGO community has had strong influence on several small- and large-scale projects around the world. They have built public awareness on the environment through conferences and other sorts of public activities. Even more important from an international relations point of view may be their activities aimed at shaping international institutions and international law.[1]

This chapter addresses this issue by analyzing the relationship between U.S. NGOs and U.S. policy regarding the environmental practice of the MDBs. The point of departure for this chapter is NGO involvement in the 1983–84 congressional hearings on MDB activity. This involvement led to a campaign aimed at making it impossible for American EDs in the MDBs to support loans for projects that could have a major impact on the environment unless an environmental impact assessment (EIA) was made available at least 120 days in advance. This campaign culminated with the Pelosi amendment, which made an EIA 120 days in advance of board consideration a requirement for U.S. support. Little more than a year after what originally started as a national campaign in the United States, this procedure was de facto turned into international law when all the MDBs made an EIA 120 days in advance of board consideration part of their standard operating procedure. The second part of this chapter is concerned with the question of whose interests the continuation of this NGO campaign served: the people in less-developed countries, the NGOs themselves, or the majority in the U.S. Congress?

The objective of this chapter is to document these processes in order to highlight the transnationalization of environment policies and the internationalization of the activities of the NGOs based in the United States, and to ask the question, Who is serving whom in these processes?

State Power, MDBs, and American NGOs

Member states constitute the most obvious avenue for external influence on MDBs. They elect the president and appoint governors and executive directors, and the votes they control are weighted in accordance with the capital subscriptions of the member state represented by the ED. The influence of individual member states is, however, not measured by their votes alone. For instance, the United States controls between 7 percent and 34 percent of the votes in the most important MDBs,[2] but in some of these institutions its influence on the president and senior staff is substantial and sometimes dominant. The United States must approve the president of all these institutions, except for the African Development

Bank (AfDB), and it controls several of the most important vice presidencies in the MDBs. Even more important, as one of the largest stockholders in the major MDBs, the United States has significant influence on the approval of proposals for increased capital subscriptions. All member states of MDBs take part in decisions to increase capital subscriptions, but only the subscriptions of wealthy countries represent effective loan resources for these institutions. The point is that most of the capital subscriptions to the MDBs are not paid in, but callable, and thus serve as a guarantee for the indebtedness of the MDBs when they borrow in international capital markets. The United States is at times outvoted, but if an MDB made a loan to which the U. S. government made objections, it could suddenly find itself in a very delicate situation because the U. S. government might begin to oppose proposals for increased capital subscriptions.

A more recent source of influence on international environmental policies and the environmental practice of the MDBs is the public of donor-member countries, whose views most often are mobilized and expressed through national and international NGOs. The 1992 Earth Summit is often seen as the international breakthrough of the NGO community, but the NGOs had in fact already for some years attracted attention from development circles and donors. As early as the end of the 1960s, when the top-down modernization approach of the public sector in developing countries started to fall into ill repute, funding increased for NGOs. The debt crisis of the 1980s led to skepticism among several donors about the wisdom of funding large public-sector projects in poor countries. Even more important, owing to the general neoclassical approach of the 1980s, NGOs gained a reputation for innovation, for promoting local participation, and for reaching the poor at the grassroots level.[3] The consequence was that during the 1980s, important donors such as the U.S. Agency for International Development (USAID) increasingly turned to the NGO community as a flexible instrument for development activities.[4] Subsequently, development funding through NGOs increased significantly, and the size of the NGO community virtually exploded.[5] Stimulated by heightened donor interest in NGOs in general and by environmental issues in particular, new environmental NGOs emerged, and originally more traditional development NGOs embraced environmental concerns as well. At the Earth Summit, more than 20,000 participants of 9,000 organizations from 171 countries were present, and more than 1,000 meetings were held between NGO representatives in a forum parallel to the official intergovernmental discussions.[6]

Another important feature of this trend is the organizational and financial growth of individual NGOs, which prominent northern NGOs in particular have experienced since the early 1980s. From 1983 to 1991, the revenues of the U.S. branch of the World Wildlife Fund (WWF) increased from $9 million to $53 million, and the number of members increased from 94,000 to nearly one million.[7] Friends of the Earth (FoE), which opened its first office in San Francisco in 1969, expanded to Paris in 1970 and to London in 1971. In the early 1970s, it began to develop the international arm of the organization called Friends of the Earth International, which grew from twenty-five member groups worldwide in 1981 to fifty-one in 1992.[8] The Sierra Club increased its number of members from 346,000 in 1983 to 560,000 in 1990 and had an annual budget of $35 million. The Natural Resources Defense Council (NRDC), established in 1972 with 6,000 members, had by 1991 grown to 170,000 members and an annual budget of $16 million. Like FoE, both the Sierra Club and NRDC broadened their international commitments and programs in the 1980s and 1990s.[9]

The multitude of NGO activity around specific projects, their impact on public opinion, and their organization of parallel conferences are evidence of a new phenomenon in international relations, but even more significant are their activities aimed at shaping international institutions and international law. For instance, the International Institute for Environment and Development (IIED) has been involved with the International Timber Organization since its establishment. For many years, the International Whaling Commission resisted public participation in its meetings, but recently it has allowed increased NGO involvement. The London Dumping Convention granted observer status to concerned NGOs in the early 1980s, and NGOs have been credited with fostering and strengthening the Montreal Protocol on Substances that Deplete the Ozone Layer.[10]

NGOs are also often given credit for putting environmental issues on MDB agendas. World Bank meetings have been a focal point of NGO activity at least since 1983, when six large U.S. NGOs pressured the World Bank to include environmental costs in its projects.[11] This event was followed by the World Bank's involvement in "scandal" projects such as the deforestation caused by the Polonoroeste project in Brazil, the soil erosion and resettlement problems related to the Narmada project in India, and the deforestation and social consequences of the Indonesian transmigration project. The controversies around these projects entailed much criticism directed against the World Bank, and even threats of reduced financial contributions emerged. NGOs based in the United States focused on and criticized the World Bank's involvement in these projects. These American NGOs lobbied both the World Bank and the U.S. Congress, and in June 1986 the first "no" vote on environmental grounds by an American ED for a World Bank project was cast.[12] At the 1991 annual meeting of the Asian Development Bank (ADB), twenty-four NGOs from Asia, the South Pacific, and North America attended and were accorded office space and access to bank officials.[13] In the AfDB, a new policy was adopted in 1991 to promote the development of African NGOs. According to this policy, the bank should provide facilities to NGOs to organize seminars, workshops, and meetings at the AfDB's headquarters. In 1992, the AfDB adopted the procedure of inviting NGOs to its annual meetings.[14]

Thus, with regard to international environmental policies, an NGO phenomenon exists. Not all NGOs are able to play—or are interested in playing—a role in the processes that are documented here, but those who do so can be compared to transnational corporations. They have a home base, they have foreign affiliates, and they often enter into strategic alliances with domestic NGOs when they operate abroad. The WWF, FoE, NRDC, Environmental Defense Fund (EDF), International Rivers Network, and Sierra Club are all examples of international environmental NGOs with the power of making their cases heard both domestically (e.g., in the U.S. Congress) and internationally in institutions such as the MDBs. The next step is to document this process by analyzing the relationship between U.S. foreign policy on the environment and the influence of the NGO community.

U.S. Foreign Environmental Policy and the NGO Community

In its foreign policy on environmental issues, a state most often plays one of four possible roles: lead state, supporting state, swing state, or veto/blocking state.[15] A lead state has strong commitments to environmental issues, makes serious attempts to move negotiation processes forward, and actively seeks support from other states for its preferred solution. A supporting state speaks and acts in favor of proposals from a lead state, whereas a swing state is one that demands substantial concessions to its point of view as the price for agreeing. A veto/blocking state is one that either openly opposes an agreement or tries to weaken the agreement to the point where it is more or less useless for effective environmental protection. The stronger a state is (economically, politically, militarily, etc.), the more able it will be to fulfil any of these four roles. Of course, the prospects for adequate leadership are somewhat different for the various items on the international environmental agenda, but the United States is the one actor without whose leadership most environmental agreements and regimes are certain to be weakened. When the United States is actively engaged in trying to forge international consensus, it can often overwhelm other states that have taken on the role of swing states or veto/blocking states. Alternatively, when the U.S. role is that of the swing state or the veto/blocking state, the agreement or regime in question is inevitably weaker. The question is, Can the NGO community push the United States to act as a lead state instead of as a swing state or veto/blocking state in its foreign policy on the environment?

The NGOs' Paths to Influence
NGOs exercise their influence through various branches of governments and directly through the MDBs. However, as we will see, direct lobbying of the MDBs is most effective if member countries, and in particular the important financial contributors, also take up the issue at hand. In the United States and other parts of the developed world, the NGOs' main path to influence is therefore to press their governments to express certain positions through the EDs represent-

ing their particular countries. What, precisely, are the NGOs' sources of bargaining leverage?

Nongovernmental groups cannot, at least formally, dictate terms to anyone. They cannot tax, legislate, adjudicate, or establish national foreign-assistance policies. But they do have influence. This influence is exercised neither bottom up nor top down, however, but by linking different policy levels—local to the international, the national to the international, and the national to the local, and so on. The bargaining leverage of NGOs is not built on traditional power resources such as territory and armies, but they do wield considerable economic strength. They can promote communication and muster support for or opposition against environmental policies. They can draw on concerned constituencies to rally support for or opposition against state policies,[16] and they can coordinate bargaining through the establishment of networks. The point we have to keep in mind is that international institutional bargaining involves extensive intraparty bargaining that occurs simultaneously with relevant interparty bargaining. States, as complex collective entities, encompass numerous groups whose interests often differ with regard to various issue areas. This variety creates potential for the development of transnational alliances among groups who favor a specific outcome of the bargaining process.[17]

Transnational alliances between environmental interest groups have played a central role in pushing through several environmental regimes.[18] With respect to the MDBs, transnational alliances between NGOs are a recent, but increasingly more important source of influence.[19] So far, the most important NGOs have been the ones from donor countries. The influence of NGOs in recipient countries has been more limited, but it is increasing, in particular when they form alliances with NGOs from the affluent part of the world. One excellent illustration of the latter is the transnational alliance between the EDF, the International Rivers Network, and the Arun Concerned Group of Nepal. This alliance accused the sponsors of the Arun III Hydroelectric Scheme for Nepal—the ADB and the World Bank—of violating World Bank policies and procedures, and eventually forced the two MDBs out of the project.[20] The next question is how the NGOs use their quite considerable nontraditional sources of power in their actual bargaining with the MDBs.

NGO Bargaining on the Environment

If we take into account that NGOs are not traditionally legitimate actors in the institutional framework of the MDBs, the NGO bargaining process must be a two-level process. First, they must use their bargaining leverage in order to gain access to the decision-making process. It is only then that they can seek to engage themselves directly in the formation and reform of international institutions. Because protests from outside MDBs have proven to be relatively ineffective,[21] NGOs must gain access to legislative process at the national level—i.e., in their home country and abroad—and to the decision-making process at the international level. In recent years, the NGO solution to the problem of access and the inadequacy of protests from outside has been to build networks and coalitions between the developed and the developing world as well as between national capitals and the grassroots in order to influence the political forces that determine the environmental policies and practices of MDBs. By linking the global and the local, NGOs seek to demonstrate that continued ecological neglect in fact could pose a threat even to the growth and survival of the MDBs. Nevertheless, whereas gathering political pressure gives indirect access and may even be seen as the first step toward direct access, getting to the table is the essential aim of the international environmental NGOs. As experienced negotiators, they have realized that in environmental negotiations there are few precedents, often an ill-defined agenda, and little predetermined structure because such negotiations are often being conducted for the first time and are thus experimental. Hence, simply sitting at the table offers the possibility of significant influence. In such situations, actors with well-prepared positions and carefully worded proposals will often be able to exercise influence far beyond their structural position.

International Environmental NGOs and the United States: The Pelosi Amendment

With regard to the MDBs, the NGOs' prime target on the administrative side of the U.S. government has been the Treasury. The secretary of the Treasury serves as the U.S. governor on the board of governors in the various MDBs, and the U.S. EDs in the MDBs are usually recruited from the Treasury as well. The assistant secretary of the Treasury for international affairs also chairs the Working Group on Multilateral Assistance, which was established in 1978 to coordinate U.S. policy on the MDBs. This group meets weekly to discuss positions on upcoming loan proposals and policies. All loans and new policy proposals are assessed on the basis of whether they are in accordance with general foreign policy, as well as whether the projects are properly conceived. The decisions reached in these meetings are transmitted to the EDs and must be followed closely.

Equally important from the NGO point of view is the monthly informal meeting between the international environmental NGOs and representatives from the Treasury, the State Department, USAID, and the Environmental Protection Agency, who review upcoming environmentally controversial loans. These meetings are informal, but they were in fact institutionalized through legislation passed by Congress in 1986 to establish an early warning system.[22] Two international environmental NGOs, the Sierra Club and the NRDC, conducted the drafting of the legislation that inscribed the Early Warning System into U.S. law. The objective of this system is to provide advanced notification about projects thought to pose environmental problems and to publish a list of these projects every six months.[23]

On the legislative side of the U.S. government, the Congress has been an important channel of influence for the NGOs. At the request of the National Wildlife Federation (NWF), the Environmental Policy Institute (EPI), and the NRDC, six different congressional subcommittees held extensive hearings on MDB activity in 1983–84. As a consequence of these hearings, the Treasury conducted a study of the environmental policies and practices of the MDBs and, in particular, those of the ADB, the Inter-American Development Bank, and the World Bank. This study was submitted to the House Banking Subcommittee on International Development Institutions and Finance. On the basis of this study, the subcommittee held a new round of hearings in close consultation with U.S.-based international environmental NGOs in order to review a series of draft recommendations concerning MDBs and the environment. The outcome of this new round of hearings was that the subcommittee urged the Treasury to strengthen its monitoring of environmental policies in the MDBs and, just as important from the NGO point of view, to expedite the flow of information between the banks, Congress, other relevant federal agencies, and the public. The individual U.S. EDs in the various MDBs were called upon to press the banks to work with NGOs. They were also urged to vote against any projects that would result in unacceptable environmental damage, which was defined by the subcommittee as unsustainable resource exploitation, species extinction, pesticide misuse, degradation of protected areas, and disturbance of the habitat of indigenous people.[24] In December 1985, Congress placed these recommendations into U.S. law.[25]

The Pelosi Amendment

Following the legislation mentioned in the previous section, the Sierra Club spearheaded a campaign with the objective of making it impossible for U.S. EDs to support funding of any proposed MDB project that could have a major impact on the environment unless an EIA was made available at least 120 days in advance of board consideration. The Sierra Club focused its lobbying on the House Banking Subcommittee on International Development Institutions and Finance, as well as on strategic members of the Congress. Among those targeted, the most important legislators to win were Representative David Obey (chair of the Appropriations Subcommittee of Foreign Relations, which controls House bills for funding MDBs) and Senator Robert Kasten (who held the same position in the Senate).

According to Larry Williams of the Sierra Club, the original idea for an EIA law came from a very conservative member of the Senate who complained to the Sierra Club that if his business constituencies had to put up with the U.S. EIA process, it should become obligatory for all World Bank projects. Larry Williams picked up this idea and took it to one of his close associates in Congress, Representative Nancy Pelosi. He suggested that she and the Sierra Club should draft a bill that would require the MDBs to adopt an EIA process in exchange for the U.S. vote.[26] The bill was written by Larry Williams and the Sierra Club, signed by Nancy Pelosi, and handed over to Congress.

The Treasury, which until then had been very supportive of the environmental concerns of the NGOs, strongly opposed legislation proposing an EIA 120 days in advance of any project. The argument of the Treasury was that the MDBs would not respond to such a law. The United States could be excluded from supporting a majority of future requests and thereby lose a considerable part of its power to influence policy and loan decisions in the MDBs. The counterargument from the Sierra Club was that none of the MDBs could afford to have the United States excluded from participation in loan decisions; the MDBs would move quickly to implement the EIA requirements rather than risk the loss of U.S. funding. In other words, U.S. NGOs seemed to be more confident of American power than was the U.S. government itself.

The Treasury objections did not stop the Sierra Club's campaign. In legislation passed in 1988, the secretary of the Treasury was directed to promote environmental reform of the MDBs by requiring the various American EDs to take recommended positions and report back to Congress on MDB compliance, and USAID was required to monitor projects likely to have an adverse environmental impact.[27] In 1989, the Sierra Club finally won when Congress passed legislation directing the secretary of the Treasury to instruct their EDs not to vote in favor of any proposed MDB action that would have a significant effect on the environment unless an EIA was completed by the borrowing country or the lending institution. The EIA had to be made available to the board members at least 120 days in advance of board consideration, and the MDB had to make the EIA or a comprehensive summary available to affected local groups and local NGOs also at least 120 days in advance of board consideration.[28]

With hindsight, it is obvious that the Sierra Club's position was the correct one. The Pelosi amendment did not exclude the United States from the policy debates in the MDBs. Rather, this case is one of the best examples of U.S. hegemonic leadership on environment policy in the MDBs. Within one year, a U.S. law was turned into standard operating procedure not only in the World Bank, but also in the AfDB and the ADB.[29] The Pelosi amendment thus demonstrates how domestic law can be turned into international "law" (practice) not by governmental leadership, as the state-centric literature on the role of hegemons in the international system suggests,[30] but by a nongovernmental organization. The EIA practice is arguably one of the best examples one can find of American leadership on environment policy in the international system. In heart and soul, however, the policy of the United States in this case was directed not by the U.S. administration, but by an external nongovernmental agent—the Sierra Club. Any genuine understanding of hegemonic power therefore has to go well beyond state capability in a narrow sense and consider the relationship between state power and domestic agents with the ability to influence international agendas and outcomes.

The Pelosi amendment and the subsequent making of U.S. law into international standard operating procedure are very important milestones in the history of environmental regulation in the multilateral system. But the enactment of this legislation did not constitute the end of NGO pressure on MDBs by way of the NGOs' relationship with and influence over state power.

International Environmental NGOs and the United States: The Case of the World Bank

The internationalization of the Pelosi amendment was a big victory for the U.S. NGO community. However, this event did not necessarily improve the relationship between the NGOs and the MDBs. In fact, many U.S.-based NGOs stayed convinced that the MDBs are basically unreliable, which resulted in the inclination to distrust any MDB activity until it had been thoroughly investigated and checked by outsiders. Subsequently, the strategy of the NGOs was to increase the pressure on the MDBs to implement new policies and guidelines, to install independent monitoring bodies, and to become more transparent and open with information. They received very critically any concessions made by the MDBs and requested more guarantees and procedures, which yet again were followed by other MDB responses, generating a dynamic of its own: MDB documents giving increased attention to the environment, and NGOs pressing for more and better environmental concern.[31] The problem with this dynamic was that both parties, in particular the U.S.-based NGOs, seemed to lose track of the broader developmental context in which the MDBs were supposed to operate. The question is, Why did this happen? If we return to the relationship between the NGOs and the United States, some underlying causes become evident.

Turning the Financial Instrument Against the MDBs: The Case of the World Bank

Over the years, U.S.-based NGOs have repeatedly turned the financial instrument against the World Bank by requesting that Congress make funding for the World Bank's International Development Association (IDA) available only on very strict conditions.[32] In 1992 and 1993, they carried out a large campaign against the tenth IDA replenishment. And, in 1992, they also objected strongly to the so-called Earth Increment (additional World Bank funding for environmental purposes). They labeled the increment as a vague and useless concept, and the EDF even argued that "Sources close to the Bank revealed that the Earth Increment was a fund-raising ploy to ensure full IDA replenishment, rather than a genuine attempt to increase environmental lending."[33] In part owing to the NGO campaign, but also in part owing to a generally more adverse attitude toward allocating financial resources, the major donors refused to honor the bank's request for ad hoc environmental funds.

In 1993, the regular U.S. contribution for IDA-10 was the prime target of American NGO action.[34] Speaking before a hearing of the House Subcommittee on Appropriations, Bruce Rich of the EDF argued,[35] "We strongly urge the Subcommittee to withhold all funding from the Bank until it has fully demonstrated in its operations, not in its rhetoric or policy proclamations, that project quality and environmental and social sustainability are the top priorities, and until it has totally reformed its restrictive policies concerning access to information by those affected by its projects as well as the public in general."[36] The U.S.-based NGOs tried to build alliances with NGOs in other countries as well. In January 1993, 140 organizations from twenty countries, including borrowing countries, issued a statement to this end. However, in spite of shared criticism of the World Bank, many African and European NGOs, developmental but also environmental, expressed strong concern about putting budgetary pressure on the bank that might affect the broader agenda of development assistance. The African NGOs' negative reaction to pleas to withhold all IDA funds led the American NGOs to moderate their position, attaching instead a number of conditions to the appropriation.[37] Subsequently, in October 1993, the U.S. Congress decided to approve IDA funds for two years instead of the regular three and reduced the 1994 pledge by $200 million. This self-imposed limit was linked to the request for increased public access to information and the creation of an appeals commission.[38]

To some extent, the criticism from the European and in particular the African NGOs taught some of the American NGOs a lesson. They were more cautious when the issue of the Global Environment Facility (GEF) emerged. When the House of Representatives discussed budget cuts in May 1994, NGOs such as Conservation International, FoE, and NRDC refused to support the Republican proposal for cuts in funding. The EDF, although not supporting the proposal, permitted the Republicans to use its objections against the GEF.[39] Nevertheless, this response showed a change of heart compared to the approach they took before the restructuring of the GEF, when the most radical NGOs lobbied the U.S. government to withhold all funds unless reforms were undertaken. However, the lessons from the criticism they received from the African NGOs seems to have been short-lived because, apart from trying to diminish funds to IDA and GEF, a growing number of NGOs soon started to advocate for the closure of the World Bank.[40] As the fiftieth anniversary of the Bretton Woods institutions came closer, more American NGOs began to support this idea in public. They created a specific campaign for the event under the banner "50 Years Is Enough," which was meant to imply not that reform was required, but that fundamental structural changes in these institutions were necessary.[41] The campaign put forward ideas such as removing IDA from World Bank management and delinking GEF from the World Bank. Some NGOs from other countries joined the campaign, but European NGOs in particular did not support these proposals, which they viewed as too extreme.[42]

At the annual meeting of the World Bank and the International Monetary Fund (IMF) in October 1994 in Madrid, the division between the "radical" and more moderate NGOs became obvious. The group that stressed the "50 years is enough" theme attracted almost all public attention, leaving little room for other positions and points of view. For instance, the Madrid Declaration of the NGO Alternative Forum called unconditionally for the closure of the Bretton Woods institutions: "It is now time to put an end to the existence of these institutions. The only thing that now needs to be discussed is the schedule and social control in dismantling the Bretton Woods institutions. This process must be initiated with the immediate reduction in their funding. It is urgent to refuse every demand to enlarge IDA-11. These programs, currently administered by the World Bank group, must be put under the immediate control of other institutions, to facilitate a rapid reorientation of their management."[43]

As the pressure on the World Bank continued from both U.S. NGOs and donor countries, the bank adopted a more offensive strategy. With respect to the NGOs, the bank singled out its most radical opponents, arguing that the American NGOs cared more about the environment than about people. Some of the EDs supported this view. For instance, the Dutch ED remarked that the NGO lobbying had resulted in the requirement of EIAs, but not of assessment on a project's impact on poor people.[44] The reply from the American NGOs was that these kinds of statements were the outcome of a deliberate World Bank effort to discredit them and were related to their campaigns against World Bank funding. To some extent, it is clear that the radical protest during the Madrid meeting strengthened the World Bank position vis-à-vis the NGOs because criticisms such as the one represented by the Alternative Forum Declaration could easily be refuted. The one-dimensional form of the analysis and the proposal undermined the plausibility of the declaration. Moreover, the allegations also angered more moderate NGOs, which feared that they would lose the influence they had acquired over the years through consultation and involvement in World Bank projects.[45]

NGOs and the United States: Who's Serving Whom?

Although U.S. NGOs in principle opposed conditionalities on aid, their campaigns clearly contributed to increased conditionality on the basis of protecting the environment. This conditionality entailed a further centralization of power in the relationship between the World Bank and borrowing countries, between governments and local organizations in the South, and within the World Bank itself.

The U.S. NGOs' exclusive focus on the MDBs and on the World Bank in particular is also evident in the installation of the so-called independent inspection panel. The opportunity to file complaints against individual projects in order to increase World Bank accountability is perhaps a desirable aim in itself, but it is highly questionable whether this approach achieves very much. If such a complaint is filed, the borrower can ignore it by simply refraining from requesting the loan and seek other funding for the project if he feels that protests become too intense.[46] The point is that many of the world's middle- and low-income countries (apart from the least-developed countries) can rely increasingly on world capital markets, and therefore they can choose more flexible lending instruments than the ones offered by the MDBs. In short, they can choose not to meet MDB requirements and environmental conditionalities. For the NGO community, in particular the U.S. NGOs, this tendency is both disturbing and contradictory. Their campaign for better environmental procedures in the MDBs might end up being ineffectual because private investors and financiers will most certainly not apply the strict environmental conditionalities that the MDBs use today.

Another development concern related to the activity of the U.S. NGOs is the reluctance of donors to replenish the various MDB development funds. In particular, the budget cuts by the United States, which to some extent were legitimized by these NGOs, have posed major challenges to the MDBs. In 1995, the World Bank even started an advertising campaign in major U.S. newspapers trying to convince American taxpayers about the value of its work and the benefits to the U.S. economy in terms of jobs and contracts.[47] Within this context, it is important to keep in mind that U.S. reservations about foreign aid were strengthened by the congressional Republican majority from 1995 onward. However, other donor countries also worried about the quality and effectiveness of the MDB project portfolio. Reconsideration of contributions to MDBs falls in line with a general tendency in Western countries to weigh the costs and benefits of foreign aid. Therefore, it was not very likely that the amount of money saved on reduced IDA contributions would be used for bilateral or other forms of aid. Thus, the NGO campaign punished the World Bank, and potential negative effects of IDA projects may have been diminished, but the overall effect of the campaign was a reduction in official development assistance (ODA). The provocative question that begs to be asked is, Did this process really serve the purpose of protecting the environment in less-developed countries, and, if not, whose interests did these cuts really serve?

Of course, one could argue that reduced economic activity in less-developed countries is good for the environment, but most people will discard such a notion for ethical reasons. The question is, then, Whom did these cuts serve? The people in the less-developed countries? Or did they serve the NGOs or the Republicans in the U.S. Congress, who suddenly achieved a new source of legitimacy for their anti-aid campaign? It is possible to argue that reduced ODA would save them from indebtedness in the future and from many ill-conceived development projects, but this view would be equivalent to arguing that all ODA is bad. Few people, even in the U.S. NGOs, would make such arguments.

The NGO campaign against the World Bank has been dominated by the *American* NGOs, not only because it is based in Washington, D.C., but also because these NGOs have access to U.S. decision makers and the United States occupies a crucial position as the major donor. U.S. NGOs tried to forge alliances with European and southern NGOs, but the U.S. NGOs were the ones that drove the debate forward and made the crucial decisions on strategy and tactics. Non-American NGOs often expressed different viewpoints, which made it difficult to keep the alliance together—the case of IDA replenishment being one obvious case. The point to be made here is that the MDB campaign in general and the IDA-replenishment campaign in particular illustrate the tendency of U.S. NGOs to focus only on the feasibility of their request.[48] The Republican anti-aid attitude and hostility toward the MDBs could effectively be translated into budget reductions for the MDBs under the pretext of environmental protection, open access to information, or the creation of an independent inspection panel. What the U.S. NGOs failed to see was that apart from some short-term common interests, their objectives differed enormously from the Republican majority's in Congress. It is therefore quite possible to make the argument that in fact it was the Republicans who used the NGOs and not vice versa. It was Republican interests that were served by the cuts in ODA, and for the first time Republicans were able to give their anti-aid campaign environmental legitimacy.

Conclusion

There is little doubt that the NGO community is a force that has to be taken into consideration with respect to international environmental policy. As stated earlier, they cannot dictate terms to anyone, nor can they tax, legislate, adjudicate, or establish foreign assistance policy. But through their membership constituencies, their knowledge of the field, and their financial resources, they do have the ability to gain access to formal decision makers. However, as we have seen here, access to formal decision makers and decision-making processes constitutes somewhat of a double-edged sword, and it is easy to become blinded by the light of power. If we look at whether the NGO community can facilitate a U.S. foreign policy on the environment that would place the United States in a lead role instead of the role of a swing state or a veto/blocking state, the double-edged nature of access becomes evident.

The campaign and the subsequent internationalization of the Pelosi amendment represent the guided use of the double-edged sword of access. In this process, the activity of the U.S. NGOs led the United States into a lead role on environmental issues in the MDBs. But the subsequent NGO campaigns against IDA and the World Bank meant that the United States actually became a veto/blocking state. The NGOs were not able to separate short-term from long-term interests, and this inability led them into an "unholy alliance" with the anti-aid campaign of the Republican majority in the U.S. Congress. Through this alliance, the U.S. NGOs gave credibility and legitimacy both to reduced levels of ODA and to increased conditionalities on the ODA that was left, which was hardly their long-term strategy.

The NGO community discussed here did not see that its access to the decision-making process constituted a double-edged sword. The actual reason why some NGOs lost track of their own agenda is difficult to identify, but one clue can be found in the main characteristic of the NGO two-level bargaining process. They must first use their bargaining leverage to gain access to the decision-making process. It is only then that they can engage in discussions on environmental reform. In these particular cases, the easiest route to access and influence was through the legislative process at the national level, into which NGOs were dragged. The final point to be made is therefore that NGOs can, as illustrated by the Pelosi amendment, push an important world policy player such as the United States into the driver's seat on environmental issues. The Pelosi amendment is one of the best examples of U.S. hegemonic leadership on environmental issues in the MDBs. However, as the second story told here illustrates, it is easy for the NGO community—as for any other group of actors— to become blinded by the light of power, and when this happens, they can propel an important player, in this case the United States, into the less-constructive role of the veto/blocking state.

Notes

1 Most approaches to environmental policies that emphasize the role of NGOs are either of the institutionalist or social-constructivist brand. What separates them is that whereas institutionalist approaches hint at the socially constructed nature of sovereignty, the social constructivists go further in understanding sovereignty as a mutable set of practices. See, for instance, R. Keohane, P. Haas, and M. Levy, eds., *Institutions for the Earth: Sources of Effective International Environmental Protection* (Cambridge, Mass.: MIT Press, 1993); R. D. Lipschutz, "Reconstructing World Politics: The Emergence of Global Civil Society," *Millennium* 21 (1992): 389–420; R. D. Lipschutz and J. Mayer, *Global Civil Society and Global Environmental Governance: The Politics of Nature from Place to Planet* (Albany: State University of New York Press, 1996); K. T. Litfin, *Ozone Discourses: Science and Politics in Global Environmental Cooperation* (New York: Columbia University Press); K. T. Litfin, "Sovereignty in World Ecopolitics," *Mershon International Studies Review* 41 (1997): 167–204; M. J. Peterson, "Transnational Activity, International Society, and World Politics," *Millennium* 21 (1992): 371–88; M. Shaw, "Global Society and Global Responsibility: The Theoretical, Historical, and Political Limits of International Society," *Millennium* 21 (1992): 421–34; and P. Wapner,

Environmental Activism and World Civic Politics (Albany: State University of New York Press, 1996).

2 The World Bank, the Asian Development Bank, the African Development Bank, and the Inter-American Development Bank.

3 See J. Tendler, *Turning Private Voluntary Organizations into Development Agencies,* USAID Programme Evaluation Discussion Paper, no. 12 (Washington, D.C.: USAID, 1982); and C. A. Meyer, "Opportunism and NGOs: Entrepreneurship and Green North-South Transfers," *World Development* 23 (1995): 1277–89.

4 USAID, *Development and the National Interest: U.S. Economic Assistance into the 21st Century* (Washington, D.C.: USAID, 1989).

5 In 1981–82, Organization for Economic Cooperation and Development (OECD) countries channeled $1.9 billion of their official development assistance through NGOs. Ten years later, in 1992, this figure had grown to $2.5 billion; see Meyer, "Opportunism and NGOs." Concerning the growth of the number of NGOs, one illustrative indicator is membership in international NGO-coordinating bodies: in 1993, the World Conservation Union listed its NGO membership at 450; the African NGOs Environment Network had 21 NGOs in 1982, but by 1990 the number of members had grown to 530, located in forty-five countries; and the Indonesian Environmental Forum, established in 1980 by 79 NGOs, increased the number of its members to more than 500 in 1992. See Mostafa Tolba, Osama El-Kholy, E. El-Hinnawi, M. V. Holdgate, D. F. McMicahel, and R. E. Munn, eds., *The World Environment 1972–1992: Two Decades of Challenge* (London: Chapman Hall, 1992), 681, 723.

6 J. Fisher, *The Road from Rio: Sustainable Development and the Nongovernmental Movement in the Third World* (Westport, Conn.: Praeger, 1993).

7 World Wildlife Fund–United States, *Annual Report* (Washington, D.C.: WWF-U.S., 1991), 3.

8 Friends of the Earth, *Newsletter of the Friends of the Earth* (Washington, D.C.: FoE, 1993), 14.

9 T. Princen and M. Finger, *Environmental NGOs in World Politics: Linking the Local and the Global* (London: Routledge, 1994).

10 Nongovernmental organizations participated directly in the preparatory and formal negotiations, but they also exerted their influence by targeting key industries. For instance, in 1988, Friends of the Earth announced a boycott of British chlorofluorocarbon-based aerosol products. Three days before the boycott was to begin, the British industry announced a phaseout in advance of the protocol's schedule. See B. J. Bramble and G. Porter, "Nongovernmental Organization and the Making of U.S. Environmental Policy," in *The International Politics of the Environment,* ed. A. Hurrell and B. Kingsbury (Oxford: Oxford University Press, 1992), 313–53.

11 P. Aufderheide and B. Rich, "Environmental Reforms and the Multilateral Banks," *World Policy Journal* 5 (1988): 301–21.

12 See H. Harboe, *Economic Development and Environmental Concern: Modeling of Environmental Consequences in Development Projects* (Oslo: NUPI, 1989).

13 Asian Development Bank, *The Environment Program and the Asian Development Bank: Past, Present, and Future* (Manila: ADB, 1994).

14 African Development Bank, *Annual Report 1993* (Abidjan, Ivory Coast: AfDB, 1994).

15 G. Porter and J. W. Brown, *Global Environmental Politics* (Boulder, Colo.: Westview, 1996).

16 For instance, in 1987, in anticipation of a World Bank vote on an Amazon development project, environmentalists in the United States, Europe, and Australia researched and wrote letters of concern jointly to their respective governments. Within one week of their coordinated and simultaneous lobbying, the World Bank cancelled the project. See Princen and Finger, eds. *Environmental NGOs.*

17 On the potential of transnational alliances, see A. Moravcsik, "Introduction: Integrating International and Domestic Theories of International Bargaining," in *Double-Edged Diplomacy: International Bargaining and Domestic Politics,* ed. P. B. Evans, H. K. Jacobson, and R. D. Putnam (Berkeley: University of California Press, 1993), 3–42; and T. Risse-Kappen, "Introduction: Bringing Transnational Relations Back In," in *Bringing Transnational Relations Back In: Non-state Actors, Domestic Structures, and International Institutions,* ed. T. Risse Kappen (Cambridge: Cambridge University Press, 1995), 3–33.

18 For example, transnational alliances between nongovernmental organizations played an important role in the establishment of the Pollution Control Regime for the Mediterranean, the Antarctic Treaty System, and the Convention on International Trade in Endangered Species. See Polar Research Board, *The Antarctic Treaty System: An Assessment* (Washington, D.C.: National Academy Press, 1986); P. Haas, "Do Regimes Matter? Epistemic Communities and Mediterranean Pollution Control," *International Organization* 43 (1989): 377–403; and L. H. Kosloff and M. C. Trexler, "The Convention on International Trade in Endangered Species: No Carrot, But Where's the Stick?" *Environmental Law Reporter* 17 (1987): 10222–236.

19 R. Mikesell and L. Williams, *International Banks and the Environment* (San Francisco: Sierra Club, 1992).

20 See *Financial Times,* 9 June 1994 and 22 October 1994; Reuters Press Release (Kathmandu, 4 August 1995); and Friends of the Earth–Japan, *NGO Guide to Japan's ODA* (Tokyo: Yen Aid Watch, 1997).

21 Aufderheide and Rich, "Environmental Reforms."

22 U.S. Public Law 99–500. 99th Cong., 2d sess., 18 October 1986.

23 Electronic communication with Larry Williams, director of the Sierra Club's International Program, 5 December 1995.

24 See B. Rich, "The Multilateral Development Banks, Environmental Policy, and the United States," *Ecology Law Quarterly* 12 (1985): 681–745.

25 U.S. Public Law 99–190. 99th Cong., 1st sess., 19 December 1985. See Mikesell and Williams, *International Banks*.

26 Williams, electronic communication.

27 U.S. Public Law 100–461. 100th Cong., 2d sess., 1 October 1988.

28 U.S. Public Law 101–240. 101st Cong., 1st sess., 19 December 1989.

29 In fact, all the multilateral development banks made the U.S. law on environmental impact assessments their internal practice.

30 See, for instance, R. Keohane, *After Hegemony: Cooperation and Discord in the World Political Economy* (Princeton, N.J.: Princeton University Press, 1984); R. Keohane, *International Institutions and State Power: Essays in International Relations Theory* (Boulder, Colo.: Westview, 1989); and J. Grieco, *Cooperation among Nations: Europe, America, and Non-tariff Barriers to Trade* (Ithaca: Cornell University Press, 1990).

31 A. Kolk, *Forests in International Environmental Politics: International Organizations, NGOs, and the Brazilian Amazon* (Utrecht: International, 1996).

32 IDA is the concessional arm of the World Bank.

33 Udall quoted in Kolk, *Forests*, 273.

34 The size of the U.S. contribution was supposed to be approximately $3.7 billion. See Kolk, *Forests*, 273.

35 Bruce Rich is with the Environmental Defense Fund, but here he appeared as the spokesman for both the Environmental Defense Fund and the Sierra Club.

36 B. Rich, *Statement Concerning FY 1994 Appropriations* (Washington, D.C.: House Subcommittee on Appropriation, 1993), 10.

37 L. Udall, "Grounds for Divorce: Why IDA Should Delink from the World Bank," in *Beyond Bretton Woods: Alternatives to the Global Economic Order*, ed. J. Cavanagh, D. Wysham, and M. Arruda (London: Pluto, 1994), 155–65.

38 This decision was proposed by Democratic Representative Frank and supported by the chairmen of the appropriations subcommittees, Representative Obey (Democrat) and Senator Leahy (Republican). See Environmental Defense Fund, *Release on WB IDA Funding*, Econet conference, available at <http://www.rainfor.worldbank>, 1 October 1993. In 1994, just before the official celebration of the fiftieth anniversary of the Bretton Woods institutions, the U.S. Congress announced comparable sanctions. Unless drastic reforms were implemented, the 1995 contribution would be cut by 50 percent. See P. Urgewald, *German Parliament Votes for World Bank Reform*, Econet conference, available at <http://www.dev.worldbank>, 7 September 1994.

39 The outcome of the debate was a limited budget cut. See P. Chatterjee and M. Finger, *The Earth Brokers: Power, Politics, and World Development* (London: Routledge, 1994).

40 The first proponent of this "radical" solution was Patricia Adams of the Canadian NGO Probe International. See P. Adams, *Odious Debts: Loose*

Lending, Corruption, and the Third World's Environmental Legacy (London: Earthscan, 1991).

41 The lead NGOs in this campaign were Environmental Defense Fund, Development GAP, Friends of the Earth–United States, and Greenpeace–United States). See Kolk, *Forests*, 275.

42 Kolk, *Forests*.

43 50 Years Is Enough, *Madrid Declaration of the Alternative Forum*, 1994, 1.

44 Kolk, *Forests*.

45 During the 1980s and 1990s, not only the number of NGOs and the span of their actions and activities expanded, but also the number of them involved in World Bank projects. See World Bank, *The World Bank's Partnership with Nongovernmental Organizations* (Washington, D.C.: World Bank, 1996).

46 This happened in the Sardar Sarovar case. See Ingunn Kroksnes, *Non-governmental Organizations and Development Policies: Identifying and Explaining Strategies—The Case of the World Bank's Narmada Dam Project*, Development and Multilateral Institutions Programme Report, no. 1 (Lysaker, Norway: Fridtjof Nansen Institute, 1997); and Friends of the Earth–Japan, *NGO Guide*.

47 This campaign cost the World Bank between $100,000 and $200,000— money that could have been spent on projects in developing countries. See R. Umoren, *NGOs Split on IDA*, Econet conference, available at <http://www.econ.saps>, 5 June 1995.

48 Kolk, *Forests*.

9 Environmental Sanctions in U.S. Foreign Policy

Elizabeth R. DeSombre

The United States has threatened sanctions for environmental goals more often than any other country, with varying but generally high degrees of success in accomplishing its stated goals. These restrictions take certain predictable forms. They almost always involve import restrictions on products that were made or obtained in a way prohibited for U.S. actors by U.S. environmental laws.

What appears to be a simple and effective foreign policy tool, however, represents in origin and implementation a number of domestic battles, and the sanctions that result take a form that, although predictable, no individual proponent would have designed. This chapter examines the domestic conflicts at three stages of U.S. environmental sanctions: their origin, application, and effects. Each of these stages represents a conflict between a set of actors, the outcome of which influences the shape of the sanctions.

Almost all of the U.S. economic sanctions for environmental protection are created by congressional legislation. At this initial stage, conflict takes place between environmentalists and industry actors, who have different goals for foreign environmental policy. Environmentalists usually hope to punish the bad environmental behavior of others, and industry actors hope for protection from foreign industries that do not have to meet the same costly environmental standards they do. The resulting form that policy takes is import restrictions that deny access to U.S. markets to those states that act in a way the United States deems environmentally unfriendly and that thereby protect domestic industries from products that are made in ways that do not require the same regulations to which U.S. industry is subject.

Although these sanctions are passed by Congress, executive branch agencies typically drag their feet when implementing them—interpreting their mandate as narrowly as possible or, when discretion is allowed, refusing to implement restrictions at all. At the same time, domestic environmental groups generally work to expand the sanctions. Several of these battles have been fought through the courts. Congress will therefore sometimes modify its original legislation to limit the degree of discretion agencies have in imposing these restrictions.

Once these sanctions have been threatened or imposed, the struggle is with the target states that resist taking the action demanded of them. States that resist giving in to U.S. demands have brought the U.S. actions before international trade dispute–settlement mechanisms. In the end, some of the domestic characteristics that influenced the shape of the sanctions affect the likelihood that the sanctions will achieve their stated goals.

The United States has used threats of unilateral trade restrictions for environmental issues with increasing frequency in the past three decades, for purposes primarily related to fisheries conservation and endangered species protection. U.S. legislation allows for sanctions, for example, against states that "diminish the effectiveness of an international fishery conservation program,"[1] do not have "effective elephant protection programs,"[2] undermine the international protection of endangered species,[3] do not protect whales in the manner the United States prefers,[4] or engage in large-scale driftnet fishing.[5] These measures have been threatened against states such as Chile, Iceland, Japan, Norway, and the Soviet Union to convince them to change their whaling practices; China, Taiwan, Singapore, and the Philippines to persuade them to join or implement policies of the Convention on International Trade in Endangered Species; and Italy, South Korea, and Taiwan to pressure them to end their use of driftnets.[6]

The highest profile U.S. environmental sanctions are those pertaining to dolphin protection under the Marine Mammal Protection Act and sea turtle protection under Section 609 of Public Law 101-162 and indirectly under the Endangered Species Act. They follow the typical pattern seen in U.S. environmental sanctions. This chapter focuses particularly on these sanctions, analyzing in depth the origins, implementation, and effects of U.S. environmental sanctions in general.

Origins of U.S. Environmental Sanctions

Most of the environmental sanctions the United States threatens have their origin in domestic regulations to which U.S. actors are bound.[7] Others relate to international agreements that the United States either wants to deepen or to provisions out of which some states have opted (functionally a similar phenomenon). The sanctions process begins with pressure from U.S. actors in the domestic arena. Industry actors that are bound by U.S. regulations work to ensure that they do not suffer competitively relative to foreign counterparts not bound by the same environmental regulations. Environmental organizations push for regulations to be applied to all actors in an issue area whose behavior can impact the resource in question, regardless of where they are located geographically. The intersection of the interests of these two diverse groups arises in the imposition of threats of economic harm against foreign actors that do not uphold the same environmental regulations U.S. actors are required to uphold.[8] Although the regulated industry would prefer to remove its own regulation, and concerned environmentalists most fervently want to convince foreign actors to adopt strict environmental standards, they both can agree on threatening with economic sanctions any states who fail to adopt environmental standards comparable to those the United States has. The form of the threatened sanctions relates to the interests of the concerned domestic actors as well: if states do not take the action the U.S. requests, goods that compete with U.S. products that have to uphold the standards in question are not allowed to enter the United States.

The first major piece of environmental sanctioning legislation the United States passed, the Pelly amendment to the Fisherman's Protective Act, clearly followed this form. The United States was party to the International Convention for the Northwest Atlantic Salmon Fisheries. Once the United States issued catch quotas for salmon, U.S. fishers had to uphold these quotas and catch fewer salmon than they might otherwise have done. Several other major salmon-fishing states in the region—West Germany, Denmark, and Norway—used the objections provision in the convention to opt out of the salmon quotas and were therefore not bound by them.[9] U.S. salmon fishers joined forces with environmentalists concerned about fisheries conservation and lobbied Congress; the resulting legislation authorized restrictions on fish imports from states that did not uphold international fishing agreements.[10] Almost identical processes were followed with respect to ensuring international participation in agreements to conserve Pacific and Atlantic tuna and relating to a wide variety of other environmental obligations U.S. actors are required to uphold. And, as seen in the two cases examined in depth here, the process happens in the same way when U.S. actors are bound by a completely domestic obligation by which their foreign counterparts are not bound.

Dolphins

Although dolphins have never been considered endangered (aside from subspecies found in China and Pakistan), they are protected under the U.S. Marine Mammal Protection Act (MMPA). The main threat to dolphins has been the tuna-fishing industry. For reasons that are still unclear, dolphins in the eastern tropical Pacific Ocean school with yellowfin tuna. Because dolphins are mammals and have to surface to breathe, tuna fishers can find the dolphins more easily than the tuna. By encircling dolphins with purse-seine nets, they can catch the tuna that school below. In the process, dolphins are caught in the nets, pulled below the surface of the water, and drown.

Under the MMPA, in 1974 the National Marine Fisheries Service (NMFS) began limiting acceptable dolphin mortality. At this point in time, most yellowfin tuna caught by U.S. fishers were caught with purse-seine nets, and annual dolphin mortality in the eastern tropical Pacific Ocean exceeded three hundred thousand.[11] Tuna fishers were outraged at the new restrictions and argued that the industry "could not survive economically" under MMPA restrictions.[12] The U.S. Pacific tuna fleet went on strike for three months in 1977 as a protest against the regulations. Stan Levitz, president of a fishing organization, noted that tuna fishers were "madder than hell."[13] Many observed that dolphin deaths by foreign tuna-fishing fleets, with which U.S. fishers competed economically, were increasing. As a story in *Forbes* explained, "The crowning irony of the tuna drama is the same one the U.S. faces in many other cases in which its environmental concerns are not shared by other countries: Foreign fishermen are not subject to U.S. law; they're operating as always."[14]

Environmental organizations thought the new regulations were insufficient. They pushed to strengthen domestic regulations and lower the number of dolphins permitted to be killed each year, and took the NMFS to court for failing to protect dolphins to the extent required under the MMPA. They, too, were concerned with foreign fishers killing dolphins, a process that was likely to become only worse as foreign tuna fleets increased their tuna catches or as U.S. tuna fishers reflagged their vessels in other states to avoid domestic regulations.

From early in the MMPA process, Congress responded to these concerns by including a sanctions process in the legislation. In the first set of MMPA regulations the NMFS created, it became illegal to import any fish into the United States if "such fish were caught in a manner prohibited by these regulations or in a manner that would not be allowed" by a person under the jurisdiction of the United States.[15] All fish, except those determined to be uninvolved with commercial fishing operations that injure or kill marine mammals, had to meet certain requirement, or they could not be imported into the United States. In order for the fish to be certified as acceptable for import, the fishing operations of the state in question had to be "accomplished in a manner which does not result in an incidental rate [of dolphin mortality] in excess of that which results from fishing operations under these regulations."[16] The most important target of the sanctions was yellowfin tuna.

Under MMPA regulations, imports of yellowfin tuna and tuna products from states known to fish in the eastern tropical Pacific Ocean (whether the particular tuna was caught there or elsewhere) are contingent upon a favorable finding by the assistant administrator for fisheries of the NMFS. The assistant administrator checks to make sure that the fishing practices of the state "are conducted in conformance with U.S. regulations and standards" or that "such fishing is accomplished in a manner which does not result in an incidental mortality and serious injury [of marine mammals] in excess of that which results from U.S. fishing operations under these regulations."[17]

The National Marine Fisheries Service also responded to concerns of environmentalists by strengthening some of the ways the MMPA was implemented—requiring, for example, that coastal spotted dolphins and northeastern offshore dolphins, considered to be more threatened than other species, receive special protection within the existing regulations. These regulations, in turn, were applied to foreign fishers, and those who did not meet them would have their tuna embargoed, even if their overall dolphin mortality rate was comparable to that of U.S. tuna fishers.

Sea Turtles

The U.S. Endangered Species Act lists all species of sea turtles as either endangered or threatened.[18] An important threat to sea turtles happens during the course of shrimp fishing when the turtles become entangled in shrimp nets and die. For that reason, Congress in October 1987 passed regulations that required U.S. shrimp trawlers in waters off the southeastern United States to use "turtle excluder devices" (TEDs) on their shrimp trawl nets.[19]

These devices act like trap doors to allow sea turtles to escape. Shrimp fishers argued that TEDs, in addition to costing up to $600 each, caused them to lose up to half of their shrimp catch because shrimp could escape through the trap door as well.[20] U.S. shrimpers staged protests against this regulation, blocking shipping lanes, threatening violence against those who tried to enforce the requirement, and picketing President George Bush when he came to speak in the Gulf Coast region.[21] In response to domestic protests, the secretary of commerce temporarily suspended the implementation of the regulation in July 1989 and allowed alternate methods of protecting sea turtles during shrimp fishing. An environmental NGO, the National Wildlife Federation, challenged this suspension in federal court, which ordered the Department of Commerce to reinstate the TED requirement.[22]

Shrimpers lobbied Congress to change the law. They argued that turtle-protection requirements cut into their profits, particularly in comparison with foreign shrimp fishers who did not have to use TEDs. At the time the regulations were initially passed, 73 percent of shrimp consumed in the United States was caught by shrimpers from other countries.[23] The president of the Texas Shrimp Association testified before Congress that foreign shrimpers were "affecting the price the American producer receives" because these shrimpers did not have to buy and use turtle excluder devices.[24] Congressional representatives from shrimping states argued that "it would be an outrage if this country imported shrimp from countries like Mexico who do not utilize these turtle-excluder devices while our shrimpers are being penalized." Others argued that "if we must use TEDs then everybody else ought to have to use TEDs as well. . . . [I]f they are not required to do that which we are required, then we should not be required to import their shrimp."[25]

Environmentalists were concerned as well about the lack of international protection for sea turtles. The Earth Island Institute initiated a publicity campaign that claimed that "Mexico's shrimp fleet is killing an estimated 11,000 sea turtles on the Endangered Species Act."[26] The chair of the wildlife program of the Environmental Defense Fund explained to Congress that "we are very sensitive to the concerns of the shrimpers with respect to foreign competition" and argued in favor of holding all shrimping states to the same standards required of U.S. shrimpers.[27]

In response to the uproar about domestic turtle-protection regulations, Congress passed Section 609 of Public Law 101-162, which took effect November 1991. This regulation required that import restrictions be applied to states that did not have turtle-protection regulations in place that could be considered equivalent to those required of U.S. shrimpers. The president (in practice, the Commerce Department) issues an annual list indicating which states have provided evidence that they undertake sea turtle–protection measures during shrimp fishing that are comparable to those required by the United States. Shrimp can be imported from countries that have been certified on this list; from all others, shrimp may not be imported.

Imposition of U.S. Environmental Sanctions

Although Congress passes sanctioning legislation, offices within the executive branch are generally charged with implementing the regulations. The agencies that have responsibility for creating the specific policies define the parameters of the regulations. They also decide which states may be potential targets of sanctions. In cases where sanctions must be imposed once it has been determined that a state is not living up to the requirements of U.S. policy, it is these agencies that collect information and determine which states meet the conditions to avoid sanctions and which do not. So the actors that make the ultimate decisions resulting in sanctions are not those who designed the original policy, and disagreements over interpretation or over intent can lead the policy to be applied in a way different than some of its original supporters prefer.

Frequently this disagreement over implementation results in legal action when claims are taken to court by those who want the sanctions process to be implemented or to be interpreted more liberally than those in charge of making this determination think it should be. For example, in the whaling sanctions process, states "diminishing the effectiveness" of the International Whaling Commission are to be certified as such, after which point the president may decide to impose sanctions on fish imports from these states. An environmental NGO, the American Cetacean Society, brought suit against the Department of Commerce for not certifying that Japan was diminishing the effectiveness of the International Whaling Commission when it was catching whales during the time the IWC was calling for a moratorium on commercial whaling. The secretary of commerce argued that the legislation did not require certification if those in charge felt it was not advisable. The case ultimately reached the Supreme Court, which decided that certification by the Commerce Department was discretionary.[28] Other examples of court cases over whether or how to implement environmental sanctions abound. In addition, Congress may modify or enhance the

College
ter
Way
8754

process has the effect it originally intended.
implementation of environmental sanctions
goals and concerns of the participants in

e was cautious in interpreting its mandate
that did not adequately protect dolphins
ngress and from domestic environmental
to foreign states. At the same time, various
modification of the regulations. Action
ourt system impacted the way the MMPA

enting the MMPA policies with respect
egulations quite broadly at the beginning.
hanged their tuna-fishing behavior when
anctions policy, no states had their tuna
tates subject to an embargo were Senegal
ie proper information. Mexican tuna was
that point Mexico could not export tuna
so there was little practical effect of such
a policy. Initially, at least, the agencies charged with holding foreign tuna fishers
to U.S. standards were not doing so.

Congress addressed its dissatisfaction with executive branch hesitance by
strengthening the legislation through amendments and by decreasing the amount
of discretion the agencies had in implementing the regulations. Amendments to
the MMPA in 1984 required that in order to be able to export tuna to the
United States, states had to document that they had adopted dolphin-conservation
programs equivalent to those in the United States and with a comparable average
dolphin mortality rate. When the lack of clarity over what would constitute
equivalent programs prevented the United States from restricting tuna in some
cases, Congress amended the act in 1988 to set the "comparable" rate at 1.25
times that of U.S. dolphin mortality.

Congress strengthened the sanctioning process in other ways. By the 1980s,
it had become clear that some foreign states were simply able to find alternate
markets for their tuna and thereby avoid having to implement U.S.-style dolphin-
protection regulations. Under the 1988 MMPA amendments, all states that
exported yellowfin tuna to the United States had to prove that they prohibited
imports of tuna from states that did not adequately protect dolphins—in other
words, from those states from which the United States had already embargoed
tuna.[29] This requirement would prevent what became known as "tuna laundering,"
or getting around the U.S. embargo by shipping tuna to an intermediary state

that would then sell it (or some other amount of tuna) to the United States. In essence, this policy required other states to adopt the same sanctions process that the United States adopted.

Environmental organizations also expressed concern that the NMFS was not adequately implementing the sanctions policy. After unsuccessful attempts to convince the NMFS to require actual change in behavior from target states, they decided to pursue their agenda through the court system. When the original embargo on Mexican tuna was dropped in the late 1980s, the domestic environmental organization Earth Island Institute, along with others, sued the secretary of commerce, arguing that the legislation required an embargo on Mexican tuna. The U.S. district court agreed and forced the renewal of the embargo.[30] The U.S. Court of Appeals for the Ninth Circuit granted the request by the Department of Commerce that it not be required to impose the sanctions, but the stay issued by that court was overturned on appeal in 1991, and the embargo was reimposed.[31]

Earth Island Institute also led a group of environmental organizations that in 1992 sued the Department of Commerce to implement and then expand the restrictions on tuna imports from "intermediary states."[32] The United States had already declared a secondary embargo the previous year on four states (Costa Rica, France, Italy, and Japan) that were known to be exporting tuna that came from the major target states for U.S. tuna sanctions, but the court ordered that all states be held to certification requirements. This order expanded the number of states by twenty that were required to provide documentation that they did not sell tuna caught by embargoed states in order to be able to sell their tuna to the United States.

Sea Turtles

The main struggles over implementation of the sanctions to protect sea turtles came over the issue of which states would be subject to the requirements in the regulations. In addition, efforts were made to increase the monitoring and enforcement of policies so it could be ensured that states claiming to meet the U.S. standards were in fact doing so. The NMFS decided that the initial legislation applied only to a group of fourteen states that catch shrimp in the Caribbean and western Atlantic. These states fished in the major migratory region of the turtles most endangered by U.S. shrimp fishing. The NMFS also allowed for a three-year period during which sea turtle protection could be phased in by target countries. These countries had to begin by supplying information and indicating a willingness to use TEDs, then indicate that they had them on a proportion of their nets, and eventually require them to be in constant use on all shrimp-fishing vessels.

A group of environmental nongovernmental organizations, led again by the Earth Island Institute, argued that sea turtles were threatened by shrimp-fishing practices anywhere in the world and that the restrictions on shrimp exports to the United States should therefore be applied to all states. They sued the Department of Commerce in the U.S. Court of International Trade, which ruled in December 1995 that the regulations must be applied to all states that catch shrimp. That expanded to seventy the number of states that must either prove that they protect sea turtles or be subject to sanctions on their shrimp.[33] Importantly, whereas the initial fourteen states were given a three-year period during which to phase in TED use, the court required that as of 1 May 1996 all shrimp-fishing states be required to have TEDs on all their nets and a comparable incidental catch rate for turtles to that of the United States.

The NMFS also increased the scrutiny with which it examined compliance by the states that received positive certification for protection of sea turtles. Initially compliance was determined by visits from U.S. officials that would inspect nets; later, states were asked to demonstrate that they enforced their TED requirements rather than simply requiring fishers to purchase the devices.

Effects of U.S. Environmental Sanctions

Sanctions are often considered an ineffective way of conducting foreign policy. Analysts have declared that sanctions do not succeed in convincing states to change their policies,[34] and that they can even be counterproductive.[35] This pessimism does not apply to the sanctions examined here. Target states of U.S. environmental sanctions frequently change their policies and undertake the action the United States demands. The United States had early success in threatening states with import restrictions on fish if they did not join the whaling regime and later success in convincing whaling states to agree to a moratorium on commercial whaling. U.S. sanctions played a role either in bringing several states into the Convention on International Trade in Endangered Species or in persuading them to adopt policies consistent with its regulations. A number of states appear to have been persuaded by threats of U.S. sanctions to join or enforce fisheries treaties relating to salmon and tuna or to end the use of high-seas driftnets.[36] And changes in fishing practices to protect dolphins and sea turtles can be traced quite directly to U.S. sanctions against those states that did not accede to U.S. policies.

Dolphins
When faced with the threat of losing their access to the U.S. tuna market, many states nevertheless resisted changing their tuna-fishing practices. Mexico, for instance, called the sanctions "a ploy to sabotage [its] tuna industry."[37] Moreover, the yardstick kept changing. Tuna fishing by foreign countries had to result in dolphin deaths comparable to that of U.S. tuna fishing to avoid being subject to sanctions, but the U.S. domestic regulations were modified and strengthened, and the comparison made at the end of a fishing year, so it was often not clear what was required of foreign fishers. In addition, the domestic battles over implementation made it difficult at times to determine how serious the threat

of sanctions was. On the whole, though, the sanctions resulted in dramatically changed fishing practices by some states and at least initial efforts by others to protect dolphins in the course of tuna fishing. Many of these polices have resulted in overall dramatic declines in dolphin mortality.

A number of states changed their tuna-fishing behavior, some immediately. Bermuda, Canada, the Cayman Islands, Costa Rica, New Zealand, the Netherlands Antilles, and Peru met the initial U.S. dolphin-protection requirements and modified their programs sufficiently so that they were never barred from exporting tuna to the United States. Ecuador and Spain resisted initially, but eventually accepted U.S.-style regulations and have for the past four years been the only states actively exporting yellowfin tuna to the United States.[38]

Other states were at least initially less willing to accept U.S. demands that they protect dolphins. Mexico, Venezuela, Vanuatu, Colombia, and Panama were prohibited from exporting tuna to the United States for some period of time. It is worth noting, however, that all these states took steps at points to meet U.S. demands, and because of changes in their tuna-fishing practices, all had periods of time when they were allowed to export tuna to the United States. Mexico, previously subject to restrictions on its tuna for other reasons,[39] did take steps in 1986 to meet U.S. dolphin-protection requirements and was allowed to export tuna to the United States from 1987 to 1989. But domestic battles within the United States described above forced the reimplementation of the embargo on Mexican tuna. Mexico did organize industry workshops on how to catch tuna in a way that would avoid the U.S. embargo,[40] and made some efforts at negotiating an international agreement with the United States and others,[41] but ultimately was not willing to make the types of changes in its fishing industry that the United States demanded.

Venezuela made some efforts at avoiding sanctions; it passed a law requiring that Venezuelan tuna fishers live up to U.S. requirements for protecting dolphins and was allowed to export tuna to the United States for much of the 1980s.[42] But since 1991, it has been unable to show that dolphin mortality from its tuna fishing is comparable to that of U.S. fishers, and its tuna has not been allowed into the United States. Panama followed a similar path; it met U.S. conditions for avoiding sanctions through most of the 1980s, and, when briefly subject to sanctions in 1988, it gave evidence of dolphin protection. In 1992, "setting on dolphins" in the course of tuna fishing was declared illegal by presidential decree, but when an international observer saw fishers encircle dolphins, sanctions were reimposed.[43]

Colombia did not attempt to export tuna to the United States during most of the early years of U.S. dolphin-protection policies. When it first did in 1992, the United States denied certification because of inadequate observer coverage to support the claim that dolphin mortality was low.[44] In 1994, Colombia submitted evidence that its incidental dolphin mortality rate was sufficiently low to meet U.S. standards and that all of its fishing vessels had international observers. As a result, the United States removed the tuna embargo.[45] The embargo was reimposed later that year, however, when U.S. policies changed to require evidence that tuna fishers never encircled northeastern offshore dolphins. Colombia did not incorporate this provision into its legislation and lost its certification.[46] Vanuatu followed a similar pattern: its tuna was embargoed in the late 1980s and again in 1991 (under the court-ordered expansion of sanctions) when it did not submit adequate information about its dolphin-protection policies but supplied evidence shortly after each episode of sanctions and was then allowed to export tuna to the United States. Vanuatu lost its ability to sell its tuna to the United States when U.S. law changed to require a particularly low mortality rate for coastal spotted dolphins in 1994, but it participated in an international observer program that put it back in compliance. Later that year, however, the embargo was reimposed when Vanuatu refused to prohibit setting on offshore spotted dolphins, as required by U.S. legislation.[47]

Changes in the tuna-fishing industry thus can be traced to the U.S. sanctions; even those states that are still subject to the embargo—such as Mexico, Venezuela, and Vanuatu—have changed their fishing practices to conform to the bulk of U.S. requirements.[48] Many other states have met U.S. demands entirely, and the dolphin population is thriving.

Sea Turtles

The threat of a shrimp embargo against states that did not adopt U.S.-style sea turtle protection had a quick and demonstrable impact on the shrimp-fishing behavior of target states. Although some states continued to resist adopting sea turtle–protection measures that would allow them to export shrimp to the United States, most did change their policies and actions in accord with the increasingly strict regulations required by the United States.

A number of the states in the initial group of fourteen subject to the restrictions met each condition as the regulations were phased in and were allowed to export shrimp to the United States throughout this period. Belize, Brazil, Colombia, Costa Rica, Guatemala, Guyana, Mexico, Nicaragua, Panama, and Venezuela all acceded to U.S. demands that they require U.S.-level protection of turtles in their shrimp-fishing operations, despite the fact that doing so meant adopting equipment and regulations they had not previously used. Mexican shrimp fishers were among the first to adopt the new turtle excluder devices, hoping to avoid the same type of embargo that their tuna-fishing counterparts had suffered for years.[49]

To a greater or lesser extent, the other four in the initial group resisted giving in to U.S. demands throughout the duration of U.S. efforts. Suriname was the first to resist; it did not provide information in 1991 on its plan for preventing incidental take of sea turtles, so imports of shrimp from Suriname were embargoed beginning 1 May 1991.[50] Suriname was certified, and the embargo lifted, when it provided the requisite information later in the year.[51] In 1992, it took the steps required of it, but in 1993 it had not met the requirement to have TEDs on 30 percent of its trawlers and so could not export shrimp to the United States.[52] It continued to hold out on accepting U.S.-style regulations on shrimp trawl nets through 1997, and shrimp exports were thus disallowed during that period. Finally, in 1998 for almost the first time since the effort at internationalization began, Suriname was deemed to have adopted sufficient turtle-protection measures and was allowed to export shrimp to the United States.[53]

Honduras initially indicated a willingness to adopt sea turtle protection and was allowed to export shrimp to the United States in 1991 and 1992, but it failed to demonstrate at the beginning of 1993 that it had installed TEDs on 30 percent of its shrimp trawl nets; its shrimp was therefore embargoed.[54] It provided the requisite evidence once sanctions were already in effect, and the embargo was removed.[55] In 1996, Honduran shrimp was again embargoed upon evidence that it was not enforcing its regulations; once it was able to convince State Department representatives that enforcement was again taking place, the embargo was dropped.[56]

Trinidad and Tobago initially agreed to adopt U.S.-style regulation of shrimp fishing. In the first year it was required to have TEDs on a proportion of its shrimp trawl nets, it did not meet the requirement initially, resulting in thirteen days of a shrimp embargo until it provided evidence that it had done so. The following year, when the United States required that TEDs be used on all shrimp trawl nets, Trinidad and Tobago failed to meet this level of regulation and was not allowed to export shrimp to the United States. This prohibition continued until 15 August 1995, when the country provided sufficient information that it had a sea turtle–protection program comparable to that in the United States.[57] Since that time, it has been able to demonstrate a level of regulation acceptable to the United States and has been allowed to export its shrimp to the United States.

French Guyana resisted internationalization efforts the most thoroughly of the initial fourteen target states. In 1991, it provided the required information about its shrimping activities and indicated a willingness to use TEDs, so it was allowed to export shrimp to the United States. It did not meet any of the subsequent requirements, however. Shrimp exports from French Guyana have therefore been embargoed since 1992, and it has not adopted U.S.-style turtle-protection regulations.

After the domestic process within the United States caused an increase in the number of states subject to sanctions, most of the new countries whose fishing environments required TEDs according to the U.S. regulations made the requisite changes in their shrimp-fishing practices, either immediately or shortly after their shrimp was embargoed. Ecuador, El Salvador, and Indonesia met the requirements as soon as the United States demanded them. Thailand, China, and Nigeria did not initially change their policies. They were therefore not allowed to export shrimp to the United States at the beginning of this period. Thailand, the largest exporter of shrimp to the United States,[58] instituted a regulation for commercial shrimp trawlers to use TEDs six months after the United States demanded that it do so.[59] China initially did not require TEDs of all its shrimp trawlers, but shortly after U.S. sanctions were imposed, it implemented a regulation requiring TEDs in fishing situations with a risk of incidental catch of sea turtles. Nigeria's Ministry of Fisheries passed a regulation requiring all shrimp trawlers operating in Nigeria's waters to use TEDs as of the end of 1996, and the U.S. State Department verified that all of Nigeria's shrimp trawlers had installed TEDs and that the country's officials were enforcing the regulations.[60]

In short, with a few exceptions, states adopted sea turtle–protection regulations shortly after being threatened with sanctions, if they did not do so initially. The timing of their policies—many changed their fishing practices shortly after their shrimp exports were cut off—indicates that the U.S. economic threat was largely the reason these states adopted the policies at issue.

International Challenges

An important additional battle in the process of U.S. environmental sanctions in both the dolphin and the sea turtle case came with international challenges to the legality of these measures. Sanctions are often seen internationally as illegitimate ways to accomplish goals (although they certainly have on occasion been instrumental in accomplishing those goals nevertheless). In a number of cases, they conflict with international trade law because they involve barriers to trade for reasons apart from trade policy. The challenged measures have not been found to be legal—although the United States has not removed the sanctions—but the process is illuminating in understanding the impact of U.S. domestic battles on the international legality of the sanctions it threatens.

Dolphins

The U.S. trade restrictions on tuna caught in ways that harm dolphins were twice brought before international dispute-settlement procedures. Mexico asked for consultations with the United States under the General Agreement on Tariffs and Trade (GATT) in 1990. After a resolution was not reached, Mexico asked in 1991 that a dispute-settlement panel be convened. Mexico argued that the MMPA embargo violated the GATT prohibition on quantitative restrictions, as well as the requirement for national treatment of like products.[61] The United States, in turn, argued that these measures were acceptable under GATT Article XX exceptions for environmental protection.

The GATT panel ruled against the United States, finding that the United States violated the principle of national treatment for like goods by discriminating against tuna imports based on how the tuna were caught. In addition, the United States was not justified in pushing domestic environmental measures unilaterally and extraterritorially. The panel found these sanctions did not meet the criteria under Article XX for trade restrictions in support of environmental policies, arguing that the particular form of the trade restriction was not "primarily aimed at" conservation because it was based not on an objective standard of resource protection, but rather on the level of dolphin mortality from the U.S. tuna fleet. Moreover, because the allowable dolphin mortality level for foreign tuna fleets was based on the U.S. fishing practices (and calculated only at the end of a given year), Mexican fishers could not know at any given point whether they were meeting the requirement to be able to export tuna to the United States.[62] Mexico never called for the panel decision to be adopted formally, however, an omission almost certainly owing to the ongoing negotiations with the United States over the North American Free Trade Agreement.

The European Union called for a dispute-settlement panel in 1992, after the failure of bilateral consultations with the United States relating to the embargo on tuna from "intermediary nations." The GATT found against the United States once again, stating that the embargo on tuna from intermediary nations was not "primarily aimed at" conservation because it embargoed all yellowfin tuna from targeted states and not just that caught in ways that harmed dolphins. More importantly, it found that neither the primary nor secondary embargo could be considered "necessary" for the protection of "human, animal, or plant life or health."[63] Once again, agreement was reached outside the institution not to bring the panel findings to a full vote.

The United States only slightly modified its implementation of the tuna sanctions in light of the panel findings, keeping the bulk of the policy intact. After the first panel report, it appears that Mexico agreed to forego further action within the GATT if the United Sates would modify the implementation of the MMPA's internationalization efforts with respect to Mexican tuna.[64] Mexico did agree to stronger dolphin-protection measures in its tuna-fishing process, but the United States held off on removing the tuna embargo, and it continued apace with respect to other target states as well. By the time of the second panel ruling, the Department of Commerce modified its interpretation of the secondary embargo requirement so that states that indicated that they did not buy tuna from embargoed states would not have to prove that annually, but the secondary embargo has continued against Costa Rica, Italy, and Japan to the present. The greatest chance for ending the sanctions has come with the negotiation of the Declaration of Panama to limit acceptable dolphin mortality worldwide in return for lifting the U.S. embargoes.[65] The international agreement implementing the declaration entered into force in 1999.

Sea Turtles

The case against U.S. shrimp sanctions for the protection of sea turtles has also been heard twice, this time by the dispute-settlement process of the new World Trade Organization (WTO). Despite meeting U.S. turtle-protection require-ments shortly after being sanctioned in 1996 and thereby becoming able to export shrimp to the United States, Thailand joined with Malaysia, India, and Pakistan to bring the United States to the dispute-settlement process of the WTO. It claimed that the widened sanctions were illegal under international trade law. A three-member panel appointed by the WTO issued an interim ruling in April 1998, finding that U.S. regulations were contrary to the prohibition on quantitative restrictions found in Article XI(1) of the GATT and were not justified under Article XX exceptions to protect the environment.[66] In particular, the panel found that because of the ruling by the U.S. Court for International Trade, the law was applied to geographic areas for which it had not been designed. It was also determined that the widened shrimp sanctions were applied in a discriminatory manner because the original fourteen target states had been allowed to phase in sea turtle protection, whereas the additional states had to meet U.S. standards immediately. And, similar to the finding of the GATT dolphin panels, the WTO panel pointed out the problem with a policy that mandated "comparable" mortality levels to United States fishing efforts. Most importantly, the panel found that the United States had not sufficiently attempted to address the protection of sea turtles multilaterally. The United States appealed the decision, but the WTO appellate body, which ruled in October 1998, did not accept the legitimacy of U.S. policy.[67]

Conclusion

Several observations can be made from the experience of U.S. environmental sanctions. An important one is that these sanctions have had a high degree of success in changing the environmental policies of target states, with little material cost to the United States. Unlike with the case of export sanctions, where U.S. actors suffer from losing foreign markets for their goods, the import sanctions threatened for environmental protection rarely harm U.S. actors economically.[68] Domestically, the policy of threatening sanctions against foreign states that do not adopt particular environmental regulations pleases a diverse group of actors, from environmentalists who applaud the internationalization of environmental policy to actors from the regulated industries who gain relatively when their competitors have to bear additional costs from environmental regulation.

The major cost borne by the United States comes from international public opinion. Charges of economic or environmental imperialism are lobbed at the United States, and international dispute-settlement processes have not found these sanctions as implemented to be legitimate ways to pursue environmental goals. It is possible that continuing to flout international trade regulations (and specific decisions by dispute-settlement bodies) will make other U.S. policy efforts more difficult in the long run.

Many of the problems the United States experiences internationally from its sanctions efforts can be traced to the domestic struggles that accompany their formation and implementation. Most obvious is the extent to which these measures have at least partly protectionist origins. Despite the justifiable environmental goals that underlie the U.S. efforts, the reason that sanctions are the instrument of choice for achieving these goals can be traced to the U.S. industry actors that want to level the international playing field when they themselves are regulated. Policies that are not "primarily aimed at" conservation are likely to result.

The requirement, for instance, that incidental dolphin deaths be "comparable" to those from U.S. tuna-fishing efforts (a policy mirrored to some extent in the sea turtle case) phrases the laudable goal of dolphin protection in terms that relate to industry actions and makes it nearly impossible for foreign states to design their fishing practices in a way that can be ensured to protect the resource sufficiently.

Even if one accepts the underlying premise of the sanctions efforts, however, other domestic struggles pervert the form they take so that they become less likely to be compatible with other international agreements. The lawsuits that forced the expansion of tuna sanctions to intermediary nations and of shrimp sanctions to states other than the original targets made both of these measures less acceptable in terms of trade law. In particular, the court-ordered expansion of the shrimp embargo left the United States open to charges of discrimination because the new target states—unlike the original fourteen states subject to the policy—were not allowed to phase in sea turtle protection.

Consideration of U.S. unilateral environmental sanctions is thus a fascinating but troubling topic. As a policy tool, the use of sanctions in this issue area has been quite effective both domestically and internationally, but the sanctions as applied have been created in a piecemeal domestic process in which no one group determines their shape. Although that process may make them effective in an organic sense on the domestic scene, it makes them problematic internationally. Similar environmental policies, even those that include the threat of sanctions, could almost certainly accomplish the same goals less objectionably if designed in a more intentional manner.

Notes

1 Public Law 219, sec. 8(a) and (b), 92 Cong., 1st sess., 23 December 1971.

2 Public Law 478, sec. 2201, 100th Cong., 2d sess., 7 October 1988.

3 Public Law 376, 95th Cong., 2d sess., 18 September 1978.

4 The legislation allowing trade restrictions for this purpose is initially the same used for states that "diminish the effectiveness of an international fishery conservation program" because whales meet the legislation's definition.

5 Public Law 627, title I, sec. 107, 101st Cong., 2d sess., 28 November 1990.

6 It is as important to study the threat of sanctions as it is to study their imposition because both are part of the same phenomenon; the most successful sanction is one that works without ever having to be imposed. Both sanctions

that are threatened and those that are imposed are considered within the topic explored in this chapter.

7 For fuller discussion of this phenomenon, see Elizabeth R. DeSombre, *Domestic Sources of International Environmental Policy: Industry, Environmentalists, and U.S. Power* (Cambridge, Mass.: MIT Press, 2000).

8 See Elizabeth R. DeSombre, "Baptists and Bootleggers for the Environment: The Origins of United States Unilateral Sanctions," *Journal of Environment and Development* 4, no. 1 (winter 1995): 53–75.

9 *U.S. Code Congressional and Administrative News* (1971), from H. Rept. 92-468, 2409.

10 The legislation is described earlier in the essay; see note 1.

11 The United States was responsible for at least 85 percent of these deaths. Alessandro Bonanno and Douglas Constance, *Caught in the Net: The Global Tuna Industry, Environmentalism, and the State* (Kansas City: University Press of Kansas, 1996), 121, 125, 127.

12 "Porpoise-Kill Limit Set by House," *Facts on File, World News Digest,* 11 June 1977, 442D3.

13 Dan Tedrick, "American Tuna Fleet," *Associated Press,* 3 May 1977 (Lexis/Nexis).

14 Bruce Coleman, "Troubled Waters," *Forbes* (1 April 1977), 56.

15 *Federal Register* 39, no. 173 (5 September 1975): 32124.

16 Ibid.

17 *Federal Register* 42, no. 247 (23 December 1977): 64558-60.

18 National Research Council, *Decline of the Sea Turtles: Causes and Prevention* (Washington, D.C.: National Academy Press, 1990), 16.

19 Public Law 478, title II, §2303, 100th Cong., 2d sess., 7 October 1988, 102 Stat. 2322; 16 U.S.C. §4242; 52 FR 24244-24262; 57 FR 18446 ff.

20 Jack Rudloe and Anne Rudloe, "Shrimpers and Lawmakers Collide over a Move to Save the Sea Turtle," *Smithsonian* 20 (December 1989), 44 ff; "U.S. Tells Shrimpers to Give Sea Turtles an Escape 'Door,' " *New York Times,* 6 September 1989, B8 (Lexis/Nexis).

21 Anthony V. Margavio and Craig J. Forsyth, *Caught in the Net: The Conflict Between Shrimpers and Conservationists* (College Station, Tex.: Texas A&M University Press, 1996), 31–34.

22 Eugene H. Buck, "Turtle Excluder Devices: Sea Turtles and/or Shrimp?" *CRS Report for Congress,* 28 November 1990, 9; Patty Curtain, "Annual Shrimping Kill: 44,000 Turtles," *St. Petersburg Times,* 18 May 1990, 1A (Lexis/Nexis); Jeff Klinkenberg, "Stubborn Shrimpers May Face Consumer Backlash Over Turtles," *St. Petersburg Times,* 8 April 1990, 5D (Lexis/Nexis).

23 Buck, "Turtle Excluder Devices," 2.

24 Harrus Lasseigne Jr., U.S. Congress, statement before the House Subcommittee on Fisheries and Wildlife Conservation and the Environment of the

Committee on Merchant Marine and Fisheries, *Sea Turtle Conservation and the Shrimp Industry*, 101st Congress, 2d sess., 1 May 1990, 13, serial no. 101-83.

25 Statements of Mr. Johnson and Mr. Breux, *Congressional Record*, Senate, 101st Congress, 1st sess., 29 September 1989, s12266.

26 Earth Island Institute, "Can We Stop Mexico's Shocking Slaughter of Endangered Sea Turtles?" (mailing, no date; also placed as advertisement in newspapers).

27 Statement of Michael Bean before the House Committee on Merchant Marine and Fisheries, *Sea Turtle Conservation and the Shrimp Industry*, 18.

28 *American Cetacean Society et al. v. Malcolm Baldridge, Secretary of Commerce, et al.*, 247 U.S. Appelant District Court 309; 768 F. 2d 426 (1985); *Japan Whaling Association v. American Cetacean Society*, Supreme Court, 478 U.S. 221, 105 C. St. 2860 (1986).

29 Public Law 711, 100th Cong., 2d sess., 23 November 1988.

30 *Earth Island Institute et al. v. Mosbacher*, U.S. District Court for the Northern District of California, No. c-88-1380-TEH, 746 F. Supp. 964, 28 August 1990; *Federal Register* 55: 42236.

31 *Earth Island Institute et al. v. Mosbacher*, U.S. Court of Appeals for the Ninth Circuit, No. 90-16581, 929 F. 2d 1449, 11 April 1991; also *Federal Register* 55: 48666.

32 *Earth Island Institute et al. v. Mosbacher et al.*, U.S. District Court for the Northern District of California, No. C 88 1380 TEH, 785 F. Supp. 826, 3 February 1992.

33 *Earth Island Institute et al. v. Warren Christopher et al.*, U.S. Court of International Trade, Court No. 94-06-00321, 913 F. Supp. 599; Humberto Marquez, "Shrimp, Next on the List for U.S. Decertification," *Inter Press Service*, 25 April 1996 (Lexis/Nexis).

34 Margaret P. Doxey, *International Sanctions in Contemporary Perspective* (New York: St. Martin's, 1987); Klaus Knorr and Frank N. Trager, eds., *Economic Issues and National Security* (Lawrence: Regents Press of Kansas, 1977).

35 Johan Galtung, "On the Effects of International Economic Sanctions: With Examples from the Case of Rhodesia," *World Politics* 19 (1967): 378–416.

36 See DeSombre, *Domestic Sources of International Environmental Policy*.

37 Katherine Ellison, "Mexican Fleet, U.S. Groups Entangled in 'Tuna War,' " *Orange County Register*, 7 November 1991, A32 (Lexis/Nexis).

38 National Oceanic and Atmospheric Administration (NOAA), National Marine Fisheries Service (NMFS), "Tuna/Dolphin Embargo Status Update," available at <http://swr.ucsd.edu/psd/embargo2.htm>, 1 June 1998.

39 Its tuna was embargoed under the Magnuson Fishery Conservation and Management Act from 1980 to 1986 for seizing U.S. tuna vessels fishing within an Exclusive Economic Zone the United States did not at that point recognize. See *Federal Register* 45, no. 137 (15 July 1980): 47562; *Federal*

Register 51, no. 157 (14 August 1986): 29183; "Mexico Terminating All Fishing Accords with United States," *New York Times*, 29 December 1980, A1 (Lexis/Nexis); Patrick McDonnell, "U.S. Reportedly Will Lift Embargo on Tuna from Mexico," *Los Angeles Times*, 6 August 1986, 3 (Lexis/Nexis).

40 Ellison, "Mexican Fleet," A32.

41 Michael Parrish and Juanita Darlin, "Mexico Backs Away from Pact on Tuna," *Los Angeles Times*, 4 November 1992, D2 (Lexis/Nexis).

42 "U.S. Might Lift Ban on Venezuelan Tuna," *Journal of Commerce*, 19 October 1988, 4A (Lexis/Nexis).

43 *Federal Register* 58, no. 4 (January 1993): 3013.

44 *Federal Register* 57, no. 82 (28 April 1992): 17858.

45 *Federal Register* 59, no. 134 (14 July 1994): 35911.

46 *Federal Register* 59, no. 245 (22 December 1994): 65974.

47 *Federal Register* 53, no. 220 (15 November 1988): 45953; *Federal Register* 59, no. 64 (4 April 1994): 15655.

48 It is also worth noting that sanctions ultimately changed the shape of the international tuna industry. Actors in a number of states simply decided to leave the industry.

49 Howard LaFranchi, "Shrimp Lovers, Take Note," *Christian Science Monitor*, 29 April 1996, 1 (Lexis/Nexis).

50 "Suriname," *Miami Herald*, 9 May 1991, A12.

51 Telephone interview with Bill Gibbons-Fly, State Department, 1 April 1994.

52 Ibid.; "U.S. Bans Some Shrimp Imports to Protect Turtles," *Miami Herald*, 6 May 1993, A14.

53 *Federal Register* 63: 30550-1.

54 Gibbons-Fly, telephone interview; "U.S. Bans Some Shrimp," *Miami Herald*.

55 Public Notice 1838, *Federal Register* 52, no. 124 (29 June 1987): 24244–24262. Exports of farm-raised shrimp from Honduras had not been embargoed, but during the embargo they were required to be accompanied by an Exporter's Declaration certifying that they were farm raised.

56 Public Notice 2423, *Federal Register* 61, no. 164 (22 August 1996): 43395.

57 Public Notice 2240, *Federal Register* 60, no. 162 (22 August 1995): 43640-1.

58 Most of Thailand's shrimp, however, comes from aquaculture and therefore was not subject to trade restrictions.

59 Public Notice 2469, *Federal Register* 61, no. 227 (22 November 1996): 59482.

60 Public Notice 2498, *Federal Register* 62, no. 21 (31 January 1997): 4826. Because the certification year runs from May through April, Nigeria's certification is considered part of the same year.

61 These claims, as well as other concerns Mexico had with the U.S. legislation, are documented and further explained in General Agreement on Tariffs and Trade, "Dispute Settlement Panel Report on United States Restrictions on Imports of Tuna [Submitted to the Parties 16 August 1991]," in *International Legal Materials* 30, 1594–623.

62 Ibid., 1616–22.

63 General Agreement on Tariffs and Trade, "United States—Restrictions on Imports of Tuna," report of Panel DS29/R, June 1994, 5.21–5.41, in *International Legal Materials* 33 (1994): 839–99.

64 Bonanno and Constance, *Caught in the Net*, 197–98.

65 "Tuna Fishing: Tuna Accord Approval Not Universal," *Europe Environment* 14 (November 1995) (Lexis/Nexis).

66 World Trade Organization, *United States—Import Prohibition of Certain Shrimp and Shrimp Products*, Interim Panel report, unpublished copy obtained from the Office of the United States Trade Representative, April 1998.

67 World Trade Organization, *United States—Import Prohibition of Certain Shrimp and Shrimp Products*, report of the Appellate Body, AB-1998-4, 12 October 1998, available at <http://www.wto.org>.

68 To the extent that they do, it is the widely dispersed actors who may have to pay a slightly higher price for some products, rather than concentrated interests that would suffer large losses.

10 The International Whaling Regime and U.S. Foreign Policy

Kristen M. Fletcher

In 1946, the United States joined fifteen other nations to determine the fate of the world's whale stocks, which had been depleted as a result of worldwide commercial harvesting.[1] The nations declared the need to assert rules to govern whaling across the globe and subsequently signed the International Convention for the Regulation of Whaling (ICRW). Under the convention, the International Whaling Commission (IWC) was created to regulate an industry facing declining demand for whale oil and severe depletions of some species of whale. By the mid-1960s, with fewer nations engaged in whaling and the addition of new nonwhaling members to the convention, the focus of the IWC became increasingly preservation oriented. This focus, along with other factors, has led to the polarization of member nations within the IWC—those favoring preservation of whale stocks conflicting with those in favor of conservation measures as well as continued consumptive and nonconsumptive uses. By 1984, these conflicts peaked when the IWC placed a ban on commercial whaling, which took effect in 1986. That ban is still in effect, although the IWC allows the taking of whales only for research purposes and for aboriginal subsistence hunts. The United States has maintained a foreign policy stance against commercial whaling, but international factors are emerging to challenge this policy. Scientists agree that several whale stocks across the globe have improved as a result of fewer commercial hunters and the international ban on commercial whaling by the IWC. Many parties on the IWC argue that these stocks are healthy enough to undergo a sustainable commercial harvest.

In recent years, IWC member nations have struggled over the limitations of the aboriginal quota and the ban on commercial whaling. Even nonwhaling nations, including the United States, support aboriginal subsistence whaling when it does not negatively impact whale stocks and when the hunt fulfills nutritional, spiritual, and cultural needs of a traditional whaling people. Yet these nations draw the line at allowing commercial trade of whale products. With Japanese markets paying the equivalent of thirty U.S. dollars per pound of whale meat, commercial trade can offer a unique economic boost to whaling communities. As a result of the continued stance by most countries against commercial whaling and the simultaneous increase in healthy stocks, whaling nations have found themselves reaching outside of the IWC for whaling policy and management. Many pro-whaling nations are forming new international bodies to promote and manage sustainable whale harvests.

As a strong international leader, the United States seems to be *reacting* to the rapidly changing international whaling regime rather than *influencing* it. Its legacy of supporting aboriginal quotas and opposing commercial whaling will certainly affect the impact of U.S. foreign policy on the global whaling policy. Although advocating for both the Alaskan Eskimo bowhead quota and the Makah Indian gray whale quota, the United States has faced notable challenges at both the domestic and international levels. Fighting science on the one hand and traditional subsistence concepts on the other, the United States has established a reputation for advocating its own interests at the expense of consistent IWC policies. It remains, however, an ardent supporter of the international ban on commercial whaling, seeking a permanent ban even though international support and science seem to be swaying toward sustainable commercial harvests. As a result of this conflicting policy, the U.S. now faces the development of regional and international bodies other than the IWC to manage whale stocks, represent whaling nations and tribes, and advocate for commercial harvests.

As whale stocks improve and the world's whaling policies change, U.S. foreign policy must evolve with them. The American reaction to these international challenges provides an opportunity to analyze U.S. whaling policy.

The U.S. Role in International Whaling Policy

The history of whaling extends back to eleventh-century practices of the Basques, who hunted whales in the Bay of Biscay for meat, bones, and oil.[2] Early technological practices kept hunters close to shore, but as coastal species became depleted, whalers sought to undertake pelagic whaling in distant waters. In the sixteenth century, these efforts were led by the British, Dutch, Germans, and French, resulting in the depletion of some whale stocks as early as the seventeenth and eighteenth centuries.[3] By the mid–nineteenth century, whaling was revolutionized by the emergence of steam-powered ships and the invention of the harpoon gun. The overharvesting threat continued into the twentieth century with the development and deployment of factory ships that made it possible to operate far from existing land stations.[4] Large-scale operations in the waters of the Antarctic were made possible by the 1925 advent of factory ships with stern slipways. By the 1930–31 season, worldwide whaling operations resulted in an annual catch of almost forty-three thousand whales, with 97.9 percent of the world whale-oil supply coming from Antarctic waters.[5]

As the whaling industry was advancing in the early twentieth century, attention turned to the international management of marine resources. Diplomats of the day recognized the need for protection against total extermination but "acknowledged their lack of technical expertise as to what type of international action was needed."[6] Seeking further information and greater participation, the League of Nations sought assistance from the International Council for the Exploration of the Seas (ICES), which reported: "the enormous expansion of the whaling industry in recent years constitutes a real menace to the maintenance of the stocks of whales and that, if the expansion continues at the present rate, there is a real risk of those stocks being so reduced as to cause serious detriment to the industry."[7] The United States, an active whaling nation at the time, was taking notice as well. Lewis Radcliffe, then deputy commissioner of the U.S. Bureau of Fisheries, reported that

> At no stage in the history of whale fisheries, have whales been so harassed in so many parts of the globe. . . . That any one who has made even a casual study of the history of the whale fisheries of the globe can honestly advance the thought that there has been little or no diminution in the number of whales in the waters of the globe, seems little short of absurdity. That the whale supply will long stand up under the losses in numbers of 18,000 whales or more killed a year, seems extremely doubtful.[8]

In the face of growing concern, the United States joined other nations convened by the League of Nations in 1930 to consider the possibility of drafting an international whaling convention. The draft convention focused on the prohibition of taking certain stocks, immature whales, and females accompanied by calves. It also called for a reduction in waste and the collection of information on each whale taken.[9] In 1931, a document was adopted as the Convention for the Regulation of Whaling, which applied to both the high seas and territorial waters. The convention entered into force by 1935, with nineteen states having ratified it, including the two principal whaling states, Norway and the United Kingdom.[10] Although it was a good start, the 1931 convention provided only limited protection against the waste seemingly inherent in the whale hunt, but it did build a foundation for the International Convention for the Regulation of Whaling, signed in 1946, which created the International Whaling Commission.[11]

Created to "protect all species of whales from further overfishing" and "provide for the proper conservation of whale stocks . . . and the orderly development of the whaling industry," the IWC began its efforts by setting quotas and drafting regulations.[12] For decades, the goal of assisting and managing the commercial whaling industry took priority over prevention of overharvesting. By the mid-1960s, the focus of the IWC began to shift.[13] Fewer nations were engaged in whaling and new nonwhaling members joined the convention, yielding a more preservation-oriented regime.[14] This focus on preservation of whale stocks, rather than on sustainable harvesting, led slowly to the polarization of member nations.

By 1982, the IWC determined that a temporary ban on commercial whaling was necessary. The ban became effective in 1986 and is still in effect today. Whaling nations' reaction to this moratorium characterized the IWC during the 1990s. Japan, Norway, and Iceland undertook ventures to uproot the preservationists on the IWC. All three unsuccessfully requested permits for the taking of whales for scientific research.[15] Without permits and despite criticism, they nevertheless set out on whale hunts for research purposes. Japan took (and is still actively taking) whales under the name of scientific research.[16] In 1992, after its request for a limited commercial hunt was denied, Iceland withdrew from the commission, claiming that a "rabid minority" controlled the organization's decision making on critical issues.[17] At the same meeting, Norway announced its intention to resume commercial whaling in 1993, and it has whaled commercially each year since.[18]

The IWC has undergone criticism for the commercial ban for several reasons. First, whaling nations acceded to the moratorium decision in 1982 with the promise that, by 1990, it would be reviewed after certain research had been completed by the IWC Scientific Committee.[19] The argument is that by keeping the ban in place after scientific evidence has shown several stocks to be recovered to a certain extent, the IWC has changed its focus to preservation and nonconsumptive uses. Second, the maintenance of the ban on commercial harvest may be outside of the terms of the International Convention for the Regulation of Whaling. By adopting and maintaining this preservationist stance, the IWC has changed its mission from regulation to preservation without amending its treaty. Third, the IWC has been criticized for failing to meet the needs of whaling nations and whaling communities that rely on whaling for sustenance. Finally, the IWC has failed to remedy its own bipolarization and may be showing its inability to provide the guidance and regulatory capacity for which it was created.

The United States has led the movement to end commercial whaling, leading some to call it the "world's leading protector of whales" and the "IWC policeman."[20] To aid in enforcing the IWC policies, the United States has imposed sanctions on violating nations and proposed conservative policies aimed at the protection of whales.[21] In fact, the 1982 vote to ban commercial whaling was not a new concept. At the United Nations Conference on the Human Environment in 1972, the United States recommended a ten-year moratorium on commercial whaling[22] and proposed a global moratorium at both the 1972 and 1973 IWC meetings.[23] The United States and Australia proposed a worldwide ban on commercial whaling in 1979. President Carter urged the IWC to take "effective action to ensure the survival of the great whales."[24] In the ensuing "whale war" between commercial harvesters and protectionists, the United States has typically sided with the latter. It has also consistently criticized both Japan and Norway for their defiance of the IWC resolutions. President Clinton recently called attention to Japan's repeated lethal research whaling activities, especially in the Southern Ocean Whale Sanctuary, directing the U.S. Department of State to convey "strong concerns" to the government of Japan.[25] The president maintained stiff opposition to Norway's commercial whale hunts, although he admitted "working through the whaling issue" with Norway.[26] Thus, international relations in this area have become strained during the years of the ban on whaling.

Aboriginal Whaling: A Hurdle in U.S. Domestic and Foreign Policy

Another hurdle for U.S. whaling policy is its sometimes inconsistent stance on aboriginal subsistence whaling. Aboriginal subsistence whaling is "[w]haling for the purposes of local aboriginal consumption carried out by or on behalf of aboriginal, indigenous or native peoples who share strong community, familial, social and cultural ties related to a continuing dependence on whaling and on the use of whales."[27] In 1981, the IWC accepted three broad management objectives for aboriginal subsistence-whaling quotas. Specifically, the aboriginal quota should "enable aboriginal people to harvest whales in perpetuity at levels appropriate to their cultural and nutritional requirements."[28] The quota must also ensure that risks of extinction to individual stocks are not seriously increased by the aboriginal whaling and that the hunts allow for sustainable populations. Intended as a narrow remedy for specific aboriginal groups, this subsistence quota has instead been stretched to further domestic policies of member nations, including the United States.

The United States first met international opposition when it advocated the continuance of the Alaskan Eskimo aboriginal exception to hunt the bowhead whale, an exception that had existed since the inception of the ICRW.[29] When the IWC became concerned about the impact of the Eskimo quota on the bowhead stock, the IWC asked the United States to conduct research on the stock and to reduce the number of bowheads struck but lost by Alaskan Eskimo whalers.[30] When the IWC finally adopted the amendment that halted the Alaskan Eskimo quota in 1977, the United States lobbied the IWC to permit a limited take of whales by the Eskimos. Even though the Scientific Committee of the IWC rejected the U.S. efforts, the IWC agreed to a "limited and strictly controlled hunt."[31] The United States continued its lobbying efforts even with increasingly stronger evidence of a decreasing population of Bering Sea bowheads.[32] Many viewed the U.S. efforts as directly contrary to its responsibilities to IWC policies and as setting bad precedent for future use of the aboriginal subsistence-whaling quota.[33]

A decade later, the United States found itself again advocating for a small constituency wishing to whale under an aboriginal quota. The Makah Indians, a Native American tribe of two thousand, located on the Olympic Peninsula in the northwest of the continental United States, trace their whaling heritage through two centuries via traditional tribal stories and the archaeological finds of a whale-dependent culture.[34] The Makah hunted gray whales for centuries until the 1920s, when commercial whaling had decimated the stocks to approximately four thousand from a peak estimated at twenty-three thousand. Having rebuilt their population for more than fifty years, gray whale numbers are estimated at more than twenty-two thousand. When the gray whale was removed from the Federal Endangered Species List in 1994,[35] the Makah Tribal Council realized the stock of the whales could accommodate a tribal hunt.

The Makah tribe requested that the U.S. government seek an aboriginal subsistence-whaling quota for them from the IWC.[36] The Makah claimed both the legal and moral right to hunt gray whales. The tribe cited the 1855 Treaty of Neah Bay reserving the Makah's traditional right to whale[37] and making the tribe eligible for the aboriginal subsistence-whaling exception.[38] The Makah also cited a moral right to whale because the tribe had depended on the whale for subsistence and their cultural heritage for centuries. They hoped that by "resurrecting this cultural and spiritual centerpiece of the tribe, the community would blossom again and the local economy might even be revived."[39]

Faced with lobbying for the Makah hunt, the United States first had to revise its own domestic regulations governing whaling by aboriginal tribes. Previously, the criteria to determine who qualified for aboriginal quotas required the demonstration of both cultural *and* subsistence needs. The revised regulations now read that there must be a demonstration of cultural *and/or* subsistence needs.[40] The change in the regulation was completed without an environmental impact statement, hearings, or public notice or input as generally required by U.S. law. Antiwhaling advocates view this revision as a major policy shift that "opened the door to cultural whaling in the United States and, by example, around the world."[41]

In 1996, the United States presented a proposal to the IWC for an aboriginal subsistence-whaling quota of five gray whales for the Makah. The proposal aroused a great deal of concern. As discussions progressed and it became evident that the IWC would not adopt the proposal by the requisite three-quarters, the United States withdrew it.[42] At the 1997 IWC meeting, the United States again lobbied for a Makah quota. Realizing it would not get the necessary support, it managed to acquire the quota by effectively "trading" whale quotas with Russia: four gray whales per year from the Russian Chukchi Eskimos' annual quota for five bowhead whales from the U.S. Alaskan Eskimo quota. The IWC voted to grant a joint whale quota of 124 eastern Pacific gray whales to the Inuit of Alaska and the Chukchi of Eastern Siberia. Under the Russia–United States agreement, the Makah were "granted" the right to take four gray whales a year. This trade prevented an IWC vote on the Makah quota and was criticized by other member nations. It led the Australian delegate to propose adding the following words to the IWC Schedule: "The only aboriginal people who are authorized to take Gray whales are those whose traditional aboriginal subsistence and cultural needs have been recognized."[43]

Though not by means of the "traditional" route for acquiring a quota, the Makah were authorized either twenty whales killed or thirty-three wounded for a period of five years, through the year 2002. With quota in hand, the Makah prepared for the hunt, recognizing that domestic legal challenges and public protest still loomed on the horizon, with one Makah member noting that "I would imagine our fight has just started."[44] Over the next year, the Makah chose a team of hunters from the tribe using both physical and spiritual guidelines. It acquired and prepared its necessary supplies, and it prepared for a hunt that no living Makah had ever experienced.

The federal government was also preparing for the hunt. The U.S. Coast Guard proposed a rule that would prevent protestors from coming within five hundred yards of a Makah whaling vessel.[45] The National Marine Fisheries Service worked with the tribe to write a whale-management plan. The government and the Makah also fought very active and heated public opposition. On behalf of the Makah, the government faced a lawsuit opposing the hunt filed by U.S., British, and Australian animal rights groups, coastal tour boat operators, kayakers, and U.S. Representative Jack Metcalf.[46] The suit challenged how federal agencies handled efforts to resume Makah whaling. However, a U.S. District Court judge dismissed the lawsuit, determining that the hunt could continue. The Coast Guard received numerous objections and requests for a public hearing in response to its five-hundred-yard rule, including a lawsuit by the Progressive Animal Welfare Society.[47] The National Guard was mobilized for potential conflicts between tribe members and protestors during the August celebration of Makah Days.[48] Conflicts did arise on 1 November 1998, when four protestors were arrested by tribal police following a confrontation that began when they trespassed onto Makah land.[49] The physical presence of the protestors became a daily feature of Makah life.[50] During training immediately before the first kill in May 1999, several groups in boats tried to disrupt outings by the tribesmen, and several arrests resulted.[51]

Regional and International Whaling Agreements: Can the United States Maintain Its Leadership?

Protestors of the Makah hunt and critics of the bowhead quota struggle of the 1970s now admit that they are more concerned about "the message this will send to Oslo, to Reykjavik, to Tokyo."[52] Ultimately, many fear the precedent on the international stage and not without reason. As the IWC reaches its fifteenth year of an international ban on commercial whaling, whaling nations are finding in traditional whaling peoples and small island nations new ambassadors for the pro-whaling message. According to a recent press report, the 1999 meeting of the IWC brought Japan's new alliance with Grenada and several other small Caribbean states into sharp focus. Those countries consistently backed every one of Tokyo's pro-whaling votes at the meeting, as they had since 1992, when Japan began sending them foreign aid that now exceeds $80 million. The votes of island states helped Japan build support for its position, after years of near isolation on whaling.[53] By gathering support from parties with aboriginal and community-based interests noted by the IWC, whaling nations may successfully introduce an increase in community whaling and simultaneously a resumption of commercial whaling.

The moratorium on commercial whaling was adopted by the IWC in part on the grounds of uncertainties surrounding the scientific knowledge of whale stocks. It was contingent upon a review of its effects to be undertaken by the year 1990, based on the comprehensive assessment of whale stocks by the IWC Scientific Committee. The Scientific Committee developed the Revised Management Procedure, which enables the long-term sustainable utilization of whales. The IWC Technical Committee is developing the Revised Management Scheme, the administrative part of the management of the stocks, but the IWC seems far from implementing the plans.[54] Critics claim this delay as evidence that the IWC is ignoring relevant science and instead allowing a few preservationist nations to determine worldwide whaling policies.[55] In the meantime, whaling nations continue to conduct research and are finding that some whale species subject to commercial whaling as recently as twenty or thirty years ago are now safe from extinction.[56] These nations struggle to refocus the whaling debate from a philosophical dilemma to the practical question of sustainable activity.[57]

While waiting for management measures to replace the moratorium on commercial whaling, Norway resumed commercial whaling in 1993. It has resumed a sustainable hunt for the minke whale in Norwegian waters. Unlike the larger species that have been slow to recover despite the ban, the minke's numbers have increased, making it by far the most numerous of the great whales. In 1997, the IWC Scientific Committee found that the minke whale population was robust enough to tolerate a limited hunt.[58] Scientists settled on an estimate that more than 900,000 minke whales are alive worldwide, with 118,000 in Norwegian waters.[59] In a move toward proven sustainability, Norway has implemented an inspection scheme that provides for inspectors on board every whaling vessel. The executive secretary of the IWC, Ray Gambell, claims that "the pro-whaling side has put forward a strong and arguable case for a resumption of commercial whaling. . . . Maybe this is time for a breakthrough."[60]

Although many nations still disapprove of Norway's hunt, Norway's image is beginning to take shape as a responsible merchant nation rather than a renegade. Some see the decreasing vehemence by international environmental and animal rights groups as evidence that sustainable commercial whaling is coming into favor.[61] In fact, Norway's two largest environmental groups have declared the minke whale hunt "sustainable."[62] Others note that the willingness of nonwhaling nations to discuss allowing a limited commercial hunt might be a sign of an international shift toward sustainable harvest of whales. However, Greenpeace spokesperson Jamie Gillies exclaimed that "Norway should abide by international agreements and stop whaling."[63] She attributes the current lull in protests to limited resources rather than to a concession of defeat.

However, the international negotiations between whaling and nonwhaling nations may be a sign of fear that commercial whaling will continue with or without sustainable harvest rules. Governments may be trying to set up regulations before there is a sharp increase in hunting worldwide.[64] Whaling nations such as Norway no longer look solely to existing international agreements for their whaling policies. Indeed, the failure of the IWC to act on management measures for the harvest of whales has led member and nonmember nations to join regional and international bodies created to promote whaling and to manage whales as sustainable resources.

For example, in 1992, the Faroe Islands, Greenland, Norway, and Iceland established a separate body, the North Atlantic Marine Mammals Commission (NAMMCO) to coordinate research and management of marine mammals, including whales, in the North Atlantic. In 1997, members of NAMMCO agreed to begin an exchange of international observers for whaling and sealing activities commencing in 1998. In addition, members exchanged research, stock-assessment reports, such as that of the north Atlantic minke whale stock, and reports on the economic implications of marine mammal and fishery interactions.[65] Similarly, in April 1998, Japanese officials announced that Japan, China, South Korea, and Russia have taken steps toward a future agreement on establishing a committee for managing whales in the northwestern Pacific region, with the objectives of cooperative research on whales and the promotion of whaling.[66]

The World Council of Whalers (WCW), formally established in 1997, offers assistance to groups wishing to resuscitate a whaling tradition.[67] The WCW held its first general assembly in March 1998, with eighteen nations represented. The purpose of the WCW is to promote the sustainable harvest of whales by community-based whalers and to include all whale-resource users such as whale watchers and researchers.[68] The council adopted a resolution supportive of efforts by Iceland, the Nuu-Chah-Nulth First Nationals of British Columbia (who announced in April 1997 their intention to hunt gray whales off the west coast of Vancouver Island for the first time in seventy years[69]), and four small whaling communities in Japan to use whales sustainably.[70] With a victory in the hands of the Makah, other tribes are following their example and seeking similar treaty rights and permits to hunt whales.

The formation of regional and international management groups aimed at the same transboundary resource is not unusual. In fact, in November 1996, seventeen governments met to negotiate and adopt the Agreement on the Conservation of Cetaceans of the Black Sea, Mediterranean Sea, and Contiguous Atlantic Area, an agreement pursuant to Article IV, paragraph 4, of the Convention on the Conservation of Migratory Species of Wild Animals.[71] The agreement specifically noted the importance of other global and regional instruments relevant to the conservation of cetaceans, such as the International Convention for the Regulation of Whaling. Rather than replace the ICRW, the nations stressed the need to promote and facilitate cooperation among states, regional economic interaction organizations, intergovernmental organizations, and the nongovernmental sector for the conservation of cetaceans. Thus, the existence of additional management regimes is not unusual and does not necessarily indicate the termination of previous agreements or regimes.

The IWC has, however, experienced a bipolarization between preservationists and conservationists, pitting antiwhaling nations against whaling nations, and has become a stage for airing conflicts. This division leaves the authority and regulatory structure of the IWC vulnerable. With a breakdown in the trust and goodwill needed to make IWC management work, it is no surprise that whalers have sought out alternative management regimes. These regimes can undermine the relevance and legitimacy of the IWC. If outside international and regional regimes provide better management and cooperation between member nations, the result may be the disintegration of the IWC, or at least a reevaluation of its mission and of the terms of the ICRW.

The rise of these regimes raises questions for the future of U.S. whaling policy. The United States can step up and guide the IWC into "regaining" control over the management of whaling, or it must begin active involvement in other whaling regimes. It is no longer adequate for the United States to send a delegation to IWC meetings once a year because the future of whale management may not be with the IWC.

Impacts of U.S. Foreign Policy on the Changing Whale Regime

U.S. foreign policy has reflected a steadfast opposition to commercial whaling in all contexts. To be sure, the United States offered support to the Makah tribe only if the hunt were to be used for nutritional and ceremonial needs, not commercial trade. Yet, the United States has sent other messages.

First, the United States has shown a willingness to ignore scientific evidence. In a 1993 letter to the International Whaling Commission, President Clinton stated that the U.S. whaling policy would continue to be based on the best scientific evidence available.[72] However, two decades prior, the United States pushed for the bowhead quota for the Alaskan Eskimo, avoiding discussion of the biological needs of the stock in order to focus on the "domestic dilemma concerning Eskimo people's subsistence rights."[73] The members of both the Panel Meeting of Experts on Aboriginal Subsistence Whaling (which met in Seattle in February 1979 to review the Alaskan aboriginal hunt) and the IWC Scientific

Committee agreed that "from a biological point of view, the only safe course is to reduce the kill . . . to zero."[74]

Despite such agreement, the United States continued to lobby for the Alaskan Eskimo quota to meet both the cultural and nutritional needs of the people. The United States, as it promised the IWC, stepped up its research efforts in the Bering Sea, resulting in increases in the IWC stock estimates.[75] Thus, when conflict arose, the United States established its own precedent favoring the aboriginal needs of a U.S. constituency over the needs of the Bering Sea bowhead whale. Decades later, the United States could flaunt the health of the gray whale stocks as support for a Makah quota and a resumption of the whale hunt.

As scientific assessment of stocks become more important in the determination of quotas and, possibly, a return to commercial whaling worldwide, the United States may find it difficult selling itself as a member nation that follows "the best scientific evidence available" in defining its whale policies.

In addition, the United States has shown a willingness to sidestep international procedures. Aware that it probably did not have the necessary votes to establish the Makah aboriginal quota, the United States took a determined step to ignore international procedure and established a new method of granting an aboriginal quota: the quota swap. Such a maneuver left fellow IWC members exasperated. After advocating proper procedure in stock assessments and changes in IWC regulations, the United States undermined its position as a credible party to the ICRW. Furthermore, it established a negative precedent on the question of aboriginal subsistence-whaling quotas. Not only may parties use a "quota swap," but they may also seek out quotas for peoples who may not meet the requirements of the ICRW for an aboriginal quota. One advocate argues that the United States has effectively created a new category of whale killing, "cultural whaling," for those peoples who have a cultural justification for whale hunting but not a subsistence need for it.[76] This precedent may return to haunt the United States in future negotiations with Japan, the IWC member that has attempted for years to secure a cultural whaling quota for four small coastal communities.[77]

As the international whaling regime undergoes changes in the coming years, the United States will have to overcome its inconsistent policies and the impact its position regarding the Alaskan Eskimo bowhead whale and the Makah gray whale quotas has had on its whaling policy.

Monaco's Prince Rainier opened the 1997 IWC meeting by stating that the "tense conflict between the whaling and anti-whaling factions seems more and more a no-win situation."[78] The failure of the IWC to follow the terms of the convention has led member and nonmember nations to join regional and international bodies created to promote and manage international whale harvests. Although not actively supporting or advocating the creation of separate international organizations to manage whale stocks, U.S. actions in support of preservation over sustainable harvest, as laid out in the ICRW, have indirectly advanced the establishment of new management bodies. Because of its influence in the IWC, some view the United States as a leader in the international preservation of whale stocks. But the IWC has transformed its role from manager of harvests to protector of whale stocks.[79] In the past, American influence might have played a role in effective conservation of whale stocks, but this harsh reality may prevent successful negotiations with whaling nations.

The Future of U.S. Whaling Policy

The United States maintains that it is an antiwhaling nation. U.S. whaling policy has been characterized by both domestic and international policies encouraging the conservation of whale species.[80] The public has long supported this position; conservationists in the United States were making efforts to halt the rapid decimation of whale stocks as early as 1920.[81] But U.S. whaling policy has entered a new era. The increase of stocks around the world, the negotiation of new international regimes to manage and promote whaling, and policy decisions to support aboriginal groups in the United States now offer sometimes competing goals for U.S. foreign policy. A good barometer for the future of foreign policy is the public opinion of the American people and the federal government's response to it.

Foreign Policy According to the American Public
In 1994, as Vice President Gore negotiated with whaling nations over the IWC Revised Management Plan, word of a compromise deal with whaling nations leaked to the U.S. press. An outraged public sent thousands of protest telegrams to Gore and President Clinton.[82] Perhaps it was these citizens who backed the groups that filed suit against the Department of Commerce for permitting the Makah gray whale hunt in U.S. waters and that challenged the Coast Guard regulation requiring protestors to keep a distance from any Makah whaling vessel. However, when faced with whale protection in their own waters, the American public can be divided. When the federal government proposed a marine sanctuary for humpback whales in Hawaii in 1996, opponents feared that new laws restricting recreational and commercial ocean activities would come along with the protected area.[83] Citizens of Hawaii and representatives from commercial and recreational users formed an organization called People Opposed to the Whale Sanctuary (POWS) to fight the designation. Members of POWS argued that the sanctuary would compete with private educational programs and impose additional regulations limiting their ability to do business.[84]

Even with these efforts, proponents of whaling assert on the one hand that the American public is "woefully ill-informed regarding whales and whaling."[85] On the other hand, the Japan Whaling Association claims that 71 percent of Americans support the regulated taking of minke whales for food by traditional whaling countries.[86] This statistic raises doubts as to whether U.S. whaling policy is truly based on the desires of the American public, as the government claims.

Foreign Policy According to the President

From early in the Clinton administration, U.S. policy has been to oppose whaling that fails to meet IWC regulations. When Norway undertook commercial whaling in 1993, the United States declined to impose sanctions immediately, although it tried "exhausting other avenues" through negotiating and encouraging voluntary compliance.[87] In 1997, the president informed Congress that Canada's permitting of aboriginal hunts outside of IWC management "jeopardizes the international effort that has allowed whale stocks to begin to recover from the devastating effects of historic whaling."[88] The president instructed the Department of State to oppose Canadian efforts to take marine mammals within the Arctic Circle and the Department of Commerce to withhold consideration of any Canadian requests for waivers to the existing moratorium on the importation of seals or seal products into the United States.[89] The administration has also consistently insisted that the U.S. position on whaling should be guided by science.[90] Consistent with this goal, President Clinton encouraged research for the health of the oceans during 1998, the International Year of the Ocean,[91] and he called on Congress to ratify the Law of the Sea Convention.[92] Furthermore, Clinton took specific steps to remedy a known threat to the northern right whale by instructing the U.S. delegation to the International Maritime Organization to propose the requirement that commercial ships entering the whale's calving and feeding areas report to the U.S. Coast Guard in order to avoid potential collisions.[93]

Foreign Policy According to the Congress

Resolutions passed in the 1990s indicate that the U.S. Congress will not soon "give in" to commercial whaling interests. Numerous congresses have passed resolutions reaffirming the U.S. position that the "continued whaling and commercialization of whale meat represent a violation"[94] of the IWC ban and that the United States should "work to strengthen the [IWC] as the indispensable organization for safeguarding for future generations the great natural resources represented by the whale stocks."[95] The Senate adopted a resolution calling for the United States to "remain firmly opposed to commercial whaling" at the 1998 meeting of the IWC and to "support the permanent protection of whale populations through the establishment of whale sanctuaries in which commercial whaling is prohibited."[96] In addition, the Senate called for the United States to "make full use of all appropriate diplomatic mechanisms, relevant international law, and agreements, and other appropriate mechanisms" to implement U.S. antiwhaling policy.[97]

Congressional commentary regarding marine mammal bills and resolutions offers a glimpse at the support for an antiwhaling policy and the contempt for whaling nations. For example, in 1992, Congressman Arthur Ravenel urged then-president George Bush to instruct the U.S. delegation to the IWC "not to wimp out under pressure from Japan, Norway, and Iceland, whose greed would turn these greatest of God's creatures into dog food and cosmetics."[98] Speaking in support of a House resolution opposing commercial whaling, Congressman Gerry Studds of Massachusetts used economics to show the value of whales as live creatures rather than as whale meat. Congressman Studds explained that "in southeastern Massachusetts, the old tradition of hunting whales for profit has been replaced by a new enterprise—watching whales for profit. This industry brings almost two million whale watchers to Massachusetts Bay each year, with a resulting tourism income for the State of over one billion dollars annually."[99]

Domestic groups and Congress consistently express definitive, if not always rational, positions against whaling. They offer impassioned arguments for the likely future of U.S. whaling policy: opposition to commercial whaling at all levels, from factory ship to aboriginal boat.

Conclusion

Since 1990, when the IWC was to reconsider the international moratorium on commercial whaling, whaling and nonwhaling nations alike have braced for the removal of the ban and a return to IWC-sanctioned whaling. As of 1998, the IWC showed signs of discussion but no signs of relenting to legalize commercial harvests.[100] Many still fear the long-term effects of a legal commercial hunt, such as creation of new incentives and rewards for expanding the harvests over time to levels that might deplete stocks again. The U.S. position on whaling adopts a cautious stance, remaining opposed to commercial whaling at all levels. But with the current divisiveness among IWC member nations, imprecise U.S. policies on the use of science-based management, and U.S. approval of aboriginal whaling, the United States may lose its position as a leader in whale protection. It has failed to recognize the current trend toward whale management. Influence over stock management may not be the only casualty. The United States must also consider its leadership in combating the wide range of new and increasing threats to whales, such as noise pollution, fishing nets and boat collisions, degradation of whale habitats by toxins, and climate change. U.S. foreign policy on whaling may have to move into line with other nations, abandoning strict conservation for international management—commercial harvesting—of the least-endangered whales. In order to lead on these future issues and to preserve the great whales, U.S. foreign policy may have to "migrate with the whales."

Notes

1 Research for this essay was sponsored in part by the National Oceanic and Atmospheric Administration, U.S. Department of Commerce (Grant No.

NA56RG0129), the Mississippi-Alabama Sea Grant Consortium, and the Mississippi Law Research Institute at the University of Mississippi Law Center. The views expressed here are my own.

2 Lawrence Juda, *International Law and Ocean Use Management: The Evolution of Ocean Governance* (London: Routledge, 1996), 68.

3 For a comprehensive review of the history of whaling, see Patricia Birnie, *International Regulation of Whaling* (New York: Oceana, 1985), 2: 65–70.

4 Juda explains that this new ability to operate in distant locales was a result, in part, of the need to find remote grounds given the depletion of more accessible stocks. Juda, *International Law*, 68.

5 Committee for Whaling Statistics, *International Whaling Statistics* (Cambridge: IWC, 1939), 12: 3, 13.

6 League of Nations, *Official Journal* (1927), 754 forty-fifth session of the council, first meeting.

7 League of Nations Archives, Economic Committee, *Report to the Council* (1929), c.307.m.106.1929.II, 7.

8 Lewis Radcliffe, *Economics of the Whale Fisheries* (n.p.: n.p, 1928), 7–8, League of Nations Archives, 3E/4010/466(1928–32), Geneva.

9 The full text of this draft convention appears in League of Nations, "Draft Convention for the Regulation of Whaling," C.353.M.146.1930.II., 1930.

10 Juda, *International Law*, 71.

11 "International Convention for the Regulation of Whaling," Treaties and Other International Acts (TIAS), 2 December 1946, *United States Treaties and Other International Agreements* [hereafter 1946 convention], no. 1849.

12 Ibid., preamble.

13 See Anthony D'Amato and Sudhir Chopra, "Whales: Their Emerging Right to Life," *American Journal of International Law* 85 (1991): 21, 29.

14 Reliance on whale products decreased during the twentieth century. For instance, in the United States, with the emergence of the petroleum industry, the whaling industry gradually declined as whale oil was replaced with the more abundant and more easily acquired petroleum. Ibid.

15 See William C. Burns, "The International Whaling Commission and the Future of Cetaceans: Problems and Prospect," *Colorado Journal of International Environmental Law and Policy* 8 (1997): 31, 53.

16 Tim Friend, "Genetic Clues Allow Watchdogs to Pinpoint Poaching of Whales," *USA Today*, 18 November 1997, D7.

17 Keith Schneider, "Balancing Nature's Claims and International Free Trade," *New York Times*, 19 January 1992, sec. 4, 5.

18 Craig R. Whitney, "Norway Is Planning to Resume Whaling Despite World Ban," *New York Times*, 30 June 1992, A1. Norway exercised the objection against the moratorium that it had taken under the International Convention for the Regulation of Whaling. See Burns, "International Whaling Commission," 50–53. In 1998, the Norwegian minke whaling season finished with

624 whales caught from a total of 671 allowed. Per Rolandsen, High North Web News (available at <http://www.highnorth.no/>), Environmental News Network (hereafter ENN) daily news, available at <http://www.enn.com>, 20 August 1998.

19 See Milton Freeman, "Is United States' Whaling Policy What the Public Wants?" in *Additional Essays on Whales and Man* (Reine i Lofoten, Norway: High North Alliance, 1995), 16–19.

20 Stephen M. Hankins, "The United States' Abuse of the Aboriginal Whaling Exception: A Contradiction in United States Policy and a Dangerous Precedent for the Whale," *University of California–Davis Law Review* 24 (1990): 489, 490.

21 Richard Kirk Eichstaedt, " 'Save the Whales' v. 'Save the Makah': The Makah and the Struggle for Native Whaling," *Animal Law* 4 (1998): 145, 150.

22 See Statement by Dr. Robert M. White, United States Delegation to the United Nations Conference on the Human Environment, reprinted in *Department of the State Bulletin* 67 (1972): 112. White explained, "We feel that strong action in restoring the world whale stocks is a matter of great urgency. . . . A moratorium would allow time for stocks to start rebuilding [and] to develop a fund of knowledge as a basis for effective long-term management." Ibid., 112–13.

23 Each year, the ban failed to win the necessary three-quarters support of the member nations. See Hankins, "United States' Abuse," 501.

24 "Opening Statement of the United States to the International Whaling Commission," *31st Meeting of the IWC* (Cambridge: IWC, 1979).

25 William J. Clinton, *Report on International Whaling Conservation Program* (Washington, D.C.: White House, Office of Communications, 1996).

26 *Remarks by President Clinton of the United States and Prime Minister Brundtland of Norway* (Washington, D.C.: White House, Office of Communications, 18 May 1994).

27 Greg Donovan, "The International Whaling Commission and Aboriginal/ Subsistence Whaling: April 1979 to July 1981," *Report of the International Whaling Commission* 83, no. 4 (1981), 4.

28 See Leesteffy Jenkins and Cara Romanzo, "Makah Whaling: Aboriginal Subsistence or a Stepping Stone to Undermining the Commercial Whaling Moratorium," *Colorado Journal of International Environmental Law and Policy* 9 (1993): 71, 77–80, quote on 77.

29 The exception is part of the original 1946 convention; see schedule 1, paragraph 2.

30 See Hankins, "United States' Abuse," 513–14.

31 "Chairman's Report of the Special Meeting, Tokyo, December 1977," *Twenty-ninth Report of the International Whaling Commission 1977–78* (Cambridge: IWC, 1978), 2.

32 "Report of the Scientific Committee of the International Whaling Commission," *Thirty-second Report of the International Whaling Commission 1980–81* (Cambridge: IWC, 1982), 43, 55–56.

33 Hankins, "United States' Abuse," 522. Hankins argues that by "persuading the IWC to grant it permission for the hunts, against all scientific evidence, the United States has forced the IWC to revert to its exploitative practices of the past." Ibid.

34 Robert Sullivan, "Permission Granted to Kill a Whale, Now What?" *New York Times Magazine*, 9 August 1998, 30, 31.

35 "Final Rule to Remove Gray Whale from Endangered Species List," *Federal Register* 59 (16 June 1994): 31094.

36 See Mark Trumbill, "Indians Hope to Harpoon New Whale Hunting Rights," *Christian Science Monitor*, 25 July 1995, 1.

37 Article IV of the Treaty of Neah Bay states that it secures the Makah "[t]he right of . . . whaling . . . at usual and accustomed grounds and stations . . . in common with all citizens of the United States." "Treaty with the Makah Tribe," *Statutes at Large* (31 January 1855), 12 Stat. 939, 940, art. IV.

38 See *Thirty-third Report of the International Whaling Commission* (Cambridge: IWC, 1983).

39 Sullivan, "Permission Granted," 32.

40 "Whaling Provisions, Consolidation and Revision of Regulations," *Federal Register* 61 (11 June 1996): 29628.

41 Will Anderson, "Makah Cultural Whaling: The Path to Commercial Whaling," statement from the Progressive Animal Welfare Society, 3 October 1998 (on file with author).

42 See Ministry of Agriculture, Fisheries, and Food, "IWC: Outcome of the International Whaling Conference," *M2 Presswire*, available at <http://www.m2.com/M2_PressWIRE/index.html/>, 8 July 1996.

43 Sea Shepherd Conservation Society, "Summary of 49th International Whaling Commission Meeting in Monaco, October 1997," available at <http://www.seashepherd.org/wh/iwc/iw97sum.html>.

44 Quoted in Scott Sunder and Ed Penhale, "Makahs Hail Go-Ahead for Whale Hunts but Legal and Other Shoals Lie Ahead," *Seattle Post-Intelligencer*, 24 October 1997, A1.

45 "Regulated Navigation Area, Strait of Juan de Fuca and Adjacent Coastal Waters of Washington," *Federal Register* 63 (22 July 1998): 39256. See also "Request for Comments," *Federal Register* 63 (1 October 1998): 52603.

46 *Metcalf v. Daley*, U.S. District Court for the Western District of Washington, Civ. No. 97-2413(HHG), 7 November 1997. The complaint alleges that the Federal National Oceanic and Atmospheric Administration (NOAA) failed to comply with federal law in permitting the taking of gray whales.

47 See Alex Tizon, "Tribe Plans Heavy Makah Days Security—Will Protestors of Whale Hunt Overrun Festival?" *Seattle Times*, 11 August 1998, B1.

48 "Makah Expect Violence over Whale Hunt," *Environmental News Network Daily News*, 11 September 1998, available at <http://www.enn.com/news>.

49 "Four Arrested in Anti-Whaling Protest," *Environmental News Network Daily News*, 2 November 1998, available at <http://www.enn.com/news>.

50 "Makah, Protestors Stay Ashore on First Day of Whale Hunting Season," *CNN Newsclip*, 2 October 1998.

51 David Usborne, "Whale Gives Indians a Taste of Their Heritage," *The Independent* (London), 19 May 1999, 18.

52 Sam How Verhovek, "Protestors Shadow a Tribe's Pursuit of Whales and Past," *New York Times*, 2 October 1998, A1, A13, quoting Paul Watson, leader of the Sea Shepherd Conservation Society.

53 Mark Fineman, "Annual Meeting Ends with Little Resolved as Some Push for More," *Los Angeles Times*, 1 June 1999, A1.

54 See Shigeko Misaki, "Responsible Management of Renewable Resources: Case for Whaling," in *Whaling for the Twenty-first Century* (Tokyo: Institute of Cetacean Research, 1996), 13, 17. Misaki argues that the slowness in implementing the management plans and the maintenance of the moratorium are based on political and cultural centrism, rather than on the needs of the stocks.

55 See "Japan Whaling Association Statement on IWC Credibility," 28 October 1997 (on file with author), which says that "the International Whaling Commission was well on its way toward losing its last vestiges of authority and credibility," and dubs the IWC the "Institution Without Credibility."

56 Milton M. R. Freeman, "Some Thoughts about the International Whaling Debate and the IWC," *Isana* 17 (1997): 11–16.

57 Freeman encourages antiwhaling nations to do just this: "In contemporary environmental terms, the critical question usually asked of any activity that consumes living resources is: 'is the activity sustainable?' " Ibid., 12.

58 For a review of the difficulties with whale stock assessments and the reliance on science in general, see Milton M.R. Freeman, "A Commentary on Political Issues with Regard to Contemporary Whaling," *North Atlantic Studies* 2 (1990): 106, 107–8.

59 Antiwhaling groups had feared the Norwegian stock to be as low as twenty thousand. Walter Gibbs, "Norwegian Whalers Defy 1986 Ban; Countries Favor Limited Whale Trade," *The Commercial Appeal*, 28 July 1997, A8.

60 Quoted in Gibbs, "Norwegian Whalers Defy 1986 Ban," A8.

61 Ibid.

62 Ibid.

63 Quoted in ibid.

64 Geoffrey Varley, "Fears Grow of Surge in Whale-Hunting," *Agence France Presse*, 21 October 1997, International News section.

65 See *High North Alliance News*, 28 August 1998.

66 Ibid., April 1998.

67 "China, Japan, Russia, and South Korea: Establishing a New North Pacific Whaling Regime?" *World Council of Whalers Fact Sheet* (18 April 1998), 3 (available from <wcw@island.net>).

68 Ibid., 2.

69 See "B.C. Indians Plan to Hunt Again" (1997), available at <http://www.oceania.org.au/soundnet/apr97/bchunt.html>.

70 Heida Diefenderfer, "World Council of Whalers Braces for Battle: To Allow Community-Based Whalers a Sustainable Harvest," *News from Indian Country*, 15 February 1997 (on file with author). Interestingly, the WCW does not automatically receive opposition from groups such as Greenpeace. Gerry Leape, Greenpeace spokesman, stated that "Greenpeace does not oppose subsistence whaling . . . but if [a hunt proposal] has a commercial element, such as selling meat to Japan, we will be in the front lines opposing it. . . . We want to shut down commercial whaling because it's the economic incentive that leads to higher and higher quotas and takes us back down the road to ruin for the whale stocks. The only reason the minke whale is not extinct is the International Whaling Commission moratorium on commercial whaling." Ibid.

71 "Final Act and Agreement on the Conservation of Cetaceans of the Black Sea, Mediterranean Sea, and Contiguous Atlantic Area," 1 July 1997, *International Legal Materials* 36, no. 4 (1997): 780–81.

72 William J. Clinton, "Message to the Congress on Whaling Activities of Norway," *Weekly Compilation of Presidential Documents* 29 (4 October 1993), 2000.

73 "Chairman's Report of the Twenty-ninth Meeting," *Twenty-eighth Report of the International Whaling Commission 1976–77* (Cambridge: IWC, 1977), 18.

74 International Whaling Commission, *Aboriginal/Subsistence Whaling* (Cambridge: IWC, 1982), 12: 4.

75 Hankins, "United States' Abuse," 519–20.

76 Ross Anderson, "Whale's Killing Stirs Intense Reactions—Some Have Conflicting Emotions on Success of Makah's Hunt," *Seattle Times*, 18 May 1999, A9, quoting Will Anderson, spokesman for the Progressive Animal Welfare Society.

77 See Milton M.R. Freeman, "A Review of Documents on Small-Type Whaling, Submitted to the International Whaling Commission by the Government of Japan, 1986–95," presented at the IWC Workshop on Japanese Community-Based Whaling, Sendai, Japan, 18 March 1997 (on file with the author).

78 Doug Mellgren, "Makah Tribe's Bid One of Tough Issues for Whaling Meeting," *News Tribune* (Tacoma), 21 October 1997, B1.

79 William Burke, interview by the author, University of Washington School of Marine Affairs, 16 March 1998.

80 See Hankins, "United States' Abuse," 498–505. Hankins offers a review of domestic laws such as the Pelly amendment to the Fishermen's Protective Act of 1967, the Packwood amendment to the Fishery Conservation and Management Act, and the Marine Mammal Protection Act.

81 Michael Bean, *The Evolution of National Wildlife Law* (Westport: Praeger, 1983), 262.

82 Polly Ghazi, "Beasts of Deep 'Betrayed': President Clinton and the Green Movement Are Under Fire After 'Selling Out' to Whalers," *Observer* (London), 24 April 1998.

83 Lisa Busch, "Saving Whales Contentiously," *Bioscience* 46 (1996), 737.

84 Ibid.

85 Milton M.R. Freeman, "Don't Need to Save Every Whale," *Plain Dealer* (Cleveland), 27 July 1993, 7B.

86 "Whaling Commission on Verge of Breakup," *Environmental News Network Daily News*, 8 May 1998, available at <http://www.enn.com/news>.

87 Dee Dee Myers, press briefing, White House Office of Communications, 17 May 1994.

88 William J. Clinton, "President Letter on Policy Versus Canadian Whaling," 11 February 1997, available via Westlaw (PRES file) or on file with the author.

89 Ibid.

90 Ibid.

91 William J. Clinton, Proclamation, "Year of the Ocean 1998, Proclamation 7065," *Federal Register* 63 (28 January 1998): 4553.

92 "Joining the Law of the Sea Convention," White House Office of Communications, 18 June 1998.

93 William J. Clinton, "Statement by the President on Northern Right Whale," White House Office of Communications, 24 April 1998.

94 United States Congress, House of Representatives, H.R. Concurrent Resolution 329, "A concurrent resolution calling for United States sanctions against nations which conduct unjustified whale research, and otherwise expressing the sense of the Congress with regard to nations which violate the International Whaling Commission moratorium on commercial whaling by killing whales under the guise of scientific research," 101st Congress, 2d sess., 2 October 1990.

95 United States Congress, House of Representatives, H.R. Concurrent Resolution 287, "A concurrent resolution for a United States policy of promoting the continuation, for a minimum of an additional 10 years, of the International Whaling Commission's moratorium on the commercial killing of whales, and otherwise expressing the sense of the Congress with respect to conserving and protecting the world's whale populations," 101st Congress, 2d sess., 29 June 1990. See also United States Congress, House of Representatives, HR. Concurrent Resolution 34, 103d Congress, 4 May 1993, claiming "there is significant widespread support in the international community for the view

that for scientific, ecological, and educational reasons, whales should no longer be hunted for profit"; and H.R. Concurrent Resolution 177, "A concurrent resolution calling for a United States policy strengthening and maintaining indefinitely the current International Whaling Commission moratorium on the commercial killing of whales, and otherwise expressing the sense of the Congress with respect to conserving and protecting the world's whale, dolphin, and porpoise populations," 102d Congress, 2d sess., 2 June 1992.

96 United States Congress, Senate, Senate Resolution 226, "Expressing the sense of the Senate regarding the policy of the United States at the 50th Annual Meeting of the International Whaling Commission," (1)(A)(E), 105th Cong., 9 May 1998.

97 Ibid., 2.

98 Ibid., H3395 and H3042 (statement of Representative Ravenel regarding the "whale-eating orgy in Japan" and the "cruel murder" of twelve hundred whales).

99 H.R. Concurrent Resolution 177.

100 Michael Canny, "Opening Statement of the Irish Delegation at the 49th Meeting of the International Whaling Commission," *Report on the 49th Meeting of the International Whaling Committee* (Cambridge: IWC, 1997), 2 (presentation of the "Irish Proposal" to allow for limited commercial whaling in coastal waters).

NATIONAL INTERESTS AND INTERNATIONAL OBLIGATIONS

11 Environment, Security, and Human Suffering: What Should the United States Do?

Paul G. Harris

For much of the twentieth century, the United States has been able to influence international affairs to its advantage by using traditional power capabilities: its strong military and the large, usually vibrant U.S. economy that supports it. However, in a globalized world, such capabilities are much less fungible; it is sometimes—or usually—difficult for the United States to translate its traditional capabilities into concrete influence. International efforts to address changes to the global environment demonstrate this changing situation. The United States, despite its superior economy and vast military arsenal, cannot force other countries to protect environments and global commons (e.g., the atmosphere and oceans) in which it, like most countries, has interests.[1]

The ongoing climate change conferences, such as those at Kyoto in 1997 and Buenos Aires in 1998, demonstrate the limitations of great power capabilities in the environmental issue area. The United States, the world's sole "superpower," could not and cannot tell the economically developing countries, "Reduce your emissions of greenhouse gases—or else." Nuclear bombs, aircraft carriers or other military capabilities—to use extreme examples—are simply of no use in this situation,[2] which suggests that the United States must find more subtle methods for influencing the behavior of other countries.

This chapter argues that the United States can more effectively achieve its foreign policy goals in the environmental issue area, and thereby protect and promote U.S. national interests, by treating other countries, particularly the developing countries, more equitably.[3] Such policies will also promote ethical imperatives, such as taking responsibility for the disproportionate adverse impacts the United States has had on the global environment. The United States is a worthwhile case to look at here, in part because it has yet to comprehend fully the changes in power capabilities inherent to contemporary international affairs and because it has the financial, technological, and diplomatic resources that can be brought to bear on problems of environment and development. It is also the world's greatest polluter, and, as such, has the greatest ethical obligation to redress the wrongs of historical and ongoing global pollution. With regard to environmentally sustainable development, the United States can further its national interests and coincidentally promote ethical goals by meeting many of the demands from developing countries for greater international equity, defined here as a fair and just distribution of the benefits, burdens, and decision-making authority associated with international environmental issues.[4]

Environment, Development, and International Equity

Effective efforts to implement sustainable economic development on a global basis require that the United States and other industrialized countries give serious consideration to demands from the developing countries for equity, and, indeed, that equity be implemented as part of global environmental protection measures.[5] Recent international environmental agreements have codified notions of equity, suggesting what "equity" could look like in reality. Examples include requirements for new and additional funds to assist developing countries in meeting the provisions of international environmental agreements; new or changed international environmental-funding institutions that give developing countries greater authority in decisions regarding the allocation of funds for sustainable development (e.g., the ozone multilateral fund and the Global Environment Facility); and requirements of the ozone and climate change regimes for developed countries to act before and more forcefully than developing countries to address these problems.

In the context of global environmental change, the United States and other industrialized countries have started to give more consideration to international equity and fairness—particularly to the demands by economically less-developed countries for greater international equity.[6] This change is clearer when contrasted with the developing countries' unsuccessful calls in the 1960s and 1970s for greater equity via what was called the New International Economic Order (NIEO). The United States is among those countries that has come to realize that the developing world usually cannot be coerced into cooperating on matters of sustainable development and global environmental protection. Rather, developing countries must be persuaded to cooperate, in part by meeting some of their demands for more equitable treatment in international environmental affairs. Toward this end, the United States has softened its historic opposition to concessional financial and technological assistance to developing countries—although too much opposition remains. To be sure, like most other developed countries, the United States has cut its foreign-assistance spending.[7] Nevertheless, funds have often been redistributed to allow increases in funding for sustainable-development programs.

Concerning climate change specifically, in 1998 the Clinton administration signed the Kyoto Protocol to the Framework Convention on Climate Change (FCCC). During the 1997 negotiations that produced the protocol, U.S. diplomats insisted that developing countries take on "new" and "meaningful" obligations, an arguably inequitable stance. Nevertheless, the United States ended up agreeing to an instrument that—at the insistence of traditionally weak countries—made no mention of such obligations.[8] Instead, the treaty requires *developed* countries to reduce their greenhouse gas emissions by about 5 percent in aggregate.[9] The United States and other developed countries appropriately agreed to take on all the initial burdens of addressing climate change.

Some great powers have realized that being seen as taking on their fair share of global environmental burdens can have benefits. The West Europeans viewed the 1992 United Nations Earth Summit as an avenue to exercise new influence on the developing world. They capitalized on the U.S. government's failure to take a leadership role at the Earth Summit. More recently, the Labour government of Tony Blair in Britain has sought to lead the industrialized world in the climate change negotiations. It insists that it will reduce its greenhouse gases largely in line with the demands of many developing countries, thereby showing its commitment to combat climate change before demanding that the developing countries take on substantial emissions limitations of their own. Of course, some developed countries have acted quite differently: using its own convoluted case for equity relative to other developed countries, Australia successfully argued during the Kyoto negotiations that it should be allowed to *increase* its greenhouse gas emissions.[10]

The U.S. government—particularly the Clinton administration—has gradually come to accept equity as an important objective of its global environmental policy. However, the degree to which it has done so has been limited and no doubt is a great disappointment to environmentalists and advocates of development assistance. In short, recent American willingness to accept the importance of equity in international environmental politics—or at least not to prevent actively and effectively its incorporation into international environmental instruments (including the climate change agreements), as happened more systematically before the advent of Clinton—is a function of many factors: concern for U.S. economic and environmental security, domestic and international political pressures, and the appeal of the notion of equity as a value in itself.[11]

U.S. policy is a response to perceived threats to the national interests from changes to the natural environment. In short, because the participation of developing countries is necessary for effective international efforts to protect the global environment on which Americans depend for their health and economic well-being (China *by itself* may produce a third or more of carbon dioxide [CO_2] emissions in the first half of the next century[12]), the U.S. government has sought to "buy" the participation of the developing countries by offering them the carrots of development aid, technology assistance, and related incentives.

The tardiness of the U.S. government's acceptance of international environmental equity as a policy goal and its failure to do more to implement this policy are largely a function of domestic political pressures. Importantly, however, actors pressuring the government operate in the midst of an emerging consensus on international equity in the context of environmental change. In the case of climate change policy, the Bush administration was receptive to automobile, fossil fuel, and electricity industry arguments against equity. In contrast, the Clinton administration joined with the efficient-energy and insurance industries (among others), as well as environment and development advocacy groups, to make equity an objective of U.S. global environmental policy. (Lobbies still thwart more activist policy, to be sure.) Admittedly, the U.S. government has not gone as far as developing countries want—and indeed as far as many other developed countries, particularly European Union member states, apparently want. But recent U.S. policy has been edging toward the emerging consensus among both developed and developing countries that equity is an important part of international environmental protection efforts.

The U.S. government has also accepted equity as an objective of its global environmental policy because the idea of international equity as a value in itself has appealed to some diplomats and policymakers involved in the process of formulating U.S. foreign environmental policy and negotiating international environmental agreements. Some American diplomats and policymakers view equity as an important objective of an ethical U.S. foreign policy, especially because they do not believe that such a policy threatens any important U.S. interests. Indeed, they see consistency between equity and U.S. national interests, a point that this chapter endeavors to highlight.[13]

Although we are far from seeing the developing countries' demands for a new international economic order realized, adverse environmental changes ranging from local problems such as water pollution and deforestation to (especially) global problems such as ozone depletion and climate change have nevertheless acted as stimuli for considerations of equity in international relations generally and in U.S. foreign policy in particular. Because the developing countries are essential to effective international environmental protection that affects the United States and indeed most countries, notions such as equity are increasingly seen as useful instruments for the creation and effectiveness of international environmental institutions.[14] This approach is unusual by historical standards, as demonstrated by the failure of the NIEO.

Ongoing deliberations regarding global environmental issues will probably be among the most important forums for serious discussions of international equity. To be sure, other international conferences have tackled considerations of international equity (e.g., the United Nations World Summit for Social Development held in Copenhagen in 1995). But it may be in the environmental issue area that the most progress is made, in large measure because so many countries may suffer the consequences of global environmental change and because the developed countries—which are best equipped to take effective action within their own jurisdictions and to finance action in less-affluent countries—have recognized the degree to which poverty and traditional industrialization in the poor countries may affect their own environmental security and economic vitality.

Environmental issues, more than any others, are compelling governments and diplomats the world over to consider equity seriously.[15] In short, environmental change and requirements for sustainable development in the global South have pushed equity onto the global political agenda.

This is not to say that the battle of developing countries has been won—far from it. Rhetoric has clearly outpaced tangible policy. Nevertheless, considerations of equity have started to take on a life of their own. Even outside the realm of international environmental relations, it is no longer easy for the United States (or other great powers) to treat weaker and poorer countries in ways that contradict commonly accepted notions of fairness. To do so may result in unfavorable responses not only from the victims, who have the capacity to hurt the United States in the long term, especially with regard to environmental matters, but also from other developed countries, thereby adversely affecting U.S. influence in international politics generally. Examples of the inclusion of equity considerations abound in the international environmental area: the Montreal Protocol on Substances that Deplete the Ozone Layer contains equity provisions (e.g., grace periods for developing countries and a multilateral development fund), and the FCCC and related agreements provide for "common but differentiated responsibility" (meaning the developed countries must act first and aid the developing countries if they are to take action)[16] in order to garner willing participation of the developing countries in these instruments.

With the foregoing in mind, the remainder of this chapter examines some of the practical and normative implications of adopting and embracing equity as an objective of global environmental policy—and, in particular, policy on global climate change—for the United States and for the world, as well as the implications that such a policy would have for American global power in the new century.[17]

Environment, Equity, and U.S. Foreign Policy: Practical Implications

By promoting considerations of international environmental equity, the United States can help protect its national interests adversely affected by environmental change and related poverty in the developing world.[18] The Clinton administration tried to move the United States in this direction, at least relative to historical standards of U.S. foreign policy. But substantial financial and diplomatic resources did not follow the administration's rhetoric. It failed to muster the robust support of the entire foreign policy establishment, and it faced tremendous hurdles, most notably in convincing the Republican-controlled Congress of the merits of funding this type of policy. The Congress has been generally opposed to new foreign aid; foreign-assistance spending continues to fall in the United States, already dipping below .08 percent of gross domestic product (GDP)—compared to more than 1.0 percent in some West European and Nordic countries.[19]

In failing to embrace international equity, the United States is developing a bad reputation in the eyes of many other international actors, logically leading to questions about the extent to which the United States can be trusted to treat them fairly and equitably in the cooperative arrangements that are increasingly important to promoting U.S. goals in international affairs. By becoming a leader with regard to considerations of international environmental equity and international equity generally, the United States could bolster its global influence and power in the coming decades.

Dangers Posed to the National Interest by Environmental Change
Although the U.S. government has slowly come to recognize that environmental changes can threaten American interests,[20] it has failed to give those threats the high priority (relative to traditional threats) that they require, and it has been slow to recognize that by promoting international environmental equity, it can reduce the likelihood that those threats will adversely affect U.S. interests.

Recent reports on climate change from the Intergovernmental Panel on Climate Change (IPCC) and the World Health Organization (WHO) have added urgency to this issue. The second assessment report of the IPCC concluded that climate change is under way, that it is at least in part the result of human activities, and that urgent action is required to prevent substantial increases in the earth's temperature during the next century.[21] The WHO report describes expected consequences to human health from climate change. According to that report, climate change, by altering local weather patterns and disturbing life-supporting natural systems and processes, will "affect the health of human populations. The range of health effects would be diverse, often unpredictable in magnitude, and sometimes slow to emerge. Adverse effects are likely to outweigh beneficial effects substantially."[22]

The WHO report concluded that climate change will likely lead to these kinds of hazards: by the middle of the next century, many major cities around the world could be experiencing up to several thousand extra heat-related deaths each year (much as Chicago experienced deadly heat waves in 1995 and 1998); a substantial increase in the proportion of the world's population living in malaria transmission zones (including southern portions of the United States); increased risk of infectious disease, asthma, and other acute and chronic respiratory disorders and deaths; an overall decrease in world cereal production (raising prices and perhaps reducing supplies in the United States);[23] changes in ocean temperatures, currents, nutrient flows, and winds that may adversely affect aquatic productivity; regional increases in frequency of droughts and heavy precipitation, leading to flooding and related deaths and injuries (this hazard applies especially to developing countries, but the United States got a taste of what might happen when it experienced nationwide damage during El Niño–related weather events in 1997 and 1998); sea-level rise leading to population displacement, lost agricultural land and fisheries, freshwater salinization, and social disruption; coastal storm surges and resulting damage to coastal infrastructure (e.g., wastewater and sanitation facilities, housing, roads); and increased exposure to ultraviolet radiation as a consequence of ozone loss exacerbated by climate change.[24]

Increasingly, the military threats to U.S. interests that characterized the Cold War are being joined or replaced by threats from environmental change and related economic changes impacting on the U.S. economy, the American way of life, and overseas interests.[25] Climate change, loss of species, ozone depletion, ocean pollution, and the like pose direct threats to the health and well-being of Americans. These local environmental changes and more can also reduce the ability of other countries, particularly developing countries, to purchase U.S. exports, thus affecting the U.S. economy. Former Secretary of State Warren Christopher pointed out that by the end of the century 80 percent of the world's consumers will live in the developing countries. He said that the United States ought to give greater attention to the "interlocking threats of insupportable population growth, endemic poverty and environmental degradation."[26] If the United States fails to do so, according to Christopher, "the result will be widespread suffering abroad and the loss of export opportunities for American companies, worker and farmers."[27] Secretary Christopher's successor, Madeleine Albright, echoed these comments when she said that "damage to the global environment, whether it is over fishing of the oceans, the build-up of greenhouse gases in the atmosphere, the release of chemical pollutants, or the destruction of tropical forests, threatens the health of the American people and the future of our economy. . . . [E]nvironmental problems are often at the heart of the political and economic challenges we face around the world."[28]

Environmental changes can contribute to migrations of large numbers of individuals to the United States and other developed countries, as well as to nearby developing countries even less able to deal with their arrival, thus contributing to domestic conflicts derived from ethnic hatreds and competition for jobs.[29] What is more, environmental changes can lead to humanitarian disasters to which the United States may feel the need to respond as compelled by domestic and world opinion. Such untended environmental threats will leave an unwanted legacy to American children in the form of a polluted, likely hotter, less-predictable global environment populated by fewer desirable species.

In an overview of the 1995 foreign affairs budget, Secretary Christopher stated that the United States

> can no longer escape the consequences of environmental degradation, unsustainable population growth, and destabilizing poverty beyond our borders. Increasingly, they threaten not just our continued prosperity but our security. Countries with persistent poverty, worsening environmental conditions, and feeble social infrastructure are not just poor markets for our products. They are likely victims of conflicts and crises that can only be resolved by costly American intervention. Supporting the developing world's efforts to promote economic growth and allevi-

ate chronic conditions of poverty serves America's interests. . . . By helping nations to emerge from poverty, we can help them become stable pillars of regions at peace, and closer partners of ours in diplomacy and trade.[30]

Similarly, in 1998, Secretary Albright said that environmental threats facing the United States "are not as spectacular as those of a terrorist's bomb or missiles. But we know that the health of our families will be affected by the health of the global environment. The prosperity of our families will be affected by whether other nations develop in sustainable ways. . . . And the security of our nation will be affected by whether we are able to prevent conflicts from arising over scarce resources."[31]

The Clinton administration gave strong *rhetorical* support to a reinterpretation of the national interest that includes environmental change and sustainable development (see chapter 3 of this volume). In 1994, Timothy Wirth, then undersecretary of state for global affairs, told an audience that the life-support systems of the planet were being undermined by human activities and that the security of Americans was "inextricably linked" with nature. The security of the United States hinged, he said, "upon whether we can strike a sustainable, equitable balance between human numbers and the planet's capacity to support life."[32] He added that U.S. security "depends on more than military might [because] boundaries are porous; environmental devastation and disease do not stop at national borders." According to Wirth,

> The primary threats to human security may not be as easy to recognize as, say, an enemy's nuclear arsenal, but they are no less deadly. These are the threats posed by the abject poverty in which one billion of the world's people live; the hunger that stalks 800 million men, women, and children; the spread of HIV/ AIDS . . . ; and the combination of violence, poverty, and environmental degradation that have forced 20 million people from their homes. Here in the United States and around the globe, we are coming to understand the close connections between poverty, the environment, the economy, and security. This historic transformation demands that we now liberate ourselves—from outworn policies, from old assumptions, from fixed views that only yesterday seemed to be the dividing and defining lines of our politics. Crises prevention and the challenge of sustainable development are among the great challenges for the remainder of this and into the next century. It is time to retool our approach to national security—recognizing that our economic and environmental futures are one and the same.[33]

Thus, U.S. officials have clearly recognized that successfully combating problems caused by environmental changes requires a redefinition and reprioritization of national interests. To be sure, threats from nuclear proliferation, terrorism, drugs, industrial espionage, and the like will and should remain high on the political and national security agenda, but it may be essential for the U.S.

government to include environmental changes alongside these more traditional concerns before the processes that are causing the environmental threats become so irreversible that no amount of U.S. effort will be enough to prevent their adverse consequences.

Defending American Interests through International Environmental Equity

Under President Clinton, the U.S. government took steps toward a redefinition of which issues constitute core security threats.[34] Policymakers were then faced (and will continue to be) with finding effective *means* to address environmental threats to U.S. interests. In conjunction with defining environmental threats as first-order threats, the U.S. government has had to look for cost-effective and efficacious ways to mitigate or reverse those threats. As suggested above, this mitigation will require the involvement of most of the world's large countries—especially the large developing countries such as China, Brazil, and India—that are rapidly outpacing the developed countries as the primary contributors to adverse global environmental changes. Indeed, it is precisely these countries that the United States wants to join commitments to one day limit their greenhouse gases in the context of the climate change negotiations.[35]

Developing countries will be more likely to participate in international environmental institutions if they believe that they are being treated with fairness and equity. This means giving due consideration to the historical consequences of industrialization, to the world's skewed consumption patterns, and to the capacities of developed countries to finance the restructuring that will be necessary to achieve sustainable development and thereby mitigate threatening environmental change. As Philip Shabecoff reminds us, recent international environmental deliberations such as the United Nations Conference on Environment and Development (UNCED, meeting as the 1992 Earth Summit), in addition to highlighting the vulnerability of the global environment, "drove home the lesson that unless we care for human needs and wants, we cannot preserve the habitability of the planet. . . . [T]he imminent threats to security were recognized [at the Earth Summit] to be the twinned crises of economic inequity and ecological destruction."[36]

Alongside a reconceptualization of core threats to the national interest, therefore, the requirements of international environmental cooperation to address global environmental changes highlight the need for a greater emphasis in U.S. foreign policy on means beyond traditional military and economic resources for protecting and advancing U.S. interests. Ideas, reputation, and the capacity to shape institutions are forms of "power" that can be convertible into achievement of U.S. objectives in international affairs. Joseph Nye points out that if a state "can help support institutions that encourage other states to channel or limit their activities in ways the dominant state prefers, it may not need as many costly exercises of coercive or hard power in bargaining situations."[37]

The United States is likely to retain its superpower status in terms of traditional power resources well into the twenty-first century. However, as Nye argues, a country's power is not found simply in material resources but in the extent to which it is able to change the behavior of other countries. "Thus the critical question for the future United States is not whether it will start the next century as a superpower with the largest supply of resources, but to what extent it will be able to control the political environment and to get other nations to do what it wants. The tasks involved in maintaining superpower status will become more complicated in the coming decades, involving a far broader range of issues and a wider variety of players."[38] U.S. "coercive" or "hard" power—a large economy and vast military arsenal—frequently cannot be converted into desired behavior by other countries and indeed by nonstate actors. Witness the intransigence of developing countries at the Kyoto climate change conference or the difficulties associated with managing the recent Asian economic crisis.

To maintain its power, the United States should find methods to persuade countries to behave in ways that promote an orderly international system conducive to its interests and that simultaneously give other countries reason to believe that their own interests will be promoted.[39] There is, according to Nye, "an indirect way to exercise power":

> A country may achieve the outcomes it prefers in world politics because other countries want to follow it or have agreed to a system that produces such effects. In this sense, it is just as important to set the agenda and structure the situations in world politics as it is to get others to change in particular situations. This aspect of power—that is, getting others to do what you want—might be called indirect or co-optive power behavior. It is in contrast to the active command power of getting others to do what you want. Co-optive power can rest on the attraction of one's ideas or on the ability to set the political agenda in a way that shapes the preferences that others express.[40]

This "soft" co-optive power complements more traditional forms of command power. Not surprisingly, "If a state can make its power legitimate in the eyes of others, it will encounter less resistance to its wishes."[41]

However, the United States seems seldom to recognize—or at least seldom to act on the recognition—that a country can bolster its long-term influence by establishing a reputation as an equitable actor. Much as people assume that other individuals will behave in ways that are similar to their past behavior, rational governments will likely expect other countries to act in ways similar to their past actions. According to Robert Keohane, if "a continuing series of issues is expected to arise in the future, and as long as actors monitor each other's behavior and discount the value of agreements on the basis of past compliance, having a good reputation is valuable even to the egoist whose role in collective activity is so small that she would bear few of the costs of her own malefactions."[42] As Keohane put it more simply, "A good reputation makes it easier for a government to enter into advantageous international agreements; tarnishing that reputation imposes costs by making agreements more difficult to reach."[43]

In his widely cited examination of international regimes, Keohane points out that morality can "pay" for governments. By adhering to accepted moral codes, states can identify themselves as "political cooperators" who are among the group of actors "with whom mutually beneficial agreements can be made." According to Keohane,

> publicly accepting a set of principles as morally binding may perform a labeling function. If the code were too passive—turn the other cheek—the moralist could be exploited by the egoist, but if the code prescribes reciprocity in a "tit-for-tat" manner, it may be a valuable label for its adherents. Each egoistic government could privately dismiss moral scruples, but if a moral code based on reciprocity were widely professed it would be advantageous for even those governments to behave as if they believed it. Vice would pay homage to virtue.[44]

Robert McElroy has argued that "equitable trust" forms the basis for the observance of moral norms in the international system.[45] States find that they can benefit by entering into continuing cooperative relationships even when the exact obligations and responsibilities of participants cannot be specified in advance. But in such arrangements states want to ensure, as much as they can, that other participants will behave equitably in those unspecified situations. Consequently, countries with reputations for equitable conduct will substantially enhance their abilities, first, to enter into cooperative relationships and, subsequently, to profit from those relationships. Importantly, the advantages that accrue for those states that have developed reputations for acting equitably are not restricted to relations between states with similar power capabilities: according to McElroy, even "a hegemon will have an interest in developing a reputation for behaving equitably in its cooperative relationships so that it can form such relationships with minimal compliance costs."[46] Thus, most or all states have an incentive to acquire the label "equitably trustworthy." Following moral norms can help states do that. Those not following international moral norms may be labeled as "nonequitable," thereby undermining their ability to join and influence subsequent cooperative arrangements—and also undermining the ability of hegemons to gain cost-effective compliance with those arrangements.

McElroy argues that "It is not really surprising that moral norms should serve this function. 'In ongoing contractual relations we find such broad norms as distributive justice, human dignity, social equality and inequality, and procedural justice' [citing Ian Macneil]. The fact that a nation follows an international moral norm can signal that the nation respects these values in its international dealings; conversely, the fact that a nation violates an international moral norm can lead other states to label it noncooperative and exploitative."[47] Such notions can be applied to contemporary security issues. Lawrence Freedman argues that Western democracies have more discretion when engaging contemporary security problems. "Credible rationales" are now critical to building support—both domestically and internationally—for security actions. These new security imperatives have, according to Freedman, "encouraged sensitivity to the normative [and] ethical dimensions of foreign policy."[48]

Many countries now seem to be seriously talking about equity, much more so than during the heyday of the NIEO—at least in the environmental issue area.[49] Among the noteworthy examples of this discussion are the equity provisions of recent international environmental agreements, such as the Montreal Protocol on stratospheric ozone depletion and the climate change and biodiversity conventions signed at the Earth Summit. Those instruments demand that developed countries provide new and additional funds to help developing countries meet the provisions of the agreements. They call for concessional technology transfers from north to south, and they make adjustments to funding arrangements to allow the least-affluent parties to take part in decisions regarding the allocation of funding to address adverse global environmental changes.[50]

Once equity becomes a common part of international discourse, it becomes a norm, and discussions turn to the subject of how to operate in that norm. Equity takes on a somewhat independent role that is beyond traditional power relationships and calculations. According to Marc Levy, Robert Keohane, and Peter Haas, "When international principles and norms have been agreed upon, they may acquire a certain legitimacy and come to be regarded as premises, or as intrinsically valuable, rather than as contestable reflections of interest-based compromises."[51] Working Group III of the Intergovernmental Panel on Climate Change observed that "A broad view of self-interest often points towards explicit consideration of equitable outcomes because of the longer-term risks that grossly inequitable behavior may pose to stability and cooperation in the international system."[52] Increasingly, it is necessary to sell one's objectives to others based on fairness. This view suggests that the contexts of international dialogue are changing, as are the frameworks underlying many international organizations and institutions. It also suggests a change in the way countries behave toward one another, albeit only marginally so far.

As already stated, the U.S. government has been slow to recognize the utility of embracing equity norms and objectives. Many participants in the 1992 Earth Summit commented that the United States—clearly the most powerful country on earth—failed to grasp the "historic opportunity to build the foundations of a new, cooperative international regime."[53] As Shabecoff points out, then-senator Al Gore said at the summit that "Every nation in the world is looking to the United States for leadership."[54] They did not get it. Commenting from the November 1999 Berlin conference of the parties to the FCCC, Philip Clapp, president of the U.S.-based National Environmental Trust, noted that the United States had not changed its ways. It continued to resist calls for it to reduce its greenhouse gas emissions: "If it continues to isolate itself from the rest of the world community by insisting on having its way at every juncture, Americans may actually get their wish. One day, they may discover that its posturing has alienated the United States from its allies, angered its trading partners, and jeopardized its leadership role in the world."[55] The advent of Clinton and Gore to the White House, although leading to a shift in policy toward modest acceptance of equity goals, did not lead to a strong embrace of equity as a policy goal in the environmental issue area—let alone in international policy more broadly.

However, the United States may be able to establish (or maintain) itself as the legitimate leader of the world in the next century by showing that it supports policies intended to bolster international environmental equity and by showing that it supports equitable arrangements in international affairs more generally. The United States can simultaneously establish a reputation as an equitable partner in international environmental politics and promote its interests in preventing or limiting environmental change.[56]

Given a successful outcome on this more limited environmental agenda, the United States might then vigorously promote considerations of equity in international relations generally, thereby establishing its reputation as not only the most "powerful" country in the world, but also one that all states can expect to deal with them fairly and equitably. Although such a policy would be a substantially new one for the United States and would be costly in terms of the financial and diplomatic resources it would require (at least compared to current meager outlays), in the long run it would likely be less costly and more conducive to the promotion of U.S. global interests than is its present policy.

Perhaps what is needed in the medium term is "enlightened" U.S. leadership— dare one use the word *hegemony?*—to prod the world in a direction that does less harm to the ecosystem on which all states and their citizens depend for survival.[57] (Within U.S. academic and policy circles, there has been much interest recently in the merits of U.S. global hegemony.[58]) But such a policy would have to be based in large part on principles of international equity if U.S. leadership were not to be resisted by other countries.

Environment, Equity, and U.S. Foreign Policy: Normative Implications

In addition to promoting U.S. global interests, a more robust acceptance by the U.S. government of international equity as an objective of global environmental policy—and indeed of foreign policy generally—has potentially beneficial implications for humankind. Implementation of the equity provisions of international environmental arrangements may reduce human suffering by helping to prevent changes to local, regional, and global environmental commons that would adversely affect people, most notably the many poor people in the economically developing countries who are least able to cope with environmental changes. Insofar as environmental protection policies focus on sustainable economic development, human suffering may be mitigated as developing countries—especially the least-developed countries—are aided in meeting the basic needs of their citizens. Economic disparities within and between countries are growing. At least one-fifth of the world's population already lives in the squalor of absolute poverty.[59] This situation can be expected to worsen in the future. If this process can be mitigated or reversed by international policies focusing on environmentally sustainable economic development, human well-being on a global scale will rise.

What is more, international cooperative efforts to protect the environment that are made more likely and more effective by provisions for international equity will help governments protect their own environment *and* the global environment if they are successful. Insofar as the planet is one biosphere—that it is in the case of ozone depletion and climate change seems indisputable—persons in every local and national community are simultaneously members of an interdependent whole. Most activities, especially widespread activities in the United States and the rest of the industrialized world, including the release of ozone-destroying chemicals and greenhouse gases, are likely to adversely affect many or possibly all persons on the planet. Efforts to prevent such harm or make amends for historical harm (i.e., past pollution, which is especially important in these examples because many pollutants continue doing harm for years and often decades) require that most communities work together. Indeed, affluent lifestyles in the United States, Western Europe, and other developed areas may harm people in poor areas of the world *more* than they will harm those enjoying such lifestyles because the poor are ill-equipped to deal with the consequences.[60] Furthermore, by concerning themselves with the consequences of their actions on the global poor and polluted, Americans and the citizens of other developed countries will be helping their immediate neighbors—and themselves—in the long run. Actualization of international equity in conjunction with sustainable development may help prevent damage to the natural environment worldwide, thereby promoting human prosperity.

The upshot is that the United States has not gone far enough in actively accepting equity as an objective of global environmental policy. It ought to go further in doing so for purely self-interested reasons. But there are more than self-interested reasons for the United States to move in this direction. It ought to embrace international equity as an objective of its global environmental policy for ethical reasons as well. We can find substantial ethical justification for the United States, in concert with other developed countries, to support politically and financially the codification and implementation of international equity considerations in international environmental agreements. The United States ought to be a leader in supporting a fair and just distribution among countries of the benefits, burdens, and decision-making authority associated with international environmental relations.[61]

To invoke themes found in the corpus of ethical philosophy (but without here assuming the burden of philosophical exegesis!), the United States ought to adopt policies that engender international equity in at least the environmental field (1) to protect the health and well-being of the human species; (2) to promote basic human rights universally; (3) to help the poor be their own moral agents (a Kantian rationale); (4) to help right past wrongs and to take responsibility for past injustices (i.e., past and indeed ongoing U.S. pollution of the global environment); (5) to aid the world's least-advantaged people and countries (a Rawlsian-like conception); (6) and to fulfill the requirement of impartiality (among other ethical reasons)[62]—all in addition to the more clearly self-interested justification that doing so will bolster U.S. credibility and influence in international environmental negotiations and contemporary global politics more generally.

One might argue, therefore, that the United States ought to be aiding the developing countries to achieve sustainable development because to do so may simultaneously reduce human suffering and reduce or potentially reverse environmental destruction that could otherwise threaten the healthy survival of the human species. Insofar as human-caused pollution and resource exploitation deny individuals and their communities the capacity to survive in a healthy condition, the United States, which consumes vastly more than necessary, has an obligation to stop that unnecessary consumption. From this basic rights perspective,[63] the U.S. government should also take steps to reduce substantially the emissions of pollutants from within the United States that harm people in other countries.[64] The United States ought to refrain from unsustainable use of natural resources and from pollution of environmental commons shared by people living in other countries—or at least make a good effort toward that end—because the people affected by these activities cannot reasonably be expected to support them (we would not be treating them as independent moral agents, to make a Kantian argument[65]). The developed countries, especially the United States, deserve the bulk of the blame for historical pollution contributing to climate change. Although the net emissions of greenhouse gases from developing countries are growing fast, the per capita emissions will remain very low relative to the United States, Australia, and other developed countries.[66] Thus, the United States ought to make sure, using Henry Shue's words, that "Poor nations ought not be asked to sacrifice in any way the pace or extent of their own economic development in order to help to prevent the climate [or other environmental] changes set in motion by the process of industrialization that has enriched others [i.e., Americans]."[67] The United States also ought to undertake policies that help the least-well-off countries and individuals in the world who are suffering from environmental changes (e.g., the people of Bangladesh and the small island states who will suffer—they argue that they already are suffering—the most from sea-level rise caused by global warming) because that is likely what Americans would expect of others were the United States in similar circumstances.[68]

And the United States ought to enter international environmental negotiations with the expectation that it should be impartial in its treatment of others, at least insofar as vital U.S. interests are not jeopardized by doing so. American statespersons ought to ask what is reasonable behavior of their government. Is it reasonable to continue to emit pollutants that contribute to climate change and that will likely have especially adverse effects in the poorest countries, and is it reasonable to deny developing countries the help they require to join in efforts to prevent climate change, especially when the United States is disproportionately at fault? The answer seems to be that it is not, leading one to conclude that the United States ought to join international agreements that place requirements on its people to change such unreasonable situations in favor of those adversely affected. In short, "The United States should aid Bangladesh [and other countries threatened or harmed by climate change] not because it is in the United States' interest to do so but because justice as impartiality suggests that the case for such aid cannot be reasonably denied."[69]

Even Hans Morgenthau, perhaps the most important "realist" theorist of international relations in this century, thought that morality could and should influence the foreign policies of nation-states, although he saw it as being much less significant than the garnering of traditional power resources to ensure national security. As he observed in *Politics among Nations,*

> if we ask ourselves what statesmen and diplomats are capable of doing to further the power objectives of their respective nations and what they actually do, we realize that they do less than they probably could and less than they actually did in other periods of history. They refuse to consider certain ends and to use certain means, either altogether or under certain conditions, not because in the light of expediency they appear impractical or unwise but because certain moral rules interpose an absolute barrier. Moral rules do not permit certain policies to be considered at all from the point of view of expediency. Certain things are not being done on moral grounds, even though it would be expedient to do them. Such ethical inhibitions operate in our time on different levels with different effectiveness. Their restraining function is most obvious and most effective in affirming the sacredness of human life in times of peace.[70]

When a country's vital interests would not be harmed by doing so, it can and should act to promote international moral norms—or at least not act in defiance of them.[71] As McElroy has argued, when the security of a country would be jeopardized by adherence to an international moral norm, the existence of that norm will have little effect on state actions. However, in the day-to-day processes of foreign policy decision making, where the economic and military security of the country are not immediately endangered by compliance with the international moral norm, "the existence of such a norm can prove decisive in determining state behavior."[72] Similarly, as argued by former U.S. national security advisor Zbigniew Brzezinski, "In a world of fanatical certitudes, morality could be seen as redundant; but in a world of contingency, moral imperatives then become the central, and even the only, source of reassurance. Recognition of both the complexity and the contingency of the human condition thus underlines the *political* need for shared moral consensus in the increasingly congested and intimate world of the twenty-first century."[73] In short, when relative security affords statespersons the freedom to choose between a variety of policy alternatives (which is the normal condition for the United States today), there will be substantial opportunities for morality to shape major foreign policy decisions.[74]

Normatively pregnant ideas can and should influence state behavior. Without the overarching threat of the Soviet Union and the perceived menace of global communism, and without any major country or force to replace them, moral principles that go beyond immediate prudential interests may become more important. In the present post–Cold War context, where knee-jerk advocacy of security at the expense of ethics seems especially out of place, morality and ethical imperatives can and probably should influence foreign policy. Especially in international politics surrounding the environmental issues that have become more salient in the wake of the Cold War, notably climate change, considerations of international ethics interact with conceptions of national interests. One lesson seems clear: by acting in its self-interest to limit adverse global environmental change, the United States can promote ethical causes such as international equity, potentially helping people suffering from squalor and environmental degradation in the poor countries of the world. By promoting nascent international moral norms of equity, the United States can promote justice in the world and reduce human suffering, while also promoting its national interests with regard to environmental change and international relations more broadly.

During the administration of President Jimmy Carter, when it was U.S. government policy to actively support and promote individual human rights the world over, albeit selectively, many American policymakers were viewed as unrealistic utopians. But with the end of the Cold War (not to mention the frequent suggestions that the human rights provisions of the Helsinki Accords helped bring it about) and the advent of the Clinton administration, human rights concerns were again a prominent component of the foreign policy debate and were reflected in U.S. policy. Policymakers that advocate human rights—especially democratic rights—are no longer reflexively labeled "utopians," as they often were during the Cold War. Human rights have become part of the national interest. Similarly, international equity is not a utopian notion restricted to the pages of moral treatises. Already, serious consideration of equity in international politics and in U.S. foreign policy in particular has been legitimized, at least in the environmental issue area. Governments and policymakers that declare themselves in support of international equity are not viewed as heretics who fail to understand the dynamics of the anarchic international system. In the real-world context of increasingly global environmental change, promoting international equity can promote national interests.

Conclusion

A more robust acceptance by the U.S. government of international equity as an important goal of global environmental policy faces many obstacles, most notably the pluralistic nature of U.S. domestic politics and of a foreign policy that permits many disparate *and* sometimes powerful actors, both domestic and foreign, to influence the policy process, as the contributors to this volume show.[75] Domestically, business and industry groups, citizens' organizations, scientists and academics, bureaucratic agencies, the media and public opinion, members of Congress and political parties, as well as influential individuals can work to oppose or support U.S. foreign policies that accept and aid in international environmental equity. Internationally, the same actors in other national jurisdictions, multinational corporations, and international governmental and nongovernmental organizations can use the American political process, the international media, and diplomatic channels to influence U.S. policy. As adverse global environmental change becomes more pronounced, rather than largely a *future* threat as it is now perceived, one would expect many of these groups to give more support—or offer less resistance—to U.S. promotion of international equity as it relates to environmental issues. Already the economically and politically powerful American insurance industry has joined with Greenpeace and other environmental groups to press the U.S. government to join the recently agreed Kyoto Protocol and its binding targets and timetables for reducing emissions of carbon dioxide and other greenhouse gases.

But many actors will feel threatened by such a policy. The American people may remain opposed to even modest foreign aid, and so might Congress. Many powerful industries will remain opposed to efforts that make the U.S. economy more environmentally benign. Thus, a more robust acceptance by the U.S. government of international equity and burden sharing as an important goal of global environmental policy will require a coalition between sympathetic agencies, diplomats, citizens groups, businesses, and the like. Most important, perhaps, will be strong leadership from the president and executive agencies, in concert with these sympathetic actors, to make clear to the American people and their congressional representatives the connections between U.S. interests and international equity, especially in the environmental field. Successful leadership efforts may also have to draw on the American people's historic willingness to "do good" in the world, especially when doing so can simultaneously promote U.S. interests.

A full understanding of the U.S. government's partial and belated acceptance of international equity as an objective of global environmental policy—and of its failure to implement such an objective more actively—requires considering the role of many state and nonstate actors, institutions and organizations, bargaining environments, and the powerful ideas that are salient in contemporary international deliberations on environmental issues, among many other factors.[76] However, although such a complex analysis would help us to understand better what has happened and is happening in international environmental politics, it may not be *sufficient* to nudge practitioners toward formulating and supporting more robust international environmental institutions that will aggressively tackle the global environmental problems we will face in the twenty-first century. What may be needed is a prescription for action that encompasses international equity as an a priori principle. To use Shue's formulation, what this means is that "ethical considerations like international justice and human rights must come in at the ground level when notions of legitimate national interests are initially shaped, not as superficial constraints that are essentially after-thoughts."[77]

A decade ago, George Kennan, the former U.S. diplomat who coined the notion of "containment" that was adapted by policymakers to guide U.S. Cold War foreign policy—and a person who is not inclined toward moral sentimentalism—noted that the world is faced with two unprecedented and "supreme" dangers: major war among the great powers and "the devastating effect of modern industrialization and overpopulation on the world's natural environment." According to Kennan,

> The need for giving priority to the averting of these two overriding dangers has a purely rational basis—a basis in national direct interest—quite aside from morality. For short of nuclear war, the worst that our Soviet rivals could do to us, even in our wildest worst-case imagining, would be a far smaller tragedy than that which would assuredly confront us (and if not us, then our children) if we failed to face up to these two apocalyptic dangers in good time. But is there not also a moral component to this necessity? . . . Is there not a moral obligation to recognize in this very uniqueness of the habitat and nature of man the greatest of our moral responsibilities, of ourselves, in our national personification, its guardians and protectors rather than its destroyer?[78]

The United States arguably has an obligation as the sole superpower, as the wealthiest country in the world, and as the greatest polluter on the planet (among other reasons) to become a leader in efforts to promote international environmental equity. A fairer and more just sharing among the world's countries of the benefits and burdens of international environmental relations such as the climate change agreements will contribute to meeting many of the reasonable demands for equity from the world's poor and weak countries and people. Managed in an efficacious manner, such a redistribution of benefits and burdens could simultaneously fulfil ethical objectives, reduce human suffering (and the suffering of other species), and protect the local, regional, and global natural environments.

These measures would also promote U.S. national interests by reducing the potential adverse economic and security consequences for the United States of environmental change and poverty in the developing world. This type of foreign policy would bolster its reputation and credibility, meaning that other countries would be more likely to turn to it for leadership and to trust it in international deliberations in other issue areas. Using the words of former president Jimmy Carter, "we should take on this global leadership role, both because it is right and because it is in our self-interest to do it."[79] In short, by doing what is right—by doing what is equitable—in its relations with the rest of the world, the United States can best promote its national interests and ensure its future status as a great power.

Notes

1 The same can be said for other countries that have "great power" status.

2 The absurdity of this example shows the limited utility of weapons of mass destruction—weapons that are, strictly speaking, the most powerful—in almost all day-to-day issue areas.

3 An earlier version of this argument first appeared as Paul G. Harris, "Environmental Security and International Equity: Burdens of America and Other Great Powers," *Pacifica Review* 11, no. 1 (1999): 25–42.

4 I have tried to elaborate this definition of international equity and to argue for its implementation largely on ethical grounds in "Affluence, Poverty, and Ecology: Obligation, International Relations, and Sustainable Development," *Ethics and the Environment* 2, no. 2 (fall 1997): 121–38. Here I focus more explicitly on prudential justifications for international equity in the context of environmental change.

5 This statement was one of the messages of the famous Brundtland Report and General Assembly resolutions underlying the 1992 United Nations Conference on Environment and Development (UNCED). See World Commission on Environment and Development (Brundtland Commission), *Our Common Future* (Oxford: Oxford University Press, 1987); United Nations General Assembly Resolution 44/228, "United Nations Conference on Environment and Development," A/44/228, 22 December 1989, available at <http://www.un.org/gopher-data/ga/recs/44/228>.

6 For an elaboration of these ideas, see Paul G. Harris, "Environment, History, and International Justice," *Journal of International Studies* 40 (July 1997): 1–33. See also James Cameron and Ruth MacKenzie, "Access to Environmental Justice and Procedural Rights in International Institutions," in *Human Rights Approaches to Environmental Protection*, ed. Alan Boyle and Michael Anderson (Oxford: Clarendon, 1998), 129–52.

7 In 1997, U.S. nonmilitary foreign aid was only $7 billion, less than one-tenth of 1 percent of gross national product (GNP) and half what it was ten years

earlier. Karen DeYoung, "U.S. Grows Stingier on Foreign Aid," *International Herald Tribune*, 26 November 1999, 1.

8 This process is detailed with regard to climate change in Paul G. Harris, *Understanding America's Climate Change Policy: Realpolitik, Pluralism, and Ethical Norms*, OCEES Research Paper (Oxford: Oxford Center for the Environment, Ethics, and Society at Mansfield College, Oxford University, June 1998). The question of U.S. Senate ratification of such an agreement is a more difficult matter. The Senate will not ratify a treaty without new "commitments" from developing countries. Hence, the Clinton administration had no plans to send the treaty for ratification without additional side agreements. The degree to which the U.S. government succumbed to the demands of the developing countries during the Kyoto climate change deliberations is described in Paul G. Harris, "Common but Differentiated Responsibility: The Kyoto Protocol and U.S. Foreign Policy," *Environmental Law Journal* 7, no. 1 (1999): 27–48.

9 The United States is required to reduce its emissions by 7 percent, with the Japanese reducing theirs by 6 percent and European Union members reducing theirs by 8 percent overall.

10 This shows that the outcomes of international environmental deliberations are, not surprisingly, more a function of political bargaining than ethics.

11 Harris, *Understanding America's Climate Change Policy*.

12 Nancy C. Wilson, "China Faces Hard Energy Choices: Booming Economy, Soaring Emissions," *Climate Alert* 6, no. 3 (May–June 1993); World Resources Institute et al., *World Resources 1996–97* (Oxford: Oxford University Press, 1996), 315–25.

13 See Harris, *Understanding America's Climate Change Policy*.

14 Paul G. Harris, "Considerations of Equity and International Environmental Institutions," *Environmental Politics* 5, no. 2 (summer 1996): 274–301.

15 Many developed countries, the United States included, have been slow to recognize the links between well-being, poverty, crime, and environmental degradation in their own backyards. However, the Environmental Protection Agency has taken notice, and it now has a program devoted to environmental justice issues. See Robert D. Buller, ed., *Unequal Protection: Environmental Justice and Communities of Color* (San Francisco: Sierra Club, 1994); Richard Hofrichter, *Toxic Struggles: The Theory and Practice of Environmental Justice* (Philadelphia: New Society, 1993); and Evan J. Ringquist, "Environmental Justice: Normative Concerns and Empirical Evidence," in *Environmental Policy*, 4th ed., ed. Norman J. Vig and Michael E. Kraft (Washington, D.C.: Congressional Quarterly, 2000), 232–56 (and works cited therein).

16 See "Montreal Protocol on Substances That Deplete the Ozone Layer," 16 September 1997, 26 ILM 1550 (1987), available at <http://www.unep.org/ozone/mont_t.htm>; "United Nations Framework Convention on Climate Change" (UN FCCC), 9 May 1992, available at <http://www.unfccc.de/

resources/docs/convkp/kpeng.html>; Jay Shulkin and Paul Kleindorfer, "Equity Decisions: Economic Development and Environmental Prudence," *Human Rights Quarterly* 17 (1995): 382–97; Harris, "Common but Differentiated Responsibility."

17 Many of the general examples here, and certainly the conclusions, apply to other traditional great powers—particularly countries that hope to remain or become "great" in the future.

18 The connections between environmental degradation and poverty are described in a vast literature. See in particular the Brundtland Commission, *Our Common Future*.

19 For a discussion, see Judy Mann, "Reviewing History's Lesson on Foreign Aid," *Washington Post*, 1 July 1998, C23.

20 National Security Council, *A National Security Strategy for a New Century* (Washington, D.C.: National Security Council, May 1997).

21 J. T. Houghton, L. G. Meiro Filho, B. A. Callander, N. Harris, A. Kattenberg, and K. Maskell, eds., *Climate Change 1995: The Science of Climate Change* (New York: Cambridge University Press, 1996).

22 World Health Organization, "Executive Summary," *Climate Change and Human Health* (Geneva: WHO Office of Global Integrated Environmental Health, 1996), 2.

23 "Some mid-continental drying in temperate zones, such as the mid-west USA . . . may occur." World Health Organization press release, "Climate Change and Human Health," WHO Office of Global and Integrated Environmental Health, 12 July 1996, 1.

24 WHO, *Climate Change and Human Health*. In July 1998, President Clinton attributed—perhaps prematurely from a scientific standpoint—widespread forest fires then afflicting Florida to climate change. "Clinton Links Fires, Global Warming," *Climate News*, 13 July 1998, available by e-mail at <climate-1@lists.iisd.ca>. See also Pim Martens, *Health and Climate Change* (London: Earthscan, 1998).

25 Thomas Homer-Dixon, "On the Threshold: Environmental Changes as Causes of Acute Conflict," *International Security* 16, no. 2 (1991): 76–116; Norman Myers, *Ultimate Security: The Environmental Basis of Political Stability* (New York: W. W. Norton, 1993).

26 Warren Christopher, "Foreign Affairs Budget That Promotes U.S. Interests," statement before the Subcommittee on Foreign Operations of the Senate Appropriations Committee, Washington, D.C., 2 March 1994, *U.S. Department of State Dispatch* 5, no. 11 (14 March 1994), available at <http://dosfan.lib.uic.edu/ERC/briefing/dispatch/index.html>.

27 Ibid.

28 Department of State, *Environmental Diplomacy: The Environment and U.S. Foreign Policy* (Washington, D.C.: Department of State, 1996), available at <http://www.state.gov/www/global/oes/earth.html>.

29 Alan Dowty and Gil Loescher, "Refugee Flows as Grounds for International Action," *International Security* 21, no. 1 (1996): 43–71; Evan Vlachos, "Environmental Threats and Mass Migrations: The Growing Challenge of Environmental Refugees," paper presented at the NATO Advanced Research Workshop, Bolkesjo, Norway, 12–16 June 1996; Myron Weiner, "Bad Neighbors: An Inquiry into the Causes of Refugee Flows," *International Security* 21, no. 1 (1996): 5–42.

30 Warren Christopher, "Overview of 1995 Foreign Policy Agenda and the Clinton Administration's Proposed Budget," statement before the Senate Foreign Relations Committee, Washington, D.C., 14 February 1995, *U.S. Department of State Dispatch* 6, no. 8 (20 February 1995), available at <http://dosfan.lib.uic.edu/ERC/briefing/dispatch/index.html>.

31 Madeleine Albright, "Earth Day 1998: Global Problems and Global Solutions," press release, Department of State, 21 April 1998, available at <http://secretary.state.gov/www/statements/1998/980421.html>.

32 Timothy E. Wirth, "Sustainable Development and National Security," address before the National Press Club, Washington, D.C., 12 July 1994, *U.S. Department of State Dispatch* 5, no. 30 (25 July 1994). The Clinton administration is aware that consumption, not just human numbers, is a major problem. President Clinton, Vice President Gore, and other administration officials have acknowledged that Americans have an obligation to reduce their disproportionately high rate of consumption (and, by implication, of pollution). See Harris, *Understanding America's Climate Change Policy*, and Harris, "Common but Differentiated Responsibility."

33 Ibid.

34 National Security Council, *A National Security Strategy*.

35 Paul G. Harris, "Les Etats-Unis: Un joueur cle," *Liaison Energy Francophonie* 39 (1998): 11–15.

36 Philip Shabecoff, *A New Name for Peace: International Environmentalism, Sustainable Development, and Democracy* (Hanover, N.H.: University Press of New England, 1996), 176–77.

37 Joseph S. Nye Jr., *Bound to Lead: The Changing Nature of American Power* (New York: Basic Books, 1990), 33. Nye subsequently went to work for the Pentagon during the Clinton administration.

38 Ibid., 175.

39 Cf. Robert W. Cox, *Production, Power, and World Order* (New York: Columbia University Press, 1987).

40 Nye, *Bound to Lead*, 31.

41 Ibid., 32.

42 Robert Keohane, *After Hegemony* (Princeton: Princeton University Press, 1984), 105–6.

43 Ibid.

44 Ibid., 127.

45 Robert W. McElroy, *Morality and American Foreign Policy* (Princeton: Princeton University Press, 1992), 48.

46 Ibid., 49.

47 McElroy, *Morality and American Foreign Policy*, 52. Ian Macneil, "Contracts: Adjustments of Long-Term Economic Relationships under Classical, Neoclassical, and Relational Contract Law," *Northwestern University Law Review* 72 (1977–78): 898.

48 Lawrence Freedman, "International Security: Changing Targets," *Foreign Policy* 110 (spring 1998): 58.

49 For example, the United States and European governments are discussing ways of relieving much or most of the international debt of the poorest countries early in the new century.

50 Harris, "Environment, History, and International Justice."

51 Marc A. Levy, Robert O. Keohane, and Peter M. Haas, "Improving the Effectiveness of International Environmental Institutions," in *Institutions for the Earth*, ed. Peter M. Haas, Robert O. Keohane, and Marc A. Levy (Cambridge, Mass.: MIT Press, 1993), 400.

52 Intergovernmental Panel on Climate Change, Working Group III, "Equity and Social Considerations," draft 8.5, mimeo (1995), 4–5.

53 Shabecoff, *A New Name for Peace*, 166 (based on Shabecoff's firsthand observation of the Earth Summit).

54 Ibid., 167 (based on Shabecoff's interview with Gore).

55 Philip E. Clapp, "America Must Act on Global Warming," *International Herald Tribune*, 4 November 1999, 9.

56 Many of the West European governments have recognized the usefulness of being seen as leaders on global environmental issues, as demonstrated by their positions during UNCED. They were and are more sympathetic than the U.S. government to the reasonable demands for equity coming from the developing countries, and presumably they understand the utility of such an attitude.

57 See John Barkdull and Paul G. Harris, "The Land Ethic: A New Philosophy for International Relations," *Ethics and International Affairs* 12 (1998): 159–77.

58 See, for example, William Pfaff, "America in History: Realists Don't Buy the Wilson Line," *International Herald Tribune*, 8 July 1998.

59 See recent issues of the World Bank's *World Development Report* (Washington, D.C.: World Bank, 2000).

60 See, for example, Robert T. Watson, Marufu C. Zinyowera, and Richard H. Moss, eds., *The Regional Impacts of Climate Change: An Assessment of Vulnerability* (Geneva: Intergovernmental Panel on Climate Change, November 1997).

61 Harris, "Affluence, Poverty, and Ecology."

62 See Mathew Paterson, "International Justice and Global Warming," in *The Ethical Dimensions of Global Change*, ed. Barry Holden (London: Macmillan, 1996), 181–201; and Chris Brown, *International Relations Theory: New Normative Approaches* (Oxford: Columbia University Press, 1992), 155–92. See, more generally, Andrew Dobson, *Justice and the Environment* (Oxford: Oxford University Press, 1998); and Robin Attfield, *The Ethics of the Global Environment* (Edinburgh: Edinburgh University Press, 1999).

63 Cf. Henry Shue, *Basic Rights*, 2d ed. (Princeton: Princeton University Press, 1996). See generally Boyle and Anderson, eds., *Human Rights Approaches*.

64 I am not suggesting that Americans ought to reduce their standard of living. Rather, they should live the good life in a more sustainable way, something modern technologies make possible. On the potential of such technologies, see, for example, Amory Lovins and Hunter Lovins, "Climate Change: Making Sense and Making Money," White Paper of the Rocky Mountain Institute (1997).

65 Cf. Onora O'Neill, *Faces of Hunger: An Essay of Poverty, Development, and Justice* (London: Allen and Unwin, 1986). See Onora O'Neill, "Kantian Ethics," in *A Companion to Ethics*, ed. Peter Singer (Oxford: Blackwell, 1993), 175–85

66 An anonymous reader points out that this important issue is illustrated by the emissions of India: in a year, all of India uses about the same amount of energy as greater Los Angeles!

67 Henry Shue, "The Unavoidability Justice," in *The International Politics of the Environment*, ed. Andrew Hurrell and Benedict Kingsbury (New York: Oxford University Press, 1992), 395.

68 This is a Rawlsian argument. See John Rawls, *A Theory of Justice* (Cambridge, Mass.: Harvard University Press, 1971).

69 Borrowing the words of Chris Brown used in general reference to impartiality regarding international distributive justice. Brown, *International Relations Theory*, 180–81. This is an argument based on impartiality. Cf. Brian Barry, *Theories of Justice* (Berkeley: University of California Press, 1989); and Brian Barry, *Justice as Impartiality* (Oxford: Clarendon, 1995).

70 Hans Morganthau, *Politics among Nations*, 6th ed., revised by Kenneth W. Thompson (New York: McGraw-Hill, 1985), 249.

71 Cf. Arnold Wolfers, *Discord and Collaboration* (Baltimore: Johns Hopkins University Press, 1962), in which Wolfers describes the spectrum of pressures influencing policymakers. On one hand is the "pole of necessity," where the state's national security will be promoted by one choice and harmed by all others. On the other hand is the "pole of choice," where the state's security is not threatened or where several possible policy choices may promote the state's security.

72 McElroy, *Morality and American Foreign Policy*, 183.

73 Zbigniew Brzezinski, *Out of Control: Global Turmoil on the Eve of the Twenty-first Century* (New York: Charles Scribner's Sons, 1993), 231, emphasis in original.

74 McElroy, *Morality and American Foreign Policy*, 184.

75 See also Paul G. Harris, *Climate Change and American Foreign Policy* (New York: St. Martin's, 2000); and Harris, *Understanding America's Climate Change Policy*.

76 Ibid.

77 Henry Shue, "Ethics, the Environment, and the Changing International Order," *International Affairs* 71, no. 3 (1995): 461.

78 George Kennan, "Morality and Foreign Policy," *Foreign Affairs* 64, no. 2 (winter 1985–86): 217.

79 Jimmy Carter, statement given before the U.S. Congress, House of Representatives, Committee on Foreign Affairs, Subcommittee on Western Hemisphere Affairs, *Hearing on the United Nations Conference on Environment and Development*, 102d Cong., 4 February 1992 (published 1993), 7.

Contributors

Braden Allenby is an environment, health, and safety vice president at AT&T; an adjunct professor at the Columbia University School of International and Public Affairs; and a former director of energy and environmental systems at Lawrence Livermore National Laboratory (LLNL).

John Barkdull is an associate professor of political science at Texas Tech University.

Jon Barnett is New Zealand Foundation for Research, Science, and Technology postdoctoral fellow at the Macmillan Brown Center for Pacific Studies, University of Canterbury.

Douglas W. Blum is an associate professor of political science at Providence College and an adjunct associate professor of international studies at the Thomas J. Watson Jr. Institute of International Studies at Brown University.

Morton Bøås is a research fellow at the Center for Development and the Environment, University of Oslo.

Elizabeth DeSombre is an assistant professor of environmental studies and government at Colby College, and a fellow at the Center for International Affairs, Harvard University.

Robert Falkner is a lecturer in international relations at the University of Kent London Centre of International Relations and an associate fellow of the Energy and Environmental Programme at the Royal Institute of International Affairs.

Kristen M. Fletcher is the director of the Mississippi-Alabama Sea Grant Legal Program, University of Mississippi Law School.

Paul G. Harris lectures at Lingnan University, Hong Kong. He is a senior lecturer in international relations at London Guildhall University. He is director of the Project on Environmental Change and Foreign Policy and an associate fellow at the Oxford Center for the Environment, Ethics, and Society at Mansfield College, Oxford University.

Srini Sitaraman is a research assistant at the Program in Arms Control and International Security, University of Illinois at Urbana-Champaign.

Index